C0-EDZ-039

Contents

Med. Phys 4B03/6B03

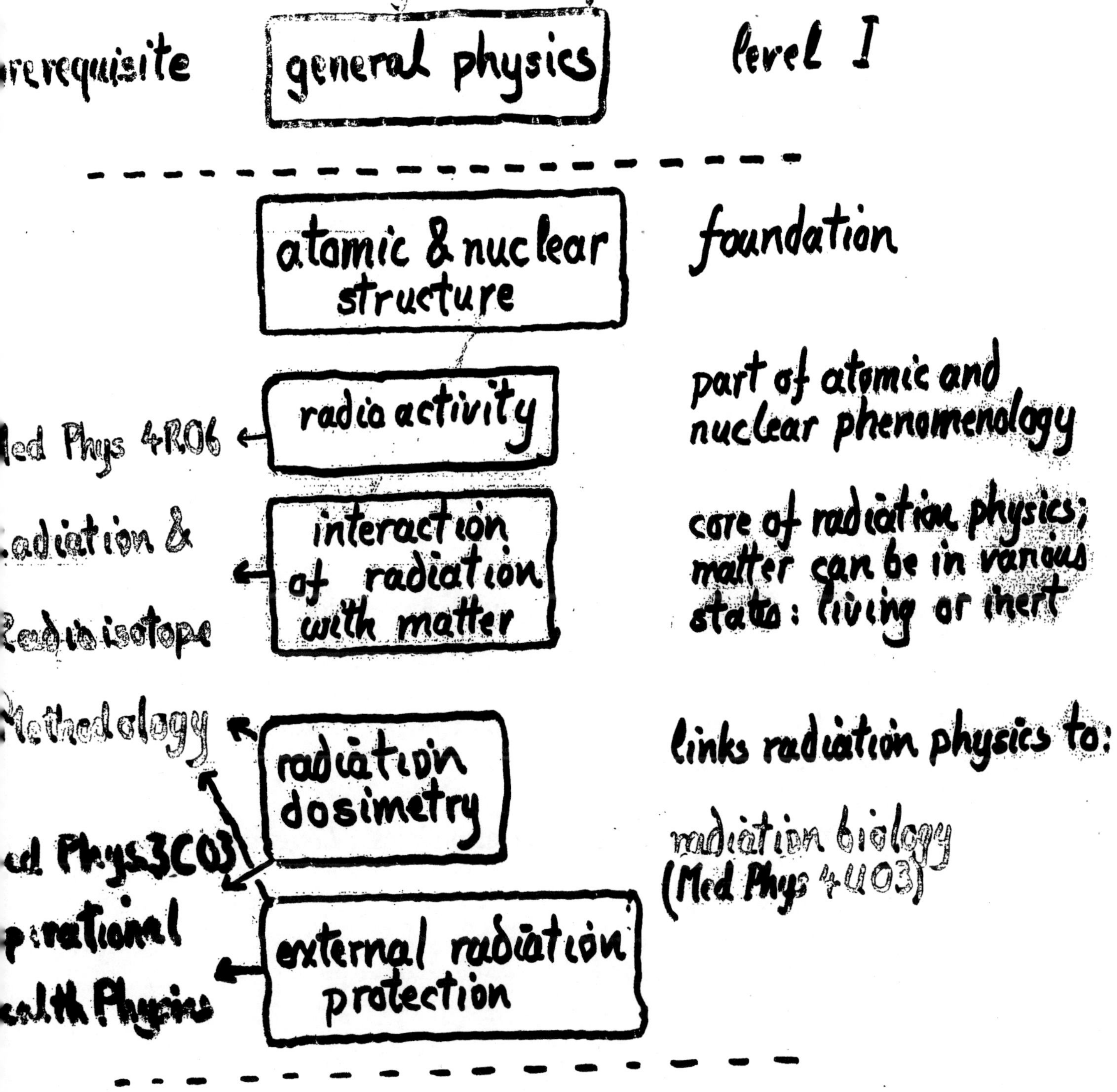

700 level courses and graduate research in

Medical Physics, Radiation Biology

Health Physics

Recommended Books

James E. Turner, "Atoms, Radiation, and Radiation Protection", 2nd edition, *John Wiley & Sons*, 1995, or 3rd edition, 2007

F. William Walker, Josef R. Parrington, Frank Feiner, "Nuclides and Isotopes", 14th edition. *GE Nuclear Energy*, 1989 (chart or book)

R.D. Evans, "The Atomic Nucleus" *McGraw-Hill*, 1955

W.E. Burcham, "Nuclear Physics, An Introduction", *Longmans*, 1963.

C.M. Lederer and **V.S. Shirley**, (eds), "Table of Isotopes" 7th (or 6th) edition, *Wiley*, 1978

H. Cember, "Introduction to Health Physics", 3rd edition, *McGraw-Hill*, 1996

H.E. Johns and J.R. Cunningham, "The Physics of Radiology", 4th edition, *Charles C. Thomas*, 1983

N.A. Dyson, "X-rays in atomic and nuclear physics", *Longman*, 1973

- Characteristic X-Rays arise from transitions between the electron energy levels;

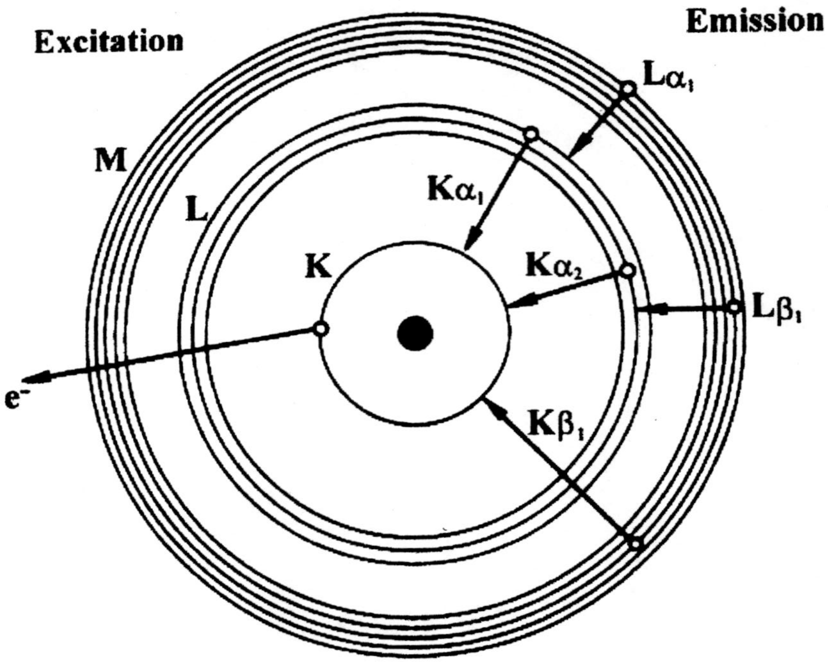

introduction: atomic model of nucleus surrounded by electrons in definite energy levels

charge on nucleus equal and opposite to summed charge of electrons

note: characteristic x-rays arise from transitions between electron energy levels, defined by energy of electron in charge field of nucleus

periodic table of elements determined by shell structure of atomic electrons

nucleus has a proton number (atomic number, z) and a neutron number

Segré chart (chart of nuclides) is plot of proton number vs neutron number, shows stable and unstable nuclei, closely linked to mass/energy

mass: define scale for convenient unit (atomic mass unit) [amu or u] based on ^{12}C

Avagadro's number of ^{12}C atoms have mass of exactly 12g and 12 amu = mass of ^{12}C

$$\text{mass of } 1\ ^{12}C \text{ atom} = \frac{12}{6.022045 \times 10^{23}} \text{ g}$$

$$= 1.992679 \times 10^{-23} \text{ g} \quad (1.992679 \times 10^{-26} \text{ kg})$$

$$\text{so } 1 \text{ amu} = 1.6605655 \times 10^{-24} \text{ g} \quad (1.6605655 \times 10^{-27} \text{ kg})$$

using energy, $E = mc^2$ (c is speed of light)

$$1 \text{ amu} = 1.6605655 \times 10^{-27} \times (2.997925 \times 10^{8})^2 \text{ J}$$

$$= 1.4924 \times 10^{-10} \text{ J}$$

$$= \frac{1.4924 \times 10^{-10}}{1.6022 \times 10^{-19}} \text{ eV}$$

$$= 931.5 \text{ MeV}$$

consider ^{12}C as $6p^{+} + 6n + 6e^{-}$, does the total equal the sum of the parts?

$$\text{mass} = 6 \times (1.6726 \times 10^{-27} + 1.6749 \times 10^{-27} + 9.1094 \times 10^{-31})$$

$$= 2.009047 \times 10^{-26} \text{ kg} \quad \text{difference, } -1.6368 \times 10^{-28} \text{ kg}$$

for ^{12}C mass difference between atom and sum of masses of separate components $= 1{\cdot}6368 \times 10^{-28}$ kg

$\equiv 91{\cdot}816$ MeV or $7{\cdot}65$ MeV per nucleon

different isotopes have different masses, therefore different binding energies – are there regularities?

semi-empirical mass formula

consider an atom of an isotope having mass number A, comprising Z protons and $A-Z=N$ neutrons

there will be Z electrons

(i) have $\underline{ZM_H + NM_n}$ where M_H is mass of hydrogen atom and M_n is mass of neutron

(ii) there is a strong attractive force, binding nucleons together

$\underline{-a_V A}$ depends on volume

(iii) surface nucleons are less tightly bound, there is a surface energy $\underline{+a_T A^{2/3}}$

(iv) symmetry, there is greater stability when $N = Z$

most apparent in light nuclei ^{4}He, ^{12}C, ^{16}O ... ^{40}Ca

expressed as instability for assymmetry

$$+ \; a_s \frac{(N-Z)^2}{A}$$

(v) nuclear charge is mutually repulsive, nuclear

volume $\propto^{al}$ A, ∴ radius $\propto^{al}$ $A^{1/3}$

Coulomb energy $\propto^{al}$ Z^2/R

$$+ \; a_c \; Z^2/A^{1/3}$$

(vi) pairing energy, even numbers of N or Z

are favoured

for odd A (ie even-odd or odd-even)

let this term = 0

even A, let term be -ve (more stable) for even-even

let term be +ve (less stable) for odd-odd

$$\delta$$

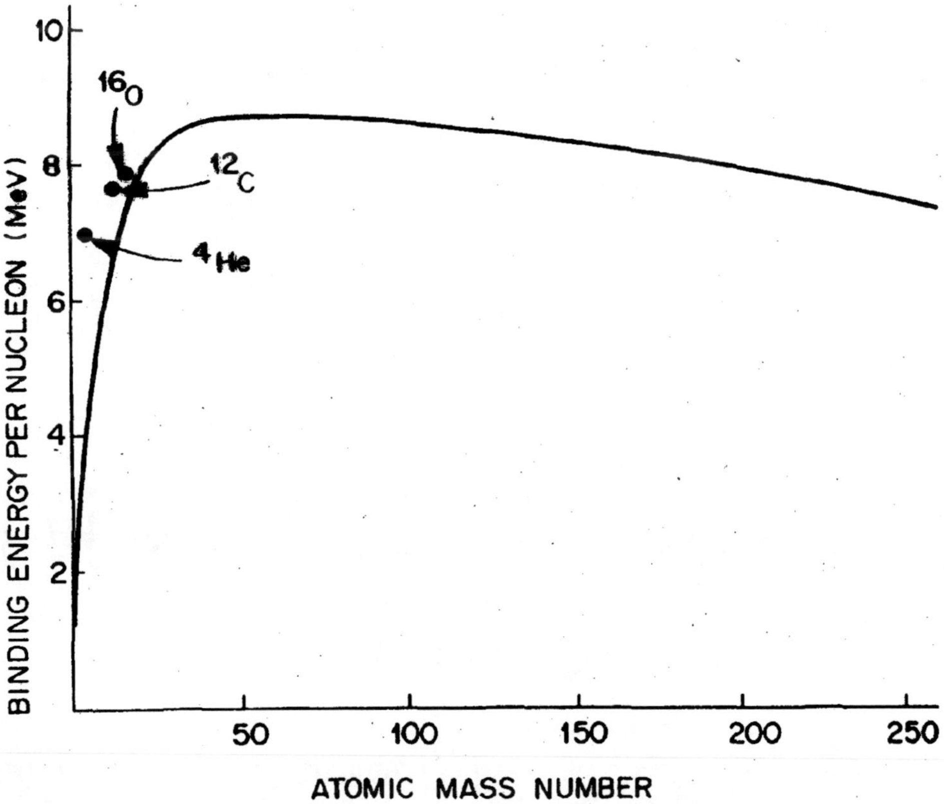

FIGURE 3.3. Average energy per nucleon as a function of atomic mass number.

so

$$M(A,Z) = Z M_H + N M_n - a_V A + a_T A^{2/3} + a_s \frac{(N-Z)^2}{A} + a_C \frac{Z^2}{A^{1/3}} \pm \delta$$

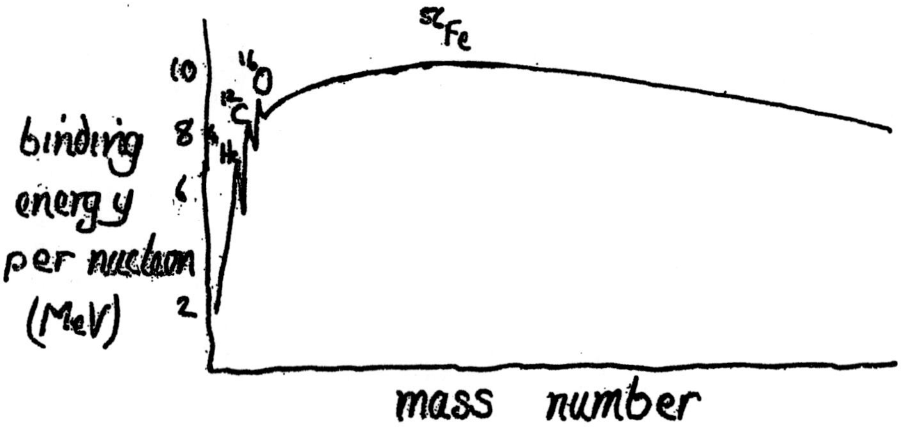

in order to make it computationally easier the mass difference (also called mass excess or mass decrement) is defined as M-A

M can be greater or less than A, depending on the binding energy

comparing to $^{12}C = 0$, by definition of amu

$$\Delta = M - A \quad \text{in MeV}$$

(Appendix D in Turner)

can use this in analysis of reactions

eg $\;{}^{1}_{0}n + {}^{14}_{7}N \rightarrow {}^{14}_{6}C + {}^{1}_{1}P$

note: mass numbers: 15 = 15
nuclear charge numbers: 7 = 7
electrons: 7 around N, 6 around C + 1 around H

nuclide	Δ (MeV)
${}^{1}_{0}n$	8.0714
${}^{1}_{1}H$	7.2890
${}^{14}_{6}C$	3.0198
${}^{14}_{7}N$	2.8637

so $\;8.0714 + 2.8637 = 3.0198 + 7.2890 + Q$

where Q is energy released

$$Q = 0.6263 \text{ MeV}$$

consider also

$${}^{1}_{0}n + {}^{10}_{5}B \rightarrow {}^{7}_{3}Li + {}^{4}_{2}He + Q \qquad {}^{10}B(n,\alpha)^{7}Li$$

Δ(MeV) $\;8.0714 + 12.052 = 14.907 + 2.4248 + Q$

$$Q = 2.7916 \text{ MeV}$$

Q needn't be positive

$$ {}^{7}_{3}Li + {}^{1}_{1}p \rightarrow {}^{7}_{4}Be + {}^{1}_{0}n + Q $$

Δ (MeV) $\quad 14{\cdot}907 + 7{\cdot}2890 = 15{\cdot}769 + 8{\cdot}0714 + Q$

$Q = -1{\cdot}6444$ MeV ie need to supply energy by accelerating proton

look at conservation of energy & momentum

a) from ${}^{10}B(n,\alpha){}^{7}Li$ $\quad E_{Li} + E_\alpha = 2{\cdot}7916$ MeV assuming E_n was negligible

also $P_{Li} = -P_\alpha \qquad E = P^2/2m$

$P_{Li}^2 = P_\alpha^2 = P^2$

so $M_{Li} E_{Li} = M_\alpha E_\alpha$

and $E_\alpha = \frac{M_{Li}}{M_\alpha} \cdot E_{Li} \simeq 7/4\, E_{Li}$

$E_\alpha = 1{\cdot}776$ MeV

$E_{Li} = 1{\cdot}015$ MeV

E_1, p_1, M_1 $\quad$ E_2, p_2, M_2 $\qquad$ E_3, p_3, M_3 $\quad$ E_4, p_4, M_4

for stationary target, $p_2 = 0$, $E_2 = 0$

so $p_1 = p_3 + p_4$, $\quad p_4 = p_1 - p_3$

from mass difference have Q -ve

so $E_1 = E_3 + E_4 - Q \qquad$ — (1)

$$E_4 = \frac{p_4^2}{2M_4} = \frac{(p_1 - p_3)^2}{2M_4} = \frac{p_1^2 + p_3^2 - 2p_1p_3}{2M_4}$$

$$p_1 = (2M_1E_1)^{1/2} \qquad p_3 = (2M_3E_3)^{1/2}$$

$$E_4 = \frac{M_1E_1 + M_3E_3 - 2(M_1E_1M_3E_3)^{1/2}}{M_4}$$

from (1) $\quad 0 = E_3M_4 + M_1E_1 + M_3E_3 - 2(M_1E_1M_3)^{1/2}E_3^{1/2} - QM_4 - M_4E_1$

$$E_3 - \frac{2(M_1E_1M_3)^{1/2}E_3^{1/2}}{M_3 + M_4} - \frac{E_1(M_4 - M_1) + M_4Q}{M_3 + M_4} = 0$$

re-express as $\quad E_3 - 2AE_3^{1/2} - B = 0$

$$E_3^{1/2} = \frac{2A \pm \sqrt{4A^2 + 4B}}{2} = A \pm \sqrt{A^2 + B}$$

$$E_3 = A^2 + A^2 + B \mp 2A\sqrt{A^2 + B}$$

$$= B + 2A^2\left(1 \pm \frac{1}{A}\sqrt{A^2 + B}\right)$$

for this to be real, $A^2 + B$ must be $\geqslant 0$

$$A^2 = \frac{M_1 E_1 M_3}{(M_3 + M_4)^2} \qquad B = \frac{E_1(M_4 - M_1) + M_4 Q}{M_3 + M_4}$$

so $$\frac{M_1 E_1 M_3}{M_3 + M_4} + E_1(M_4 - M_1) + M_4 Q \geqslant 0$$

$$E_1\left(M_1 M_3 + M_3 M_4 + M_4^2 - M_1 M_3 - M_1 M_4\right) + M_4(M_3 + M_4)Q \geqslant 0$$

$$E_1 \geqslant -\frac{Q(M_3 + M_4)}{M_3 + M_4 - M_1}$$

in this case: $Q = -1.6444$ MeV

$M_1 = 1$ amu, $M_3 \simeq 7$ amu, $M_4 \simeq 1$ amu

$$E_1 \geqslant \frac{1.6444(8)}{7} \geqslant 1.879 \text{ MeV}$$

b) $^{56}Fe(n, p)^{56}Mn$

Δ (MeV) $-60.604 + 8.071 = -56.909 + 7.289 + Q$

$Q = -2.913$

$E_1 \geq \dfrac{-Q(M_3 + M_4)}{M_3 + M_4 - M_1}$; $M_3 = 56,\ M_4 = 1,\ M_1 = 1$

$E_1 \geq \dfrac{+2.913(56+1)}{56+1-1} = 2.965$ MeV

Fission, shape of binding energy curve **shows that** it is energetically favourable to move from **high A** to medium A

consider the reaction

$$^{235}_{92}U + {}^{1}_{0}n \longrightarrow {}^{236}_{92}U^{*} \longrightarrow {}^{140}_{54}Xe + {}^{93}_{38}Sr + 3\,{}^{1}_{0}n + Q$$

Δ (MeV) $40.9164 + 8.0714 = 42.4420 + * = -73.18 - 80.28 + 3 \times 8.0714 + Q$

$* = 6.5458$ MeV

$Q = 178.234$ MeV

but $^{140}_{54}Xe$ and $^{93}_{38}Sr$ are both radioactive and eventually decay to $^{140}_{58}Ce$ and $^{93}_{41}Nb$

Δ(MeV) −88·081 −87·209

eventual Q = 200·064 MeV

alternatively $^{236}_{92}U^* \rightarrow \,^{97}_{39}Y + \,^{137}_{53}I + 2\,^{1}_{0}n + Q$

Δ (MeV) = −75·61 −76·72 + 2×8·0714 + Q

Q = 185·175 MeV

eventually $^{97}_{42}Mo$ $^{137}_{56}Ba$

Δ(MeV) −87·544 −87·733

eventual Q = 208·122 MeV

Fusion: shape of binding energy curve shows that it is energetically favourable to move from low to meduim A

consider $^{2}_{1}H + \,^{3}_{1}H \rightarrow \,^{4}_{2}He + \,^{1}_{0}n + Q$

Δ(MeV) 13·1359 + 14·9500 = 2·4248 + 8·0714 + Q

Q = 17·5897 MeV

alternatively

$$^{2}_{1}H + ^{2}_{1}H = ^{3}_{2}He + ^{1}_{0}n + Q$$

$$\Delta\ (MeV)\quad 13{\cdot}1359 + 13{\cdot}1359 = 14{\cdot}9313 + 8{\cdot}0714 + Q$$

$$Q = 3{\cdot}2691\ MeV$$

or $$^{2}_{1}H + ^{2}_{1}H = ^{3}_{1}H + ^{1}_{1}H + Q$$

$$\Delta\ (MeV) \qquad = 14{\cdot}9500 + 7{\cdot}2890 + Q$$

$$Q = 4{\cdot}0328\ MeV$$

but the nuclei have to reach each other before the reaction can take place

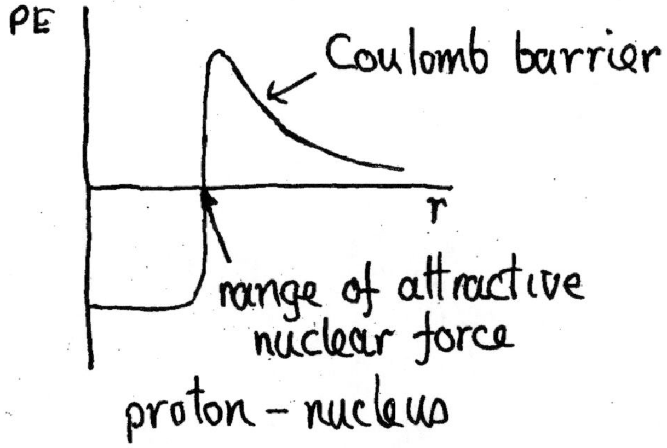

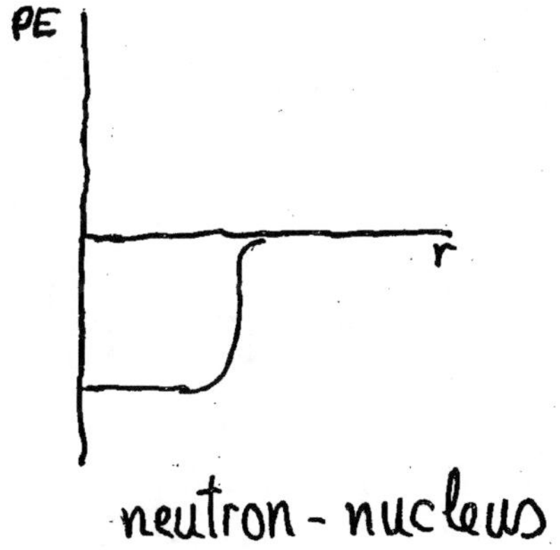

height of Coulomb barrier is potential energy arising from 2 charges (cf Turner p 56)

$PE = \frac{k_0 Z_1 Z_2}{r}$ J where Z_1 & Z_2 are the two charges (C), r is the distance between the charges (m)

(Turner appendix C)

k_0 is const $= 8.99 \times 10^9$ N m^{2}C^{-2}

need to know r

for $^3H(d,n)^4He$ require $r_t + r_d$

$r = 1.3 A^{1/3} \times 10^{-15}$ m (Turner equ'n 2.2)

$r_t = 1.3 \times 3^{1/3} \times 10^{-15}$ m $\qquad r_d = 1.3 \times 2^{1/3} \times 10^{-15}$ m

$= 1.87 \times 10^{-15}$ m $\qquad = 1.64 \times 10^{-15}$ m

so $PE = \frac{8.99 \times 10^9 \times (1.6 \times 10^{-19})^2}{3.51 \times 10^{-15}}$

$= 6.55 \times 10^{-14}$ J $= 0.409$ MeV

for $^2H(d,n)^3He$ require $r_d + r_d$

$PE = \frac{8.99 \times 10^9 \times (1.6 \times 10^{-19})^2}{3.28 \times 10^{-15}} = 7.03 \times 10^{-14}$ J

$= 0.439$ MeV

for reaction to be self sustaining need high temperature

average energy in Boltzmann distⁿ = $\frac{3}{2} kT$

$$T = \frac{2E}{3k}$$

$$= \frac{2 \times 0.44 \times 1.6 \times 10^{-13}}{3 \times 1.38 \times 10^{-23}}$$

$$= 3.4 \times 10^{9} \text{ K}$$

~0.01% will have E > 0.44 MeV at 10^7 K

how much energy could $^2_1$H, $^2_1$H fusion yield?

if two branches are equally probable

4 $^2_1$H atoms could yield 7.30 MeV

natural abundance of ^{2}H is 1.48×10^{-4}

1 kg water contains $\frac{1}{9}$ kg H

no. of H atoms = $\frac{1}{9} \times 6 \times 10^{26}$ of these 1.48×10^{-4} are ^{2}H

energy release $= \frac{1}{9} \times 1.48 \times 10^{-4} \times 6 \times 10^{26} \times \frac{7.3 \times 1.6 \times 10^{-13}}{4}$

$= 2.88 \times 10^{9}$ J

Coulomb barrier when a charged particle is emitted

$^{56}Fe(n, p)^{56}Mn$

p is repulsed by ^{56}Mn and at infinity has energy

$$\frac{k_0 Z_1 Z_2}{r} \simeq \frac{8.99\times10^{9}\times1\times25\times(1.6\times10^{-19})^2}{1.3\times10^{-15}(1 + 56^{1/3})}$$

$$= 9.171\times10^{-13} \text{ J}$$

$$= 5.732 \text{ MeV}$$

$Q = -2.913$ MeV, so Coulomb barrier places further constraint on this reaction

$^{10}B(n, \alpha)^{7}Li$

$$\text{Coulomb barrier} = \frac{8.99\times10^{9}\times2\times3\times(1.6\times10^{-19})^2}{1.3\times10^{-15}(4^{1/3} + 7^{1/3})\times1.6\times10^{-13}} \text{ MeV}$$

$$= 1.897 \text{ MeV}$$

$Q = +2.792$ MeV, so there is sufficient energy to overcome the Coulomb barrier

modes of radioactive decay — Turner, chapter 3

alpha decay

in general: $^{A}_{Z}X \rightarrow ^{A-4}_{Z-2}Y + ^{4}_{2}He + Q$

eg $^{226}_{88}Ra \rightarrow ^{222}_{86}Rn + ^{4}_{2}He + Q$

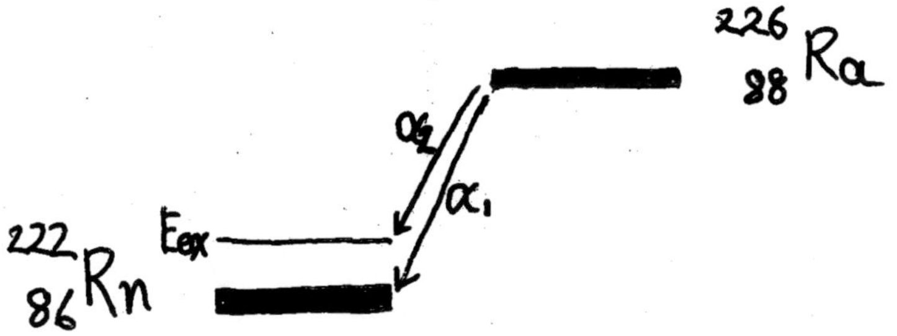

nuclide	Δ(MeV)
^{226}Ra	23·69
^{222}Rn	16·39
^{4}He	2·4248

$Q = 4.8752$ MeV (to ground state of ^{222}Rn)

$= E_\alpha + E_{Rn}$; $P_\alpha = -P_{Rn}$

$P_\alpha^2 = P_{Rn}^2 = 2 M_\alpha E_\alpha = 2 M_{Rn} E_{Rn}$

$$E_{Rn} = \frac{M_\alpha}{M_{Rn}} E_\alpha$$

$Q = E_\alpha \left(1 + \frac{M_\alpha}{M_{Rn}}\right)$; $E_\alpha = \frac{Q}{\left(1 + \frac{4}{A-4}\right)} = Q\left(1 - \frac{4}{A}\right)$

A is mass of parent nuclide (Ra)

A = 131 (EB; CML)

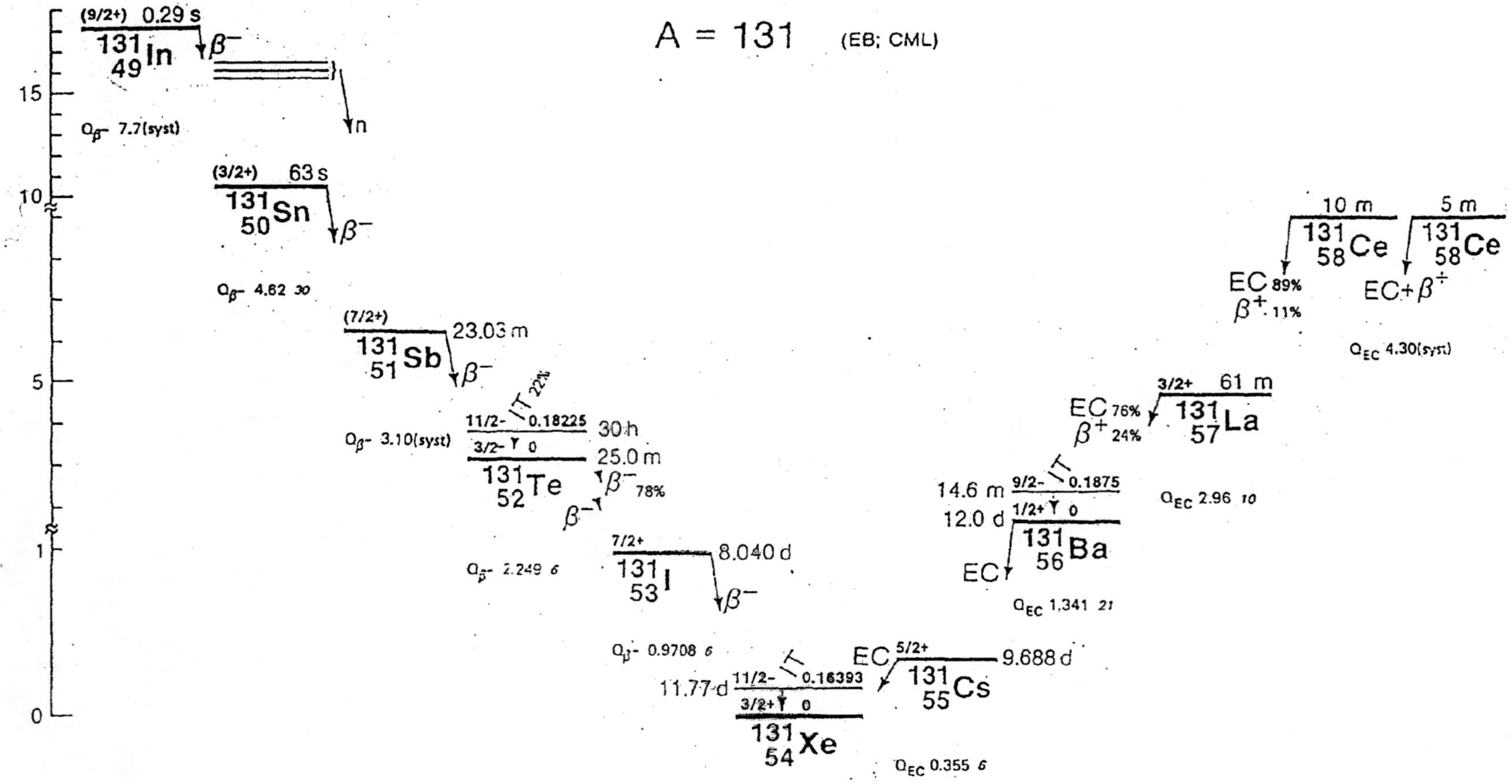

(9/2+) 0.29 s
131 49 In
β−
n
Qβ− 7.7(syst)
(3/2+) 63 s
131 50 Sn
β−
Qβ− 4.82 30
(7/2+) 23.03 m
131 51 Sb
β−
Qβ− 3.10(syst)
11/2− 0.18225 30 h
3/2− 0 25.0 m
131 52 Te
IT 22%
β− 78%
β−
Qβ− 2.249 6
7/2+ 8.040 d
131 53 I
β−
Qβ− 0.9708 6
11.77 d 11/2− 0.16393
3/2+ 0
131 54 Xe
IT
EC 5/2+ 9.688 d
131 55 Cs
QEC 0.355 6
14.6 m 9/2− 0.1875
12.0 d 1/2+ 0
131 56 Ba
EC
IT
QEC 1.341 21
EC 76%
β+ 24%
3/2+ 61 m
131 57 La
QEC 2.96 10
10 m
131 58 Ce
EC 89%
β+ 11%
5 m
131 58 Ce
EC+β+
QEC 4.30(syst)
15
10
5
1
0

A = 126 (JMD; CML)

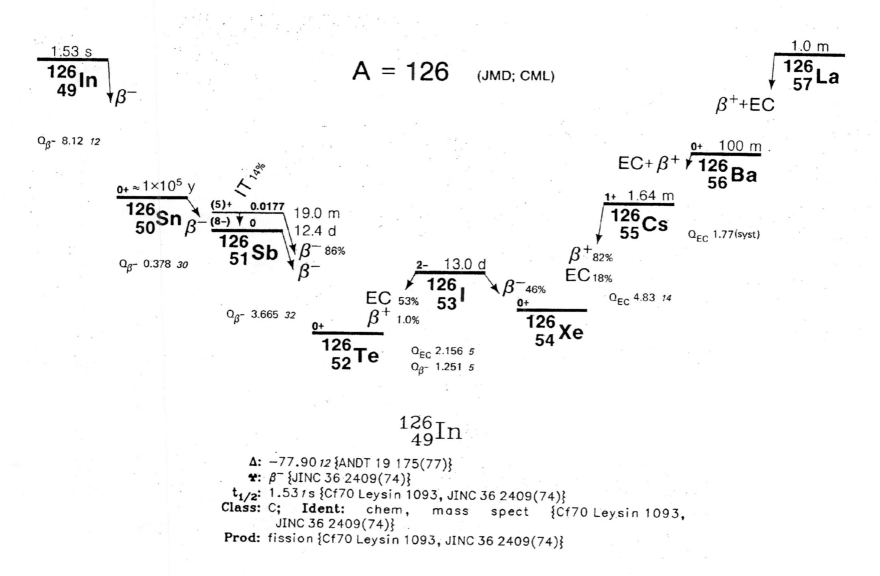

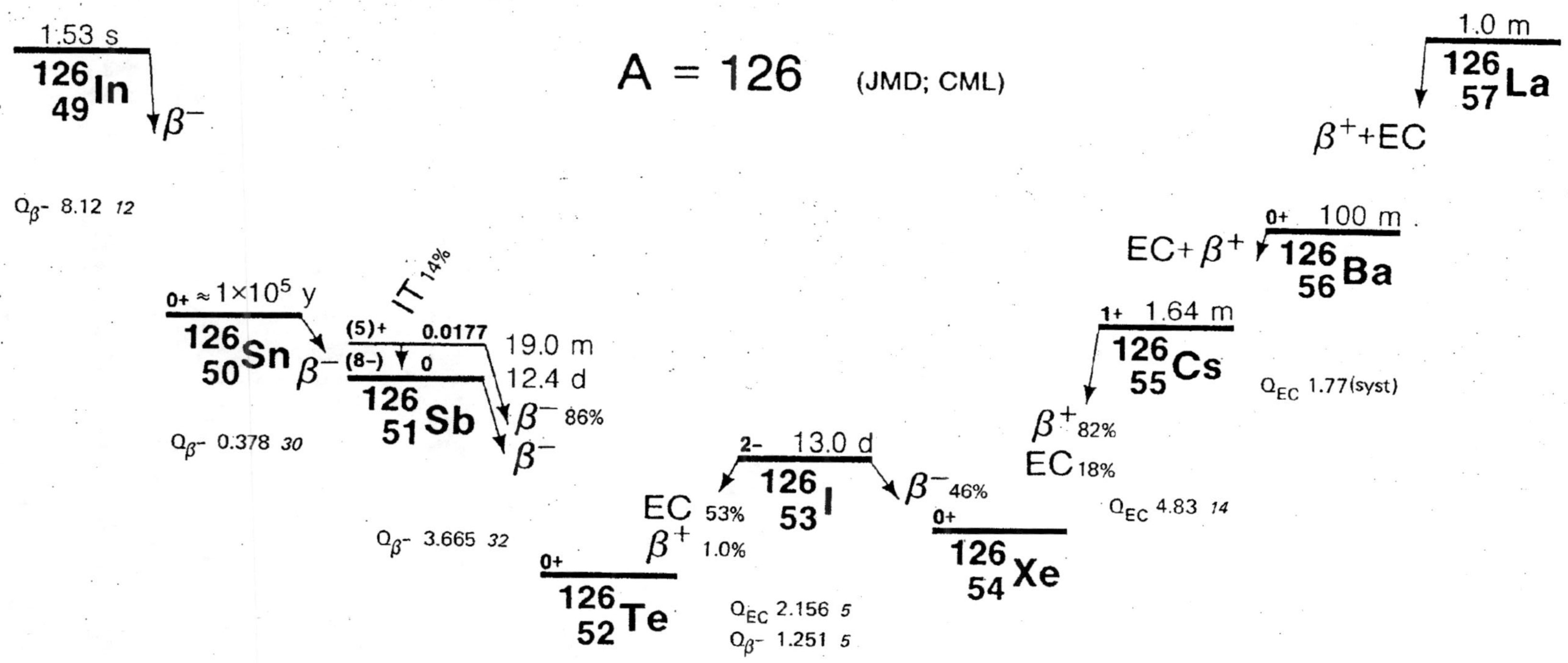

$^{126}_{49}$In

Δ: −77.90 *12* {ANDT 19 175(77)}
☢: β^- {JINC 36 2409(74)}
$t_{1/2}$: 1.53 *1* s {Cf70 Leysin 1093, JINC 36 2409(74)}
Class: C; **Ident:** chem, mass spect {Cf70 Leysin 1093, JINC 36 2409(74)}
Prod: fission {Cf70 Leysin 1093, JINC 36 2409(74)}

if decay is to excited state

$$E_\alpha = (Q - E_{ex})\left(1 - \frac{4}{A}\right)$$

for ^{226}Ra, $E_{\alpha_1} = 4.8752\left(1 - \frac{4}{226}\right)$

$= 4.789$ MeV

$E_{\alpha_2} = (4.8752 - 0.1862)\left(1 - \frac{4}{226}\right)$

$= 4.606$ MeV

beta decay

a) β^- decay $\quad n \rightarrow p + e^- + \bar{\nu}_e$

$$^A_Z X \rightarrow {}^A_{Z+1}Y^+ + {}^0_{-1}\beta^- + {}^0_0\bar{\nu}_e$$

in order for Y to be electrically neutral, an electron from the medium will be attracted, so the overall effect of the two steps, the decay then the neutralisation of the atom is:

$$e^- + {}^{A}_{Z}X \rightarrow {}^{A}_{Z+1}Y + {}^{0}_{-1}\beta^- + {}^{0}_{0}\bar{\nu}_e$$

and this is reflected in the energy balance, for example ${}^{28}_{13}Al$

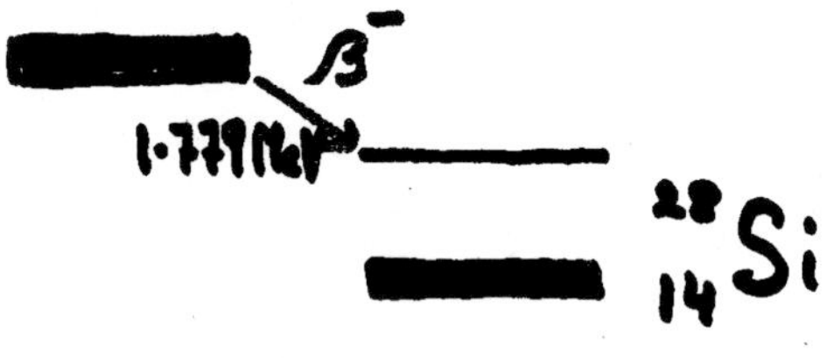

$$e^- + {}^{28}_{13}Al \rightarrow {}^{28}_{14}Si + {}^{0}_{-1}\beta^- + {}^{0}_{0}\bar{\nu}$$

$$\Delta\,(\text{MeV}) \quad 0{\cdot}511 - 16{\cdot}848 = -21{\cdot}491 + 0{\cdot}511 + Q$$

$Q = 4{\cdot}643$ MeV, decay is to excited state (1·779 MeV), $E_{\beta max} = 2{\cdot}864$ MeV

$$\bar{E}_\beta \simeq 0{\cdot}3 \rightarrow 0{\cdot}4\ E_{\beta max}$$

b1) β^+ decay $\qquad p \rightarrow n + e^+ + \nu_e$

$$ {}^{A}_{Z}X \rightarrow {}^{A}_{Z-1}Y + {}^{0}_{1}\beta^+ + {}^{0}_{0}\nu$$

but X had z atomic electrons, whereas Y will only retain z-1 atomic electrons so the overall effect of the decay then the atomic rearrangement is

$${}^{A}_{Z}X \longrightarrow {}^{A}_{Z-1}Y + {}^{0}_{1}\beta^{+} + e^{-} + {}^{0}_{0}\nu_e$$

the β^+ then annihilates with an electron in the medium and two photons are observed, each of energy 0·511 MeV

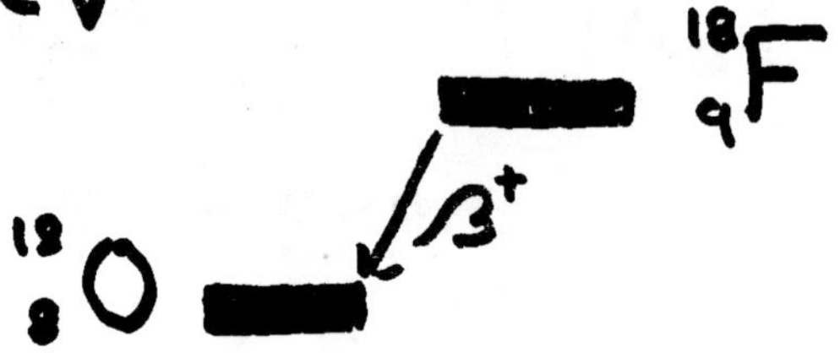

$${}^{18}_{9}F \longrightarrow {}^{18}_{8}O + {}^{0}_{1}\beta^{+} + e^{-} + {}^{0}_{0}\nu_e$$

$$\Delta(\text{MeV})\ 0{\cdot}8725 = -0{\cdot}7830 + 0{\cdot}511 + 0{\cdot}511 + Q$$

$$Q = 0{\cdot}6335 \text{ MeV} = E_{\beta^{+}_{max}}$$

b2) orbital electron capture

$$e^{-} + {}^{A}_{Z}X \longrightarrow {}^{A}_{Z-1}Y + {}^{0}_{0}\nu_e$$

but X had z atomic electrons, whereas Y will only retain z-1 atomic electrons; so the overall effect of the decay then the atomic

^{18}F

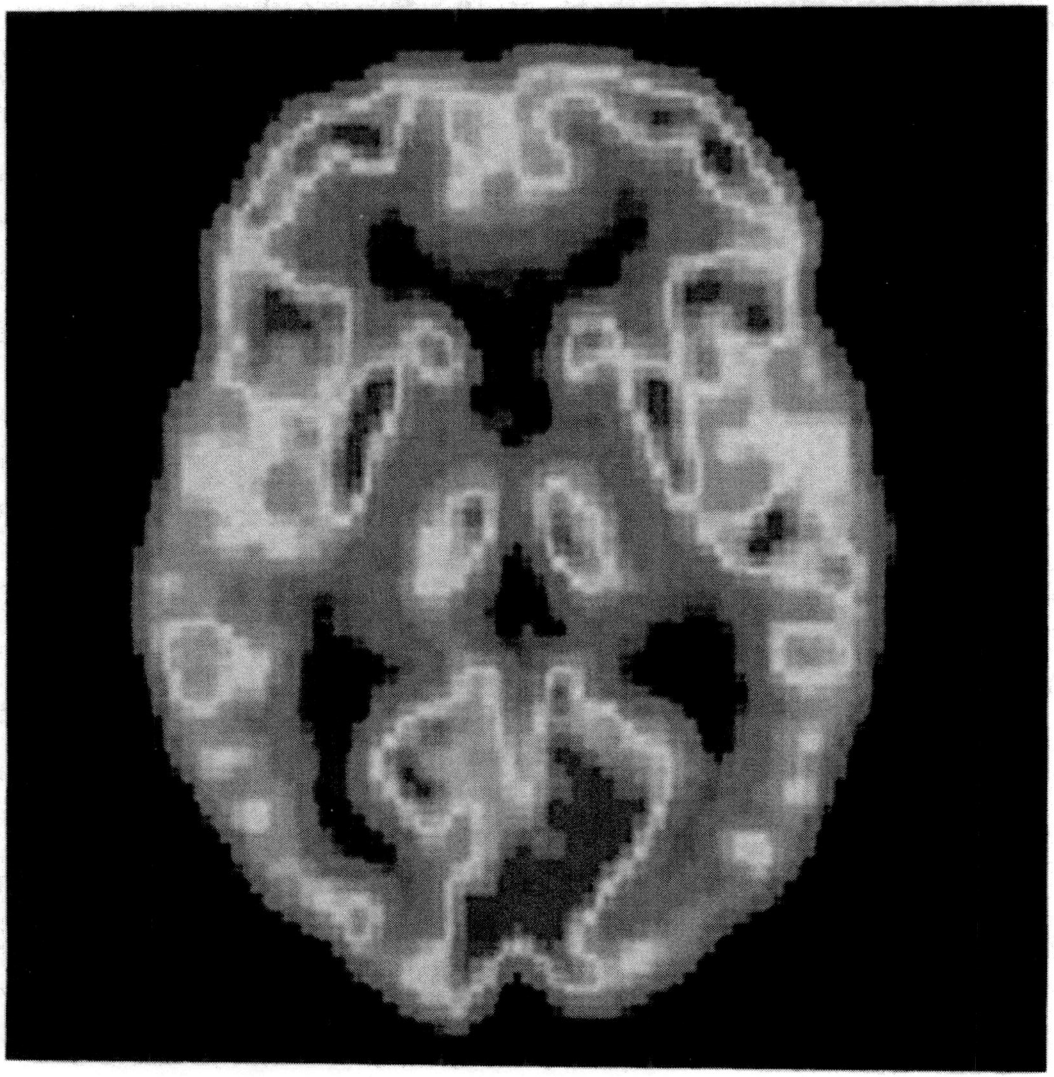

rearrangement is

$$^{A}_{Z}X \longrightarrow {}^{A}_{Z-1}Y + {}^{0}_{0}\nu$$

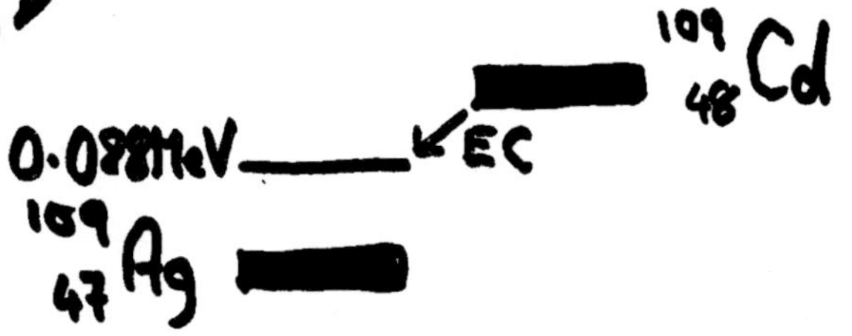

$$^{109}_{48}Cd \longrightarrow {}^{109}_{47}Ag + {}^{0}_{0}\nu$$

$$\Delta\,(\text{MeV}) \quad -88.540 = -88.722 + E_{be} + Q$$

K shell binding energy for Cd = 0.0267 MeV

$Q = 0.1553$ MeV, but it goes to excited state, so

$$E_{\nu_e} = 0.0673 \text{ MeV}$$

(E_{ν_e} would be higher if an L shell electron were captured, rather than a K shell electron) for β^- and β^+ decay

$$E_\beta + E_\nu = Q - E_{er}$$

β spectra have shape

$\Rightarrow$ non-conservation of energy or

an 'unknown' particle

neutrino rest mass near zero

orbital electron capture leaves vacancy in (usually) K shell of atom, as vacancy filled energy released, either as characteristic x-rays or by ejecting loosely bound (valence) electron(s) (Auger effect)

probability for x-ray emission, λ_x

probability for Auger electron emission, λ_A

define fluorescence yield, $\omega = \dfrac{\lambda_x}{\lambda_x + \lambda_A}$

ω can take values $0 \rightarrow 1$

$$\omega_K = \frac{Z^4}{a + Z^4} \qquad a = 1.12 \times 10^6$$

Z	8 (O)	26 (Fe)	47 (Ag)	82 (Pb)
ω_K	0·36%	29%	81%	98%

spontaneous fission $\quad Z_1 + Z_2 = Z; \; A_1 + A_2 + k = A$

in general $\quad {}^{A}_{Z}X \rightarrow {}^{A_1}_{Z_1}Y_1 + {}^{A_2}_{Z_2}Y_2 + k\,{}^{1}_{0}n$

consider $\quad {}^{252}_{98}Cf \longrightarrow {}^{142}_{54}Xe + {}^{108}_{44}Ru + 2\,{}^{1}_{0}n$

Δ (MeV) $\quad 76{\cdot}031 = -66{\cdot}05 - 83{\cdot}82 + 2\times 8{\cdot}0714 + Q$

$Q = 209{\cdot}758$ MeV

this isn't the final figure: a) decay

b) neutrino loss

for ^{252}Cf $\quad$ 3% $\quad$ spontaneous fission

97% $\quad$ α particle emission

nuclear de-excitation

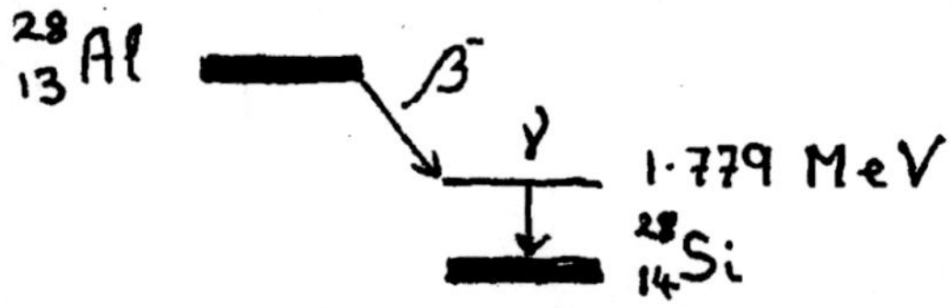

total energy available = E_{ex} = 1·779 MeV

momentum of γ-ray (P_γ) = E_γ/c

$P_M = -P_\gamma$; $E_{ex} = E_M + E_\gamma$; $E_M = \frac{P_M^2}{2M} = \frac{P_\gamma^2}{2M} = \frac{E_\gamma^2}{2Mc^2}$

so $E_{ex} = E_\gamma + \frac{E_\gamma^2}{2Mc^2}$

and $E_\gamma = Mc^2\left(\sqrt{1+\frac{2E_{ex}}{Mc^2}} - 1\right)$

for this example $Mc^2(^{28}Si) = 28 \times 931{\cdot}5$ MeV

E_{ex} = 1·779 MeV

E_γ = 1·778 938 MeV

recoil loss = 62 eV

nuclear resonant scattering

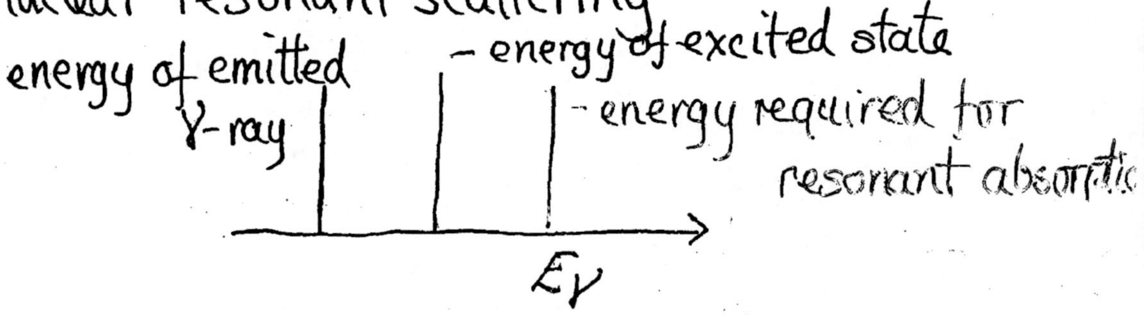

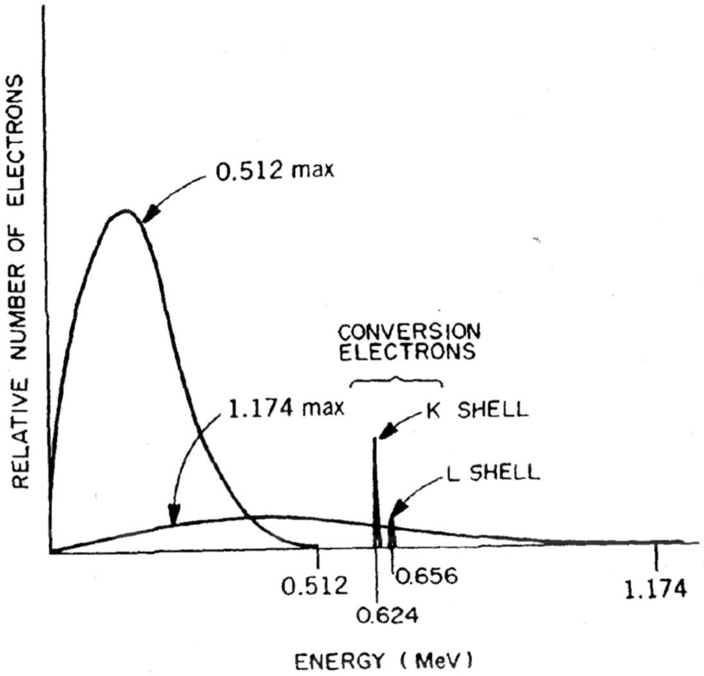

FIGURE 3.9. Sources of electrons from $^{137}_{55}Cs$ and their energy spectra. There are two modes of β^- decay, with maximum energies of 0.512 MeV (95%) and 1.174 MeV (5%). Internal-conversion electrons also occur, with discrete energies of 0.624 MeV (from the K shell) and 0.656 MeV (L shell) with a total frequency of 10%. See decay scheme in Fig. 3.8. The total spectrum of emitted electrons is the sum of the curves shown here.

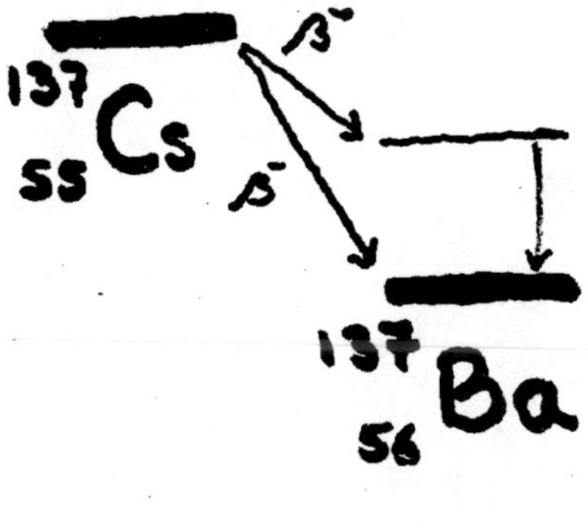

internal conversion

a nuclear excited state can de-excite by emission of an atomic electron (usually K or L) as an alternative to a photon

tends to occur for high Z ($\sim Z^3$), low E_{ex} and long lived states

internal conversion produces an electron with discrete energy

$$E_e = E_{ex} - B_e \,,$$ where B_e is the K or L shell electron binding energy

see Turner p 70 for ^{137}Cs

transition probabilities λ_e and λ_γ

internal conversion coefficient, $\alpha = \lambda_e / \lambda_\gamma$

α can take values from 0 to ∞

total transition probability $= \lambda_e + \lambda_\gamma$

leaves atomic electron vacancy => characteristic x-rays

production of characteristic x-rays following electron capture decay and internal conversion

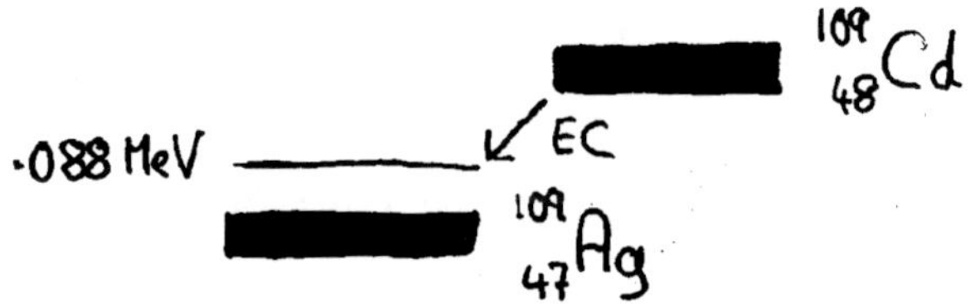

every decay goes via electron capture (EC)

every decay goes to the 0·088 MeV 1st excited state of ^{109}Ag

each EC decay produces a vacancy in an atomic electron shell of Ag

this vacancy can be in the K, L, M ---- shell

from data tables (Lederer and Shirley, 1978, Table of Isotopes)

$$EC(L+M+\cdots)/EC(K) = 0{\cdot}228$$

so

$$\frac{EC(K)}{EC(total)} = \frac{EC(K)}{EC(L+M+\cdots)+EC(K)} = \frac{1}{0{\cdot}228+1}$$

$$= 0{\cdot}814 \ (81{\cdot}4\%)$$

the vacancy is filled by a less tightly bound atomic electron, this results

either in characteristic x-ray emission

or in Auger (outer shell, valance) electron emission

the K shell fluorescence yield (ω_K) is the proportion of K shell vacancies which results in characteristic x-ray emission

$$\omega_K = \frac{Z^4}{1.12 \times 10^6 + Z^4}$$

in this case, Ag, $Z = 47$ and

$$\omega_K = \frac{47^4}{1.12 \times 10^6 + 47^4} \simeq 0.813$$

so, characteristic K x-ray emission following EC

proportion of EC resulting in K shell vacancy $\times \omega_K$

$$= 0.814 \times 0.813 = 0.662$$

+ internal conversion

internal conversion

every decay of ^{109}Cd goes to the first excited state (.088 MeV) of ^{109}Ag, the internal conversion coefficient for this state, $\alpha = e/\gamma = 26.4$

so $\lambda_e/\lambda_\gamma = 26.4$; $\lambda_e = 26.4\lambda_\gamma$; $\lambda_{total} = \lambda_e + \lambda_\gamma = 27.4\lambda_\gamma$

so $\lambda_e = \frac{26.4}{27.4}\lambda_{total}$ and $\lambda_\gamma = \frac{1}{27.4}\lambda_{total} = .0365$

from data tables $e_K/\gamma = 11.4$ or $\lambda_{e_K}/\lambda_\gamma = 11.4$

so the proportion of all de-excitations resulting in a K shell vacancy

$$\lambda_{e_K} = 11.4\,\lambda_\gamma = \frac{11.4}{27.4} = 0.416$$

(alternatively, from data tables:

$K/L_1/L_2/L_3/M/N+O+\cdots = 100/5.5/48.1/53.6/21.0/3.55$

this gives relative proportions of electron shell vacancies for internal conversion

simplifying gives $K/L+M+N+O = 100/131.75$

or $\lambda_{e_K}/\lambda_{e_{L+\dots}} = 100/131.75$

so $\lambda_e = \lambda_{e_K} + \lambda_{e_{L+\dots}}$ and $\lambda_{e_K} = \frac{100}{100+131.75}\lambda_e$

$= 0.4315\,\lambda_e$

but $\lambda_e = \frac{26.4}{27.4}\lambda_{total}$, so $\lambda_{e_K} = 0.4315 \times \frac{26.4}{27.4} = 0.416$)

once there is a vacancy, again consider fluorescence yield

$\omega_K = 0.813$

so characteristic K x-ray emission following internal conversion $= 0.416 \times 0.813 = 0.338$

and total K x-ray emission from EC + internal conversion

$= 0.662 + 0.338 = 1.00$

Natural radioactivity

cosmogenic $^{14}_{7}N(n, p)^{14}_{6}C$

$^{14}_{7}N(n, t)^{12}_{6}C$ $[t \equiv {}^{3}_{1}H$

$$e^- + {}^{3}_{1}H \longrightarrow {}^{3}_{2}He + \beta^- + \bar{\nu}$$

Δ(MeV) 14·950 = 14·931 + Q

$$Q = E_{\beta max} = 0\cdot019 \text{ MeV}$$

for d,t fusion fuel cycle can also produce $^{3}_{1}H$ from $^{6}Li(n,\alpha)^{3}H$

$$e^- + {}^{14}_{6}C \longrightarrow {}^{14}_{7}N + \beta^- + \bar{\nu}$$

Δ(MeV) 3·020 = 2·863 + Q

$$Q = 0\cdot157 \text{ MeV}$$

primordial $^{40}_{19}K$, note δ term in semi-empirical mass formula, ^{40}K has Z = 19, N = 21 it will be more stable as Z = 20, N = 20 ⇒ $^{40}_{20}Ca$ or Z = 18, N = 22 ⇒ $^{40}_{18}Ar$

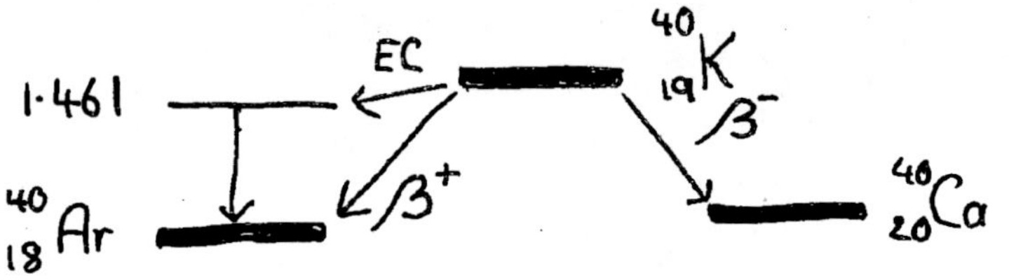

β^-	.893
EC	.107
β^+	.000010

nuclide	^{40}K	^{40}Ca	^{40}Ar
Δ (MeV)	−33.535	−34.847	−35.040

for β^- $\quad Q = -33.535 + 34.847 = 1.312$ MeV

for β^+ $\quad Q = -33.535 + 35.040 - 2 \times .511 = 0.483$ MeV

for EC $\quad Q = -33.535 + 35.040 - 0.004$ (K_K BE)

$= 1.501$ MeV

$E_\nu = 1.501 - 1.461 = 0.040$ MeV

γ-ray 1.461 MeV, 10.7% of decays, used to measure body potassium

$^{238}_{92}U \xrightarrow{\text{eventually}} {}^{206}_{82}Pb$

change in $A = 32 \implies 8 \times \alpha$

$8 \times \alpha \implies -16$ in Z

so need $+6$ in Z

$\implies 6 \times \beta^-$

$^{238}_{92}U$

α

$^{234}_{90}Th \xrightarrow{\beta^-} {}^{234}_{91}Pa \xrightarrow{\beta^-} {}^{234}_{92}U$

α

$^{230}_{90}Th$

α

$^{226}_{88}Ra$

α

$^{222}_{86}Rn$

α

$^{218}_{84}Po \xrightarrow{\beta^-} {}^{218}_{85}At \xrightarrow{\beta^-} {}^{218}_{86}Rn$

$\alpha \quad \alpha \quad \alpha$

$^{214}_{82}Pb \xrightarrow{\beta^-} {}^{214}_{83}Bi \xrightarrow{\beta^-} {}^{214}_{84}Po$

$\alpha \quad \alpha$

$^{210}_{81}Tl \xrightarrow{\beta^-} {}^{210}_{82}Pb \xrightarrow{\beta^-} {}^{210}_{83}Bi \xrightarrow{\beta^-} {}^{210}_{84}Po$

$^{206}_{80}Hg \xrightarrow{\beta^-} {}^{206}_{81}Tl \xrightarrow{\beta^-} {}^{206}_{82}Pb$

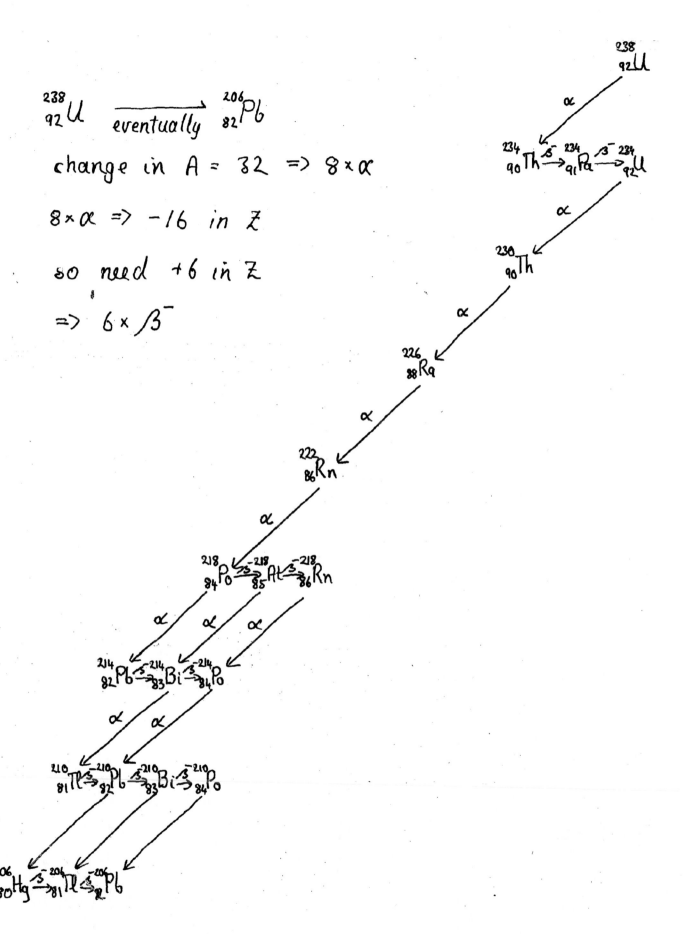

$^{235}_{92}U \xrightarrow[\text{eventually}]{} {}^{207}_{82}Pb$

change in A = 28 $\Rightarrow$ $7 \times \alpha$

$7 \times \alpha \Rightarrow -14$ in Z

so need +4 in Z

$\Rightarrow 4 \times \beta^-$

$^{235}_{92}U \xrightarrow{\alpha} {}^{231}_{90}Th$

$^{231}_{90}Th \xrightarrow{\beta^-} {}^{231}_{91}Pa$

$^{231}_{91}Pa \xrightarrow{\alpha} {}^{227}_{89}Ac$

$^{227}_{89}Ac \xrightarrow{\beta^-} {}^{227}_{90}Th$

$^{227}_{89}Ac \xrightarrow{\alpha} {}^{223}_{87}Fr \qquad {}^{227}_{90}Th \xrightarrow{\alpha} {}^{223}_{88}Ra$

$^{223}_{87}Fr \xrightarrow{\beta^-} {}^{223}_{88}Ra$

$^{223}_{87}Fr \xrightarrow{\alpha} {}^{219}_{85}At \qquad {}^{223}_{88}Ra \xrightarrow{\alpha} {}^{219}_{86}Rn$

$^{219}_{85}At \xrightarrow{\beta^-} {}^{219}_{86}Rn$

$^{219}_{85}At \xrightarrow{\alpha} {}^{215}_{83}Bi \qquad {}^{219}_{86}Rn \xrightarrow{\alpha} {}^{215}_{84}Po$

$^{215}_{83}Bi \xrightarrow{\beta^-} {}^{215}_{84}Po \xrightarrow{\beta^-} {}^{215}_{85}At$

$^{215}_{84}Po \xrightarrow{\alpha} {}^{211}_{82}Pb \qquad {}^{215}_{85}At \xrightarrow{\alpha} {}^{211}_{83}Bi$

$^{211}_{82}Pb \xrightarrow{\beta^-} {}^{211}_{83}Bi \xrightarrow{\beta^-} {}^{211}_{84}Po$

$^{211}_{83}Bi \xrightarrow{\alpha} {}^{207}_{81}Tl \qquad {}^{211}_{84}Po \xrightarrow{\alpha} {}^{207}_{82}Pb$

$^{207}_{81}Tl \xrightarrow{\beta^-} {}^{207}_{82}Pb$

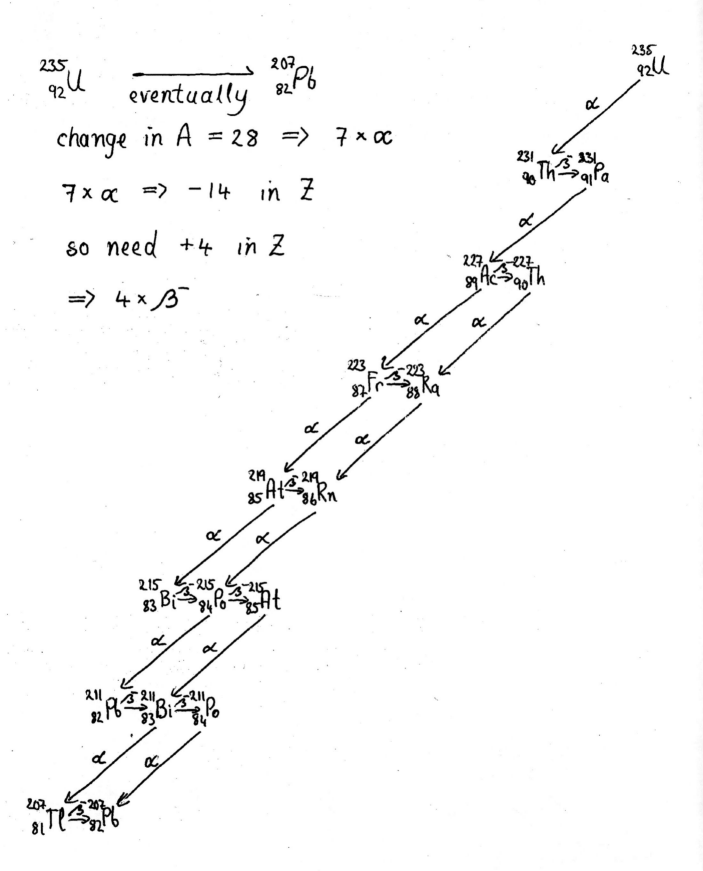

$$^{232}_{90}Th \xrightarrow{\text{eventually}} ^{208}_{82}Pb$$

change in $A = 24 \Rightarrow 6 \times \alpha$

$6 \times \alpha \Rightarrow -12$ in Z

so need $+4$ in Z

$\Rightarrow 4 \times \beta^-$

$^{232}_{90}Th$

α

$^{228}_{88}Ra \xrightarrow{\beta^-} ^{228}_{89}Ac \xrightarrow{\beta^-} ^{228}_{90}Th$

α

$^{224}_{88}Ra$

α

$^{220}_{86}Rn$

α

$^{216}_{84}Po$

α

$^{212}_{82}Pb \xrightarrow{\beta^-} ^{212}_{83}Bi \xrightarrow{\beta^-} ^{212}_{84}Po$

α α

$^{208}_{81}Tl \xrightarrow{\beta^-} ^{208}_{82}Pb$

Pb isotope ratios vary from one geological deposit to another

can tell where a sample of Pb came from

Turin Pb in gasoline experiment

Pb isotope ratios in blood

half-lives

^{40}K	1.277×10^{9}	y
^{238}U	4.468×10^{9}	y
^{235}U	7.038×10^{8}	y
^{232}Th	1.41×10^{10}	y

decay kinetics

each process is governed by a transition probability λ (s^{-1})

if X decays to Y and there are $N_X(0)$ atoms of X at time 0

$$\frac{d\,N_X(t)}{dt} = -\lambda N_X(t)$$

(if Y is stable, $\frac{d\,N_Y(t)}{dt} = +\lambda N_X(t)$)

$$\frac{d\,N_X(t)}{N_X(t)} = -\lambda\,dt$$

$$\int \frac{dN_X(t)}{N_X(t)} = \int -\lambda\,dt$$

$$\ln(N_X(t)) = -\lambda t + C$$

$$N_X(t) = e^{-\lambda t} \cdot e^{C}, \quad e^{C} = N_X(0)$$

$$N_X(t) = N_X(0)\,e^{-\lambda t} \quad \text{or } N = N_0\,e^{-\lambda t}$$

half life, what is t such that $N_X(t) = \frac{N_X(0)}{2}$

$$\tfrac{1}{2} = e^{-\lambda t}, \quad \lambda t = \ln 2$$

$$t_{1/2} = \frac{\ln 2}{\lambda}$$

define unit of activity becquerel (Bq)

$1\ \mathrm{Bq} \equiv 1$ disintegration s^{-1}

old unit Curie (Ci)

$1\ \mathrm{Ci} \equiv 3{\cdot}7 \times 10^{10}$ disintegration s^{-1}

was originally defined as 1g radium

activity $= N\lambda$

${}^{226}_{88}\mathrm{Ra}$, $t_{1/2} = 1{\cdot}6 \times 10^{3}\,y$, $\lambda = \ln 2 / t_{1/2}$

1g contains $\dfrac{6{\cdot}0221 \times 10^{23}}{226}$ atoms $= N$

$N\lambda = 3{\cdot}66 \times 10^{10}$ disintegrations s^{-1}

specific activity - activity per unit mass

$\mathrm{Bq\ kg^{-1}}$ $(\mathrm{Ci\ g^{-1}})$

for pure ${}^{238}U$ $t_{1/2} = 4.47 \times 10^{9}\,y$

1 kg ${}^{238}U$ contains $\dfrac{6{\cdot}0221 \times 10^{23}}{238} \times 10^{3}$ atoms

$N\lambda = 1{\cdot}24 \times 10^{7}\ \mathrm{Bq\ kg^{-1}}$ $(0{\cdot}336\,\mu\mathrm{Ci\ g^{-1}})$

^{40}K is 0·0118% abundant, $t_{1/2}$ $1{\cdot}28 \times 10^9$ y

1 kg of natural potassium has $\frac{6{\cdot}0221 \times 10^{26}}{39{\cdot}0983}$ atoms

of these $1{\cdot}18 \times 10^{-4}$ are ^{40}K

$N\lambda = 3{\cdot}12 \times 10^4$ Bq (kg natural K)$^{-1}$

human body contains ~ 140 g K

⇒ 4,366 Bq (467 1·46 MeV γ-rays s^{-1})

^{238}U - abundance 99·28% half life $4\cdot 47 \times 10^{9}$ y

^{235}U 0·72% $7\cdot 04 \times 10^{8}$ y

$$N_{238}(t) = N_{238}(0)\, e^{-\lambda_{238} t} \quad , \quad N_{235}(t) = N_{235}(0)\, e^{-\lambda_{235} t}$$

if $N_{238}(0) = N_{235}(0)$

$$N_{238}(t) / N_{235}(t) = e^{(\lambda_{235} - \lambda_{238}) t}$$

$$t = \frac{\ln\left(\frac{N_{238}(t)}{N_{235}(t)}\right)}{\lambda_{235} - \lambda_{238}} = 5\cdot 9 \times 10^{9}\ y$$

chain decay

$$a \rightarrow b \rightarrow c$$

eg natural series or $^{99}Mo \xrightarrow{67h} {}^{99m}Tc \xrightarrow{6h} {}^{99}Tc$

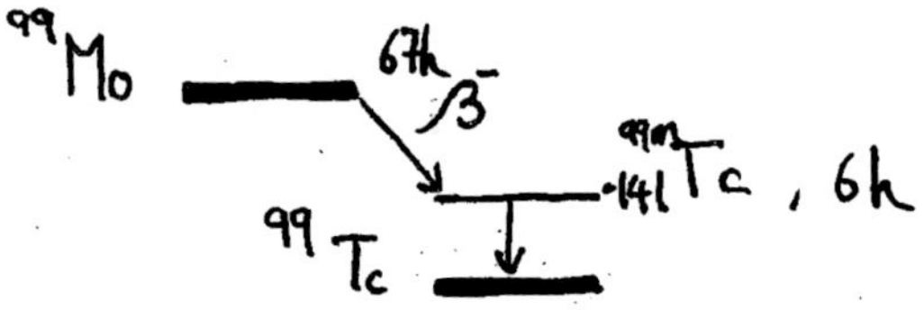

$$N_a(t) = N_a(0)\, e^{-\lambda_a t}$$

$$\frac{dN_b}{dt} = \lambda_a N_a - \lambda_b N_b$$

$$\frac{dN_b}{dt} + \lambda_b N_b = \lambda_a N_a(0)\, e^{-\lambda_a t}$$

use integrating factor. $I = \int \lambda_b\, dt = \lambda_b t$, multiply by $e^{\lambda_b t}$

How is Tc-99m Produced?

1. NRU irradiates small quantities of highly enriched uranium to produce Mo-99;
2. Mo-99 us extracted from irradiated uranium at CRL;
3. Mo-99 shipped to MDS Nordion for processing and purification;
4. MDS Nordion exports Mo-99 to generator manufacturers;
5. Manufactured generators shipped to hospitals;

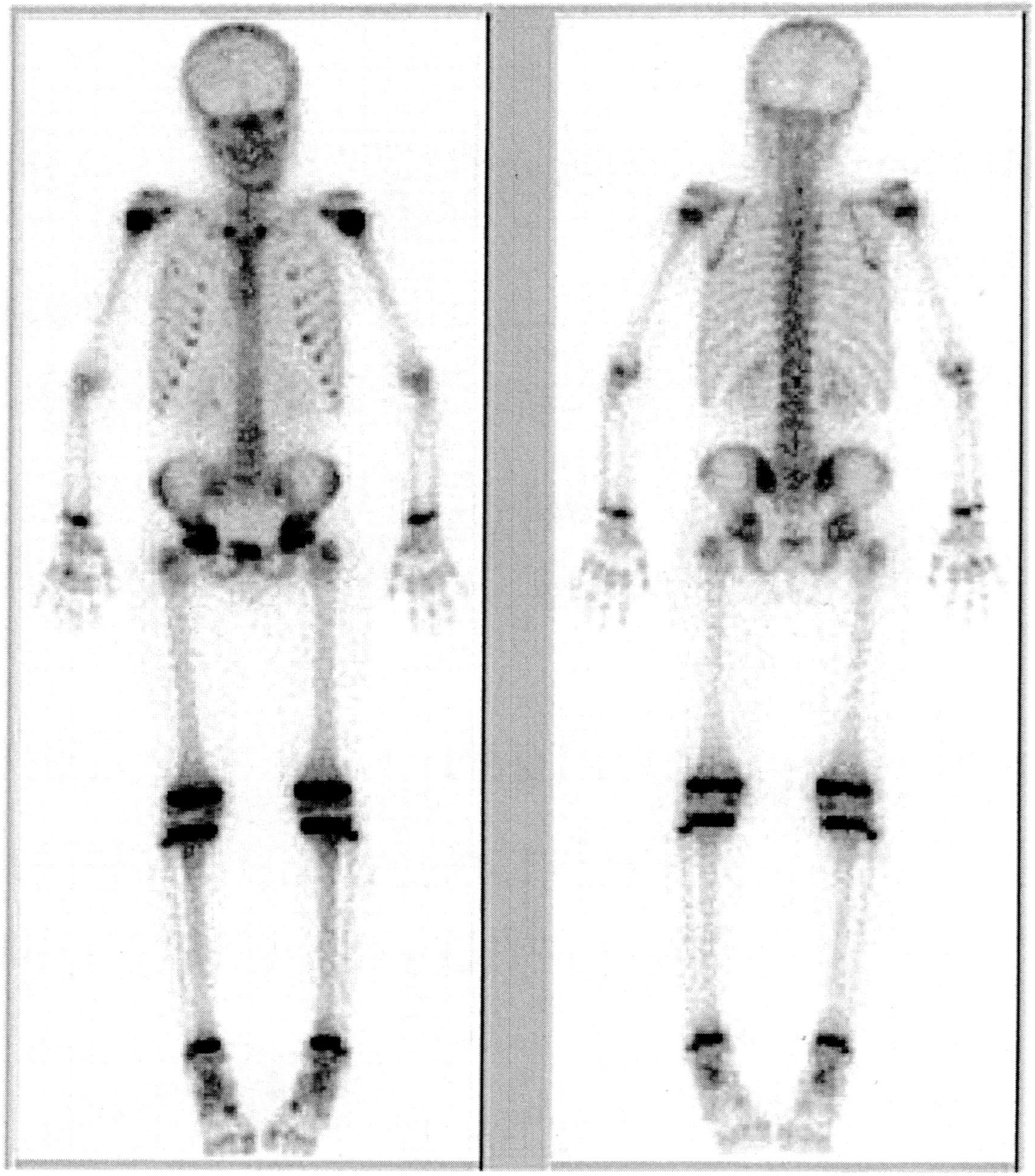

$$e^{\lambda_b t}\left(\frac{dN_b}{dt} + \lambda_b N_b\right) = \lambda_a N_a(0)\, e^{-\lambda_a t} e^{\lambda_b t}$$

$$\frac{d\,(N_b e^{\lambda_b t})}{dt} = \lambda_a N_a(0)\, e^{(\lambda_b-\lambda_a)t}$$

$$N_b e^{\lambda_b t} = \frac{\lambda_a N_a(0)}{\lambda_b-\lambda_a} e^{(\lambda_b-\lambda_a)t} + c$$

at $t=0$, $N_b = N_b(0)$

$$N_b(0) = \frac{\lambda_a N_a(0)}{\lambda_b-\lambda_a} + c$$

$$c = N_b(0) - \frac{\lambda_a N_a(0)}{\lambda_b-\lambda_a}$$

$$N_b = N_b(0)\, e^{-\lambda_b t} + \frac{\lambda_a N_a(0)}{\lambda_b-\lambda_a}\left(e^{-\lambda_a t} - e^{-\lambda_b t}\right)$$

if $N_b(0) = 0$, then $\dfrac{N_b \lambda_b}{N_a \lambda_a} = \dfrac{\lambda_b}{\lambda_b-\lambda_a}\left(1 - e^{-(\lambda_b-\lambda_a)t}\right)$

for $\lambda_b > \lambda_a$ (daughter shorter lived than parent)

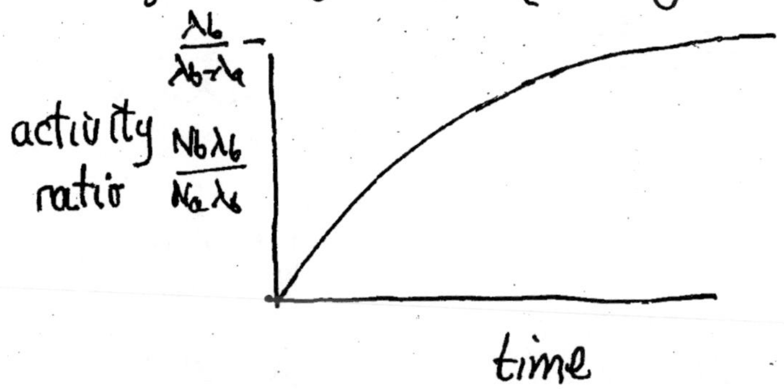

called 'transient equilibrium'

if $\lambda_a t << t$, ie a is very long lived eg ^{238}U

activity ratio $\Rightarrow 1$ & have 'secular equilibrium'

so $\lambda_a N_a(0) = N_b \lambda_b = N_c \lambda_c$ etc

for $\lambda_b < \lambda_a$ ie daughter longer lived than parent

activity ratio does not asymptote ∵ exponential term is +ve

consider when daughter activity is max

$$(N_b \lambda_b)_{max} = \lambda_b (N_{b\,max})$$

$$N_b = \frac{\lambda_a N_a(0)}{\lambda_b - \lambda_a} \left(e^{-\lambda_a t} - e^{-\lambda_b t} \right)$$

$$\frac{dN_b}{dt} = \frac{\lambda_a N_a(0)}{\lambda_b - \lambda_a} \left(-\lambda_a e^{-\lambda_a t} + \lambda_b e^{-\lambda_b t} \right)$$

$$\frac{dN_b}{dt} = 0 \quad \text{for} \quad \lambda_a e^{-\lambda_a t} = \lambda_b e^{-\lambda_b t} \quad (\text{max for } \lambda_b < \lambda_a)$$

$$\frac{N_b \lambda_b}{N_a \lambda_a} = \frac{\lambda_b}{\lambda_b - \lambda_a} \left(1 - e^{-(\lambda_b - \lambda_a)t} \right)$$

$$= \frac{\lambda_b - \lambda_b e^{-\lambda_b t} e^{\lambda_a t}}{\lambda_b - \lambda_a} = \frac{\lambda_b - \lambda_a}{\lambda_b - \lambda_a}$$

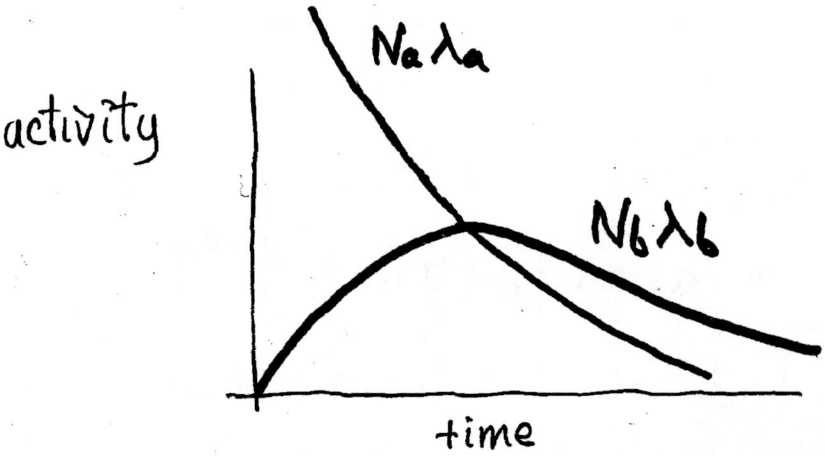

for $N_b(0) = 0$ and $\lambda_b < \lambda_a$

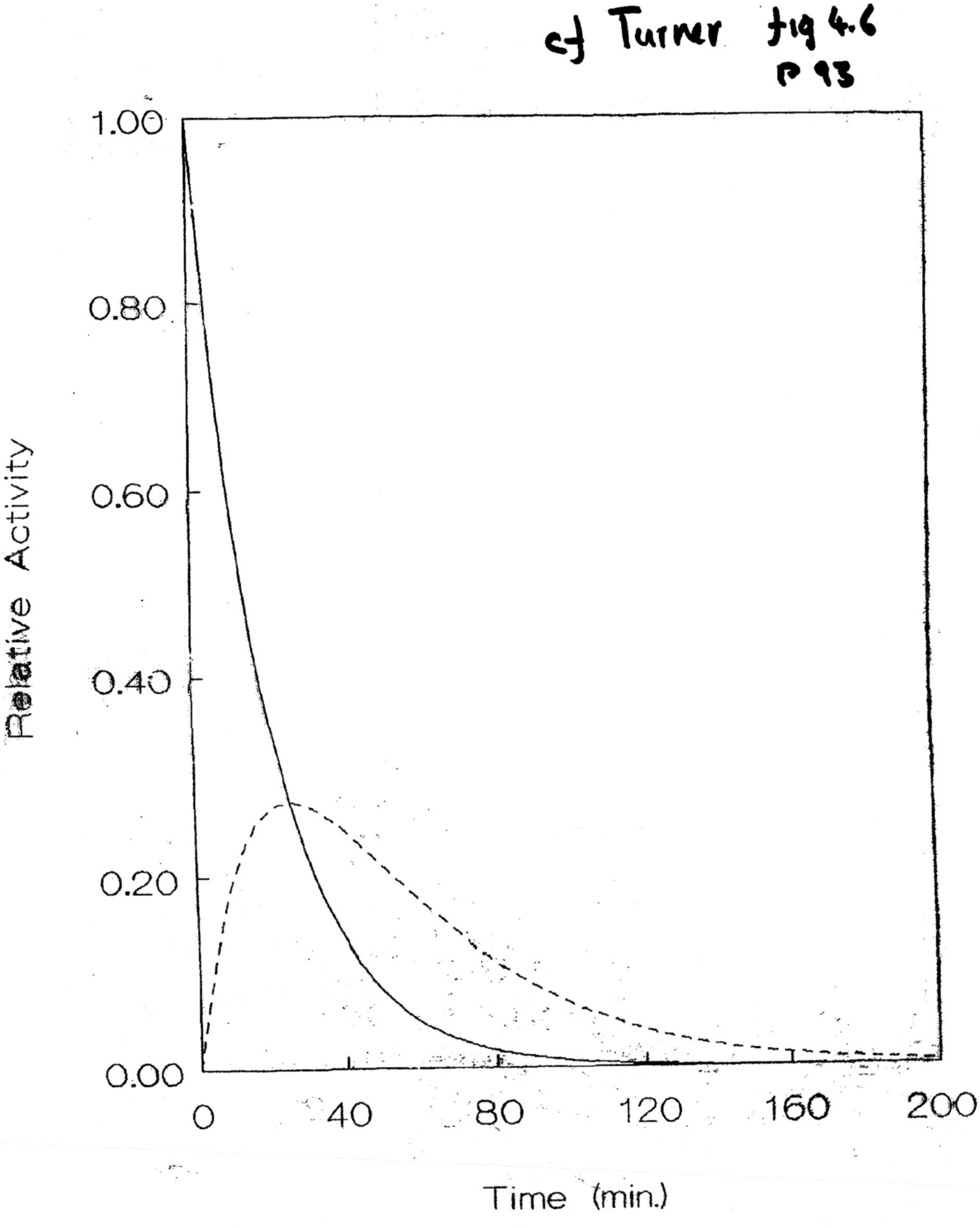
cf Turner fig 4.6
p 93
1.00
0.80
0.60
0.40
0.20
0.00
Relative Activity
0
40
80
120
160
200
Time (min.)

production of radio isotopes

- constant rate of formation
- decay of product radio isotope

$$\frac{dN}{dt} = k - \lambda N$$

$$= -\lambda\left(N - k/\lambda\right)$$

$$\frac{dN}{\left(N - k/\lambda\right)} = -\lambda \, dt$$

$$\ln\left(N - k/\lambda\right) = -\lambda t + c$$

$$N - k/\lambda = e^{-\lambda t} . e^{c}$$

if $N = 0$ at $t = 0$ then $e^{c} = -k/\lambda$

$$N = k/\lambda \left(1 - e^{-\lambda t}\right)$$

what is k? number of target nuclei $\frac{m.a.N_A}{A}$
flux of bombarding particles, ϕ
probability of interaction, σ

$$N = \phi\sigma \frac{m.a.N_A}{A\lambda}\left(1 - e^{-\lambda t}\right)$$

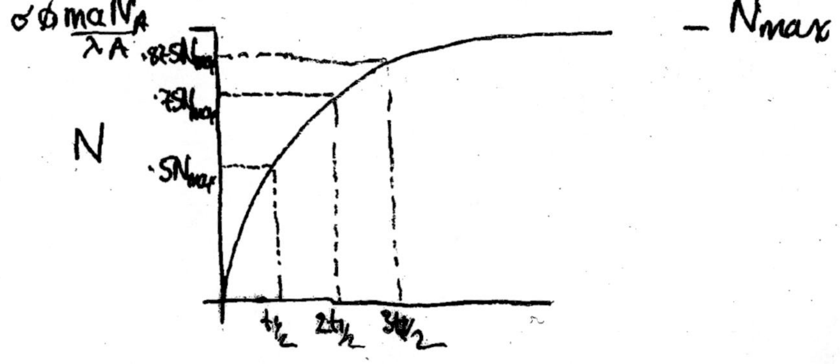

Interaction of Radiation with matter

charged particles	neutral particles
heavy – p, α	photons
light – β	neutrons

regardless of energy loss mechanism can calculate maximum energy transfer in a single interaction

consider frame of reference in which target particle is at rest

kinetic energy: $\frac{1}{2} m_1 v_1^2 = \frac{1}{2} m_1 v_1'^2 + \frac{1}{2} m_2 v_2'^2$

$$m_1 (v_1^2 - v_1'^2) = m_2 v_2'^2 \qquad ①$$

momentum: $m_1 v_1 = m_1 v_1' + m_2 v_2'$

$$m_1 (v_1 - v_1') = m_2 v_2' \qquad ②$$

divide ① by ② $\quad v_1 + v_1' = v_2'$

so $m_1 v_1 = m_1 v_1' + m_2 v_1 + m_2 v_1'$

$$v_1' = \frac{(m_1 - m_2) v_1}{(m_1 + m_2)}$$

$$\tfrac{1}{2} m_2 v_2'^2 = \tfrac{1}{2} m_2 (v_1 + v_1')^2 = \tfrac{1}{2} m_2 \left(v_1 + \frac{v_1(m_1 - m_2)}{m_1 + m_2}\right)^2$$

$$= \frac{\tfrac{1}{2} m_2 v_1^2}{(m_1 + m_2)^2} \left(m_1 + m_2 + m_1 - m_2\right)^2$$

$$= \frac{\tfrac{1}{2} m_1 v_1^2 4 m_1 m_2}{(m_1 + m_2)^2}$$

$$= \frac{4 m_1 m_2 E}{(m_1 + m_2)^2}$$

where E is the initial kinetic energy

most interactions are with atomic electrons

for non-relativistic proton, E_p, maximum energy transfer $= \dfrac{4 \times 931.5 \times 0.511\, E_p}{(931.5 + 0.5)^2}$

$$= 2.2 \times 10^{-3} \times E_p$$

for non-relativistic α, E_α, maximum energy transfer $= \dfrac{4 \times 4 \times 931.5 \times 0.511\, E_\alpha}{(4 \times 931.5 + 0.5)^2}$

$$= 5.5 \times 10^{-4}\, E_\alpha$$

for β particles the two rest masses (incident particle and target atomic electron) are equal.

the non-relativistic formula gives maximum energy transfer as the full energy

in practice protons & α's lose energy in large number of small energy transfer interactions

β's lose energy in small number of large energy transfer interactions

heavy charged particle (α, p)

light charged particle (β)

can define average energy lost per collision Q_{avg} and probability per unit distance travelled that an interaction occurs, μ

then stopping power $-\frac{dE}{dx} = \mu Q_{avg}$

Thurs 20th.
Fri 21st

what does energy transfer depend on?

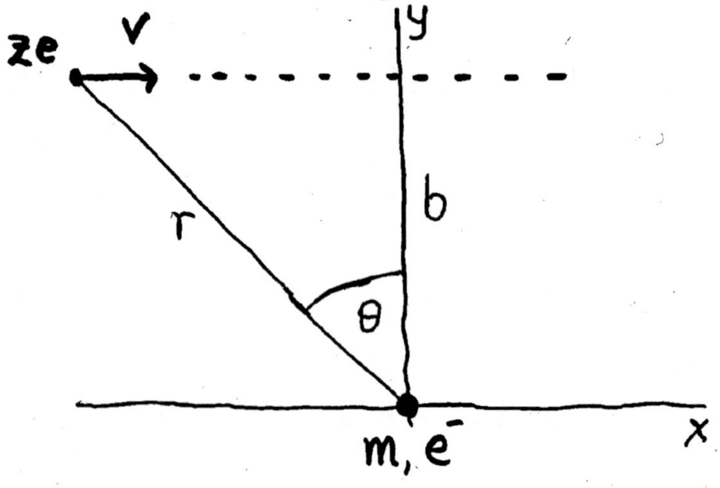

charged particle moving past electron, closest approach is impact parameter, b

electron initially free and at rest

interaction takes place rapidly

there is a Coulomb force between charged particle and electron

$$F = \frac{k_0 z e^2}{r^2}$$

F_x is symmetrical and results in no net energy transfer, however $F_y = F\cos\theta$

momentum transferred to electron

$$p = \int_{-\infty}^{\infty} F_y \, dt = \int_{-\infty}^{\infty} F \cos\theta \, dt$$

$$= k_0 z e^2 \int_{-\infty}^{\infty} \frac{\cos\theta}{r^2} \, dt$$

$$\int_{-\infty}^{\infty} \frac{\cos\theta}{r^2} \, dt = 2 \int_0^{\infty} \frac{b}{r} \cdot \frac{1}{r^2} \, dt$$

$$= 2b \int_0^{\infty} \frac{dt}{(b^2 + V^2 t^2)^{3/2}}$$

$$= \frac{2b}{V^3} \int_0^{\infty} \frac{dt}{\left(\frac{b^2}{V^2} + t^2\right)^{3/2}}$$

$$= \frac{2b}{V^3} \left[\frac{t}{\frac{b^2}{V^2}\left(\frac{b^2}{V^2} + t^2\right)^{1/2}} \right]_0^{\infty}$$

$$= 2b \left[\frac{t}{b^2 (b^2 + V^2 t^2)^{1/2}} \right]_0^{\infty}$$

$$= \frac{2b}{V b^2} \left[\frac{Vt}{(b^2 + V^2 t^2)^{1/2}} \right]_0^{\infty}$$

$$= \frac{2}{Vb} \left[\sin\theta \right]_{0^\circ}^{90^\circ} = \frac{2}{Vb}$$

so $p = \dfrac{2 k_0 z e^2}{V b}$

and energy transferred, $Q = \dfrac{p^2}{2m} = \dfrac{2 k_0^2 z^2 e^4}{m V^2 b^2}$

so, energy transferred per collision needs to be adjusted for number target electrons to get energy loss per unit path length, if n electrons per unit volume

$$-\frac{dE}{dx} \propto \frac{k_0^2 z^2 e^4 n}{m V^2} \times \text{distance terms}$$

z - atomic number of bombarding particle

e - magnitude of electron charge

n - target electron density

m - (<u>target</u>) electron rest mass

V - velocity of <u>bombarding</u> particle

full relativistic quantum mechanical treatment (Bethe formula) gives

$$-\frac{dE}{dx} = \frac{4\pi k_0^2 z^2 e^4 n}{m c^2 \beta^2} \left[\ln\left\{ \frac{2mc^2\beta^2}{I(1-\beta^2)} \right\} - \beta^2 \right]$$

c - speed of light in vacuum

β - V/c (bombarding particle)

I - mean excitation energy of medium

└ avg. energy to take e⁻ away in medium

consider a 5 MeV α-particle in air

$$-\frac{dE}{dx} = \frac{5.08 \times 10^{-31} z^2 n}{\beta^2}\left[\ln\left\{\frac{1.02\times10^6 \beta^2}{I_{(eV)}(1-\beta^2)}\right\} - \beta^2\right] \text{ MeV cm}^{-1}$$

(props of bombarding particle: z^2, β^2; prop of medium: n)

put $F(\beta) = \ln\left\{\frac{1.02\times10^6\beta^2}{1-\beta^2}\right\} - \beta^2$

then $$-\frac{dE}{dx} = \frac{5.08\times10^{-31} z^2 n}{\beta^2}\left[F(\beta) - \ln I_{(eV)}\right] \text{ MeV cm}^{-1}$$

(Turner eq'n 5.32–5.34)

need to find: z^2, n, β^2, I

and calculate $F(\beta)$

for α, $z = 2$, $\underline{z^2 = 4}$

for 5 MeV α, kinetic energy, $T = m_\alpha c^2\left(\frac{1}{\sqrt{1-\beta^2}} - 1\right)$

$$5 = 931.5 \times 4\left(\frac{1}{\sqrt{1-\beta^2}} - 1\right)$$

$$\underline{\beta^2 = 2.678 \times 10^{-3}}$$

think of $\frac{M}{E}$ if v. small, not v. relativistic.

for n_{air}: 1 m^3 air has mass 1.29×10^3 g

of this ~0.8 is nitrogen and ~0.2 is oxygen

electrons m^{-3} = $6.02\times10^{23} \times 1.29\times10^3 \left(\frac{.8\times7}{14} + \frac{.2\times8}{16}\right)$

$$\underline{n = 3.88 \times 10^{26} \text{ m}^{-3}}$$

$\left(e^-/m^3\right)$

Turner equns 5.24 → 5.26 gives

$$I = \begin{cases} 19.0 & \text{for } Z = 1 \\ 11.2 + 11.7Z & 2 \le Z \le 13 \\ 52.8 + 8.71Z & Z > 13 \end{cases} \text{ eV}$$

approx

2 ways to do it (most cases doesn't matter which)

$I_{air} = 0.8 I_N + 0.2 I_O$
$= 0.8 \times 93.1 + 0.2 \times 104.8$
$= 95.44$

$\ln I = 4.558$

$$\ln I_{air} = \frac{.8 \times 7}{.8 \times 7 + .2 \times 8} \ln I_N + \frac{.2 \times 8}{.8 \times 7 + .2 \times 8} \ln I_O$$

$$= \frac{5.6}{7.2} \ln(93.1) + \frac{1.6}{7.2} \ln(104.8)$$

$= 4.560$

for some this is better

$$F(\beta) = \ln\left\{\frac{1.02 \times 10^6 \times 2.678 \times 10^{-3}}{1 - 2.678 \times 10^{-3}}\right\} - 2.678 \times 10^{-3}$$

$F(\beta) = 7.913$

so $$-\frac{dE}{dx} = \frac{5.08 \times 10^{-31} \times 4 \times 3.88 \times 10^{26}}{2.678 \times 10^{-3}} (7.913 - 4.558)$$

$$= 0.988 \text{ MeV cm}^{-1}$$

as α energy decreases, stopping power increases

eg for 3 MeV α-particle $\beta^2 = 1.608 \times 10^{-3}$

$F(\beta) = 7.403$

$$-\frac{dE}{dx} = 1.395 \text{ MeV cm}^{-1}$$

note even air is a radiation sheild against α particles

5 MeV α-particle in graphite

$z^2 = 4$, $\beta^2 = 2.678 \times 10^{-3}$ as before

$n_{graphite}$: 1 m^3 graphite has mass 1.9×10^6 g

(all Carbon

$$n = 1.9 \times 10^6 \times 6.02 \times 10^{23} \times \frac{6}{12}$$

$$= 5.719 \times 10^{29} \; m^{-3}$$ ← not suprising, graphite more dense than air.

$I = 81.4$ eV $\quad \ln I = 4.399$

$$-\frac{dE}{dx} = \frac{5.08 \times 10^{-31} \times 4 \times 5.719 \times 10^{29}}{2.678 \times 10^{-3}} (7.913 - 4.399)$$

$$= 1525 \text{ MeV cm}^{-1} \quad (= 0.15 \text{ MeV } \mu m^{-1})$$

for materials of similar atomic number, stopping power varies mostly with density

so $-\frac{dE}{dx}/\rho \approx$ const

5 MeV α in air $\quad -\frac{dE}{dx}/\rho = 766$ MeV $cm^2 g^{-1}$

5 MeV α in graphite $\quad -\frac{dE}{dx}/\rho = 803$ MeV $cm^2 g^{-1}$

can extend to more complicated mediums based on density (ex. tissue)

Range

evaluate numerically, $-\frac{dE}{dx}$ for 5 MeV α in air

$= 0.987 \text{ MeV cm}^{-1}$ => will lose 0.5 MeV in $\simeq$ 0.507

energy (MeV)	β^2	$F(\beta)$	$-\frac{dE}{dx}$ (MeV cm^{-1})	distance for E interval (cm)	cumulative distance (cm
5.0	2.68×10^{-3}	7.913	0.987		
4.5	2.41×10^{-3}	7.808	1.062	0.507	0.507
4.0	2.14×10^{-3}	7.690	1.151	0.471	0.978
3.5	1.88×10^{-3}	7.557	1.259	0.434	1.412
3.0	1.61×10^{-3}	7.403	1.394	0.397	1.809
2.5	1.34×10^{-3}	7.221	1.565	0.359	2.168
2.0	1.07×10^{-3}	6.998	1.792	0.319	2.487
1.5	8.05×10^{-4}	6.710	2.107	0.279	2.766
1.0	5.37×10^{-4}	6.305	2.564	0.237	3.003
0.5	2.68×10^{-4}	5.612	3.091	0.195	3.198
0.25	1.34×10^{-4}	4.919	2.109	0.081	3.279
0				0.119	3.398

since stopping power scales approximately as density for materials of similar z, range will to

for 5 MeV α in air ~ 34 mm

in soft tissue, range $34 \times 1000 \times \frac{1.29 \times 10^{-3}}{1}$ μ

$= 44\ \mu m$

very small.

range 44 μm in $\rho = 1\,g\,cm^{-3}$ tissue

can also express as $4.4\,mg\,cm^{-2}$

skin has minimum thickness of $\sim 7\,mg\,cm^{-2}$

in general α-particles from radioactive decay cannot penetrate the skin

---

range straggling   thought experiment

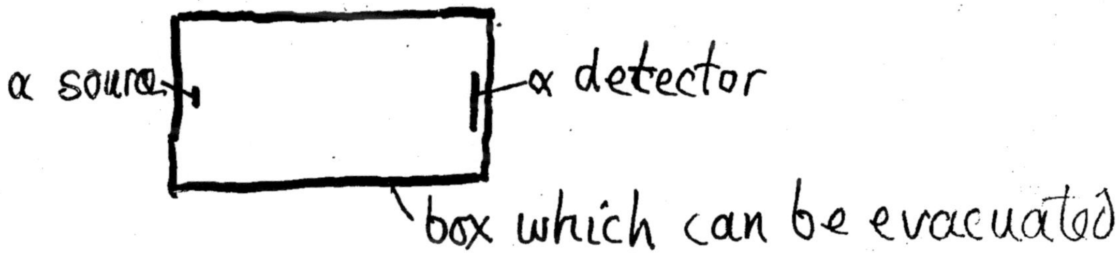

evacuate box and count α-particles

allow some air in, count again; repeat

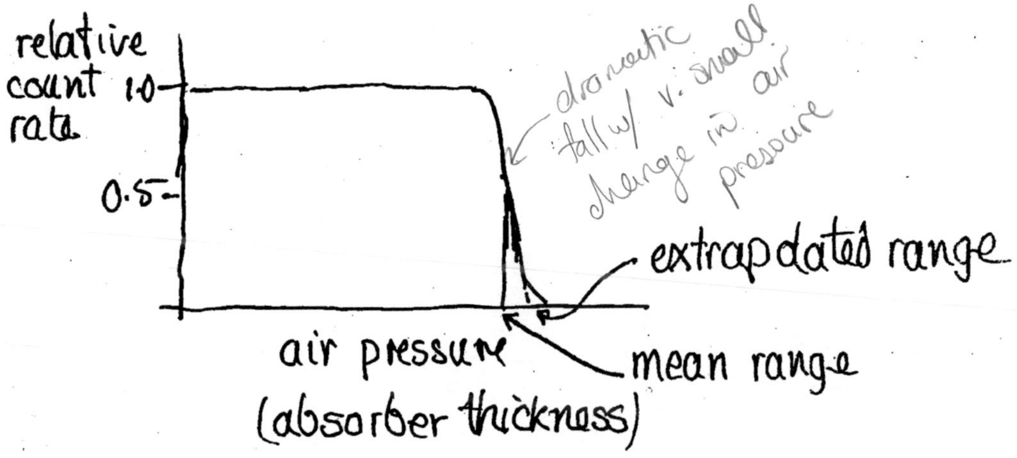

α energy spectrum observed by detector as
pressure rises (absorption increases)

$\frac{N(E)}{dE}$ a) no pressure E_α ↗energy of detected particles

$\frac{N(E)}{dE}$ b) let a little air in E_α

$\frac{N(E)}{dE}$ c) more pressure E_α

$\frac{N(E)}{dE}$ d) even more pressure E_α ← right of edge of graph on previous page

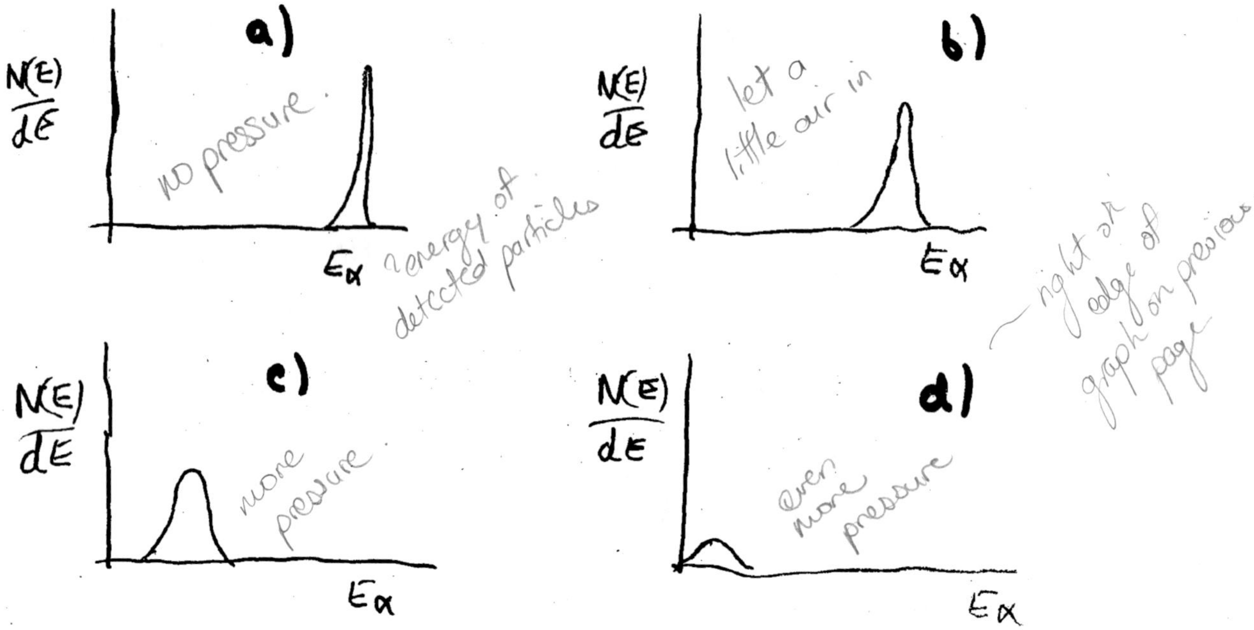

a) in vacuum, b) & c) successively increasing
   pressure   area is same for a), b), c)

d) absorption corresponding to mean range,
   area is half that in a), b), c)

fri 21st

light charged particle $-\beta^{\pm}$

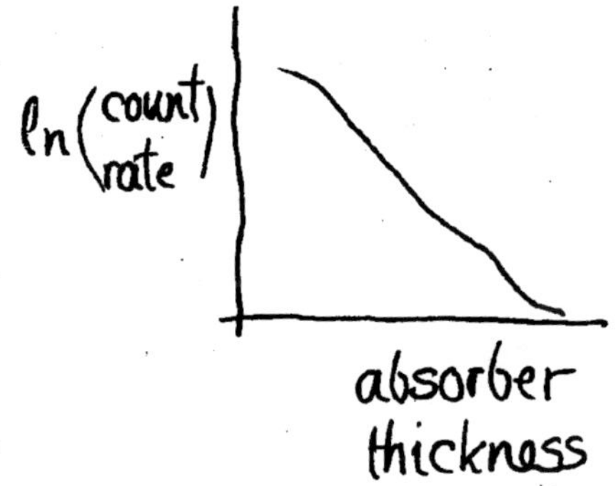

count rate not flat because β spectra are not monoenergetic also straggling at end as in α absorption

for electrons need to consider collision (Coulomb interactions, as with p & α) also radiative energy loss, as charge (electron) undergoes significant acceleration in Coulomb interaction

$$\left(-\frac{dE}{dx}\right)^{\pm}_{total} = \left(-\frac{dE}{dx}\right)^{\pm}_{collision} + \left(-\frac{dE}{dx}\right)^{\pm}_{radiative}$$

collision stopping power is similar to that for heavy charged particles

Turner eq'n 6.1

$$\left(-\frac{dE}{dx}\right)^{\pm}_{col} = \frac{4\pi k_0^2 e^4 n}{mc^2\beta^2}\left[\ln\left(\frac{mc^2\tau\sqrt{\tau+2}}{\sqrt{2}\,I}\right) + F^{\pm}(\beta)\right]$$

$$\tau = T/mc^2 = E_\beta / 0.511\,(\text{MeV})$$

$F^{\pm}$ represents two factors, F^- and F^+ which apply to electrons and positrons respectively; and they are different

one reason is that β^- and target electron are identical particles, after a collision can't tell which was which before collision

β^+ is not identical to target electron

$$F^-(\beta) = \frac{1-\beta^2}{2}\left[1 + \frac{\tau^2}{8} - (2\tau+1)\ln 2\right]$$

$$F^+(\beta) = \ln 2 - \frac{\beta^2}{24}\left[23 + \frac{14}{\tau+2} + \frac{10}{(\tau+2)^2} + \frac{4}{(\tau+2)^3}\right]$$

Turner equ'ns 6.2, 6.3

this can again be made (slightly) more convenient computationally by putting

$$G^{\pm}(\beta) = \ln\left(3.61\times10^5\,\tau\sqrt{\tau+2}\right) + F^{\pm}(\beta)$$

equ'n 6.6

and

$$\left(-\frac{dE}{dx}\right)^{\pm}_{col} = \frac{5.08\times10^{-31} n}{\beta^2}\left[G^{\pm}(\beta) - \ln(I_{eV})\right] \text{ MeV cm}^{-1}$$

equ'n 6.5

what about a 1 MeV β-particle in air

consider both β^- and β^+

$n_{air} = 3.88\times10^{26}$ m^{-3} $\qquad \ln(I_{air}) = 4.558$

$\beta^2 = 1 - (1+\tau)^{-2} = 1 - \left(1 + \frac{E}{.511}\right)^{-2} = 0.8856$

$\tau = 1.957 \qquad F^-(\beta) = -0.110$; $F^+(\beta) = -0.312$

$G^-(\beta) = 14.046$; $G^+(\beta) = 13.844$

$$\left(-\frac{dE}{dx}\right)^{-}_{col} = 2.112\times10^{-3}\ \text{MeV cm}^{-1} \qquad \left(-\frac{dE}{dx}\right)^{+}_{col} = 2.067\times10^{-3}\ \text{MeV cm}^{-1}$$

$$\left(-\frac{dE}{dx}\right)^{+}_{col} \Big/ \left(-\frac{dE}{dx}\right)^{-}_{col} = 0.979$$

now consider 1 MeV $\beta^{\pm}$ in graphite

$$n_{graphite} = 5.719\times10^{29}\ m^{-3} \qquad \ln(I_{graphite}) = 4.399$$

$$\left(-\frac{dE}{dx}\right)^{-}_{col} = 3.165\ \text{MeV cm}^{-1} \qquad \left(-\frac{dE}{dx}\right)^{+}_{col} = 3.098\ \text{MeV cm}^{-1}$$

what about variation of stopping power with energy?

in air

E_e (MeV)	$\left(-\frac{dE}{dx}\right)^{-}_{col}$ (MeV cm^{-1})	$\left(-\frac{dE}{dx}\right)^{+}_{col}$ (MeV cm^{-1})
1	2.11×10^{-3}	2.07×10^{-3}
0.338	2.54×10^{-3}	2.54×10^{-3}
0.1	4.60×10^{-3}	4.78×10^{-3}
0.01	0.0248	0.0275
10^{-3}	0.126	0.153

Bremsstrahlung

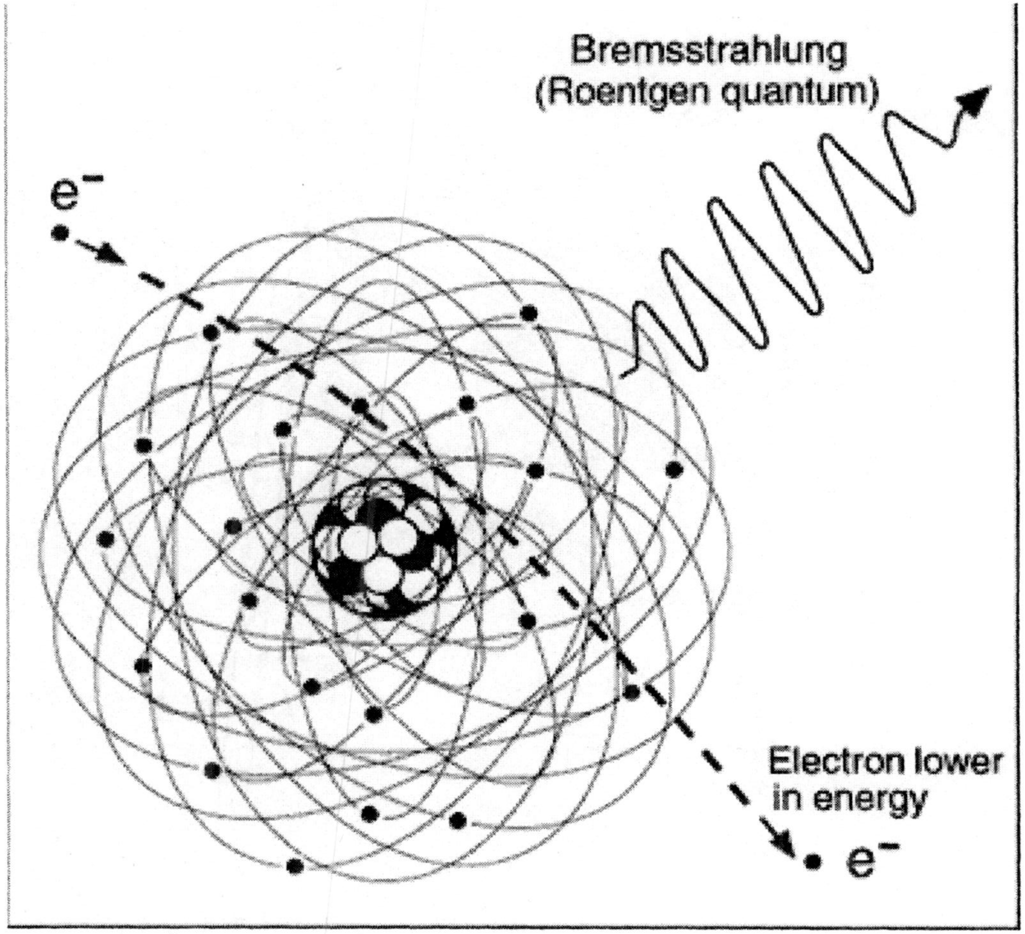

The energy the beta particle loses as it is slows down or changes direction has to go somewhere.

It leaves the interaction as a photon.

Simple Schematic of an X-Ray Tube

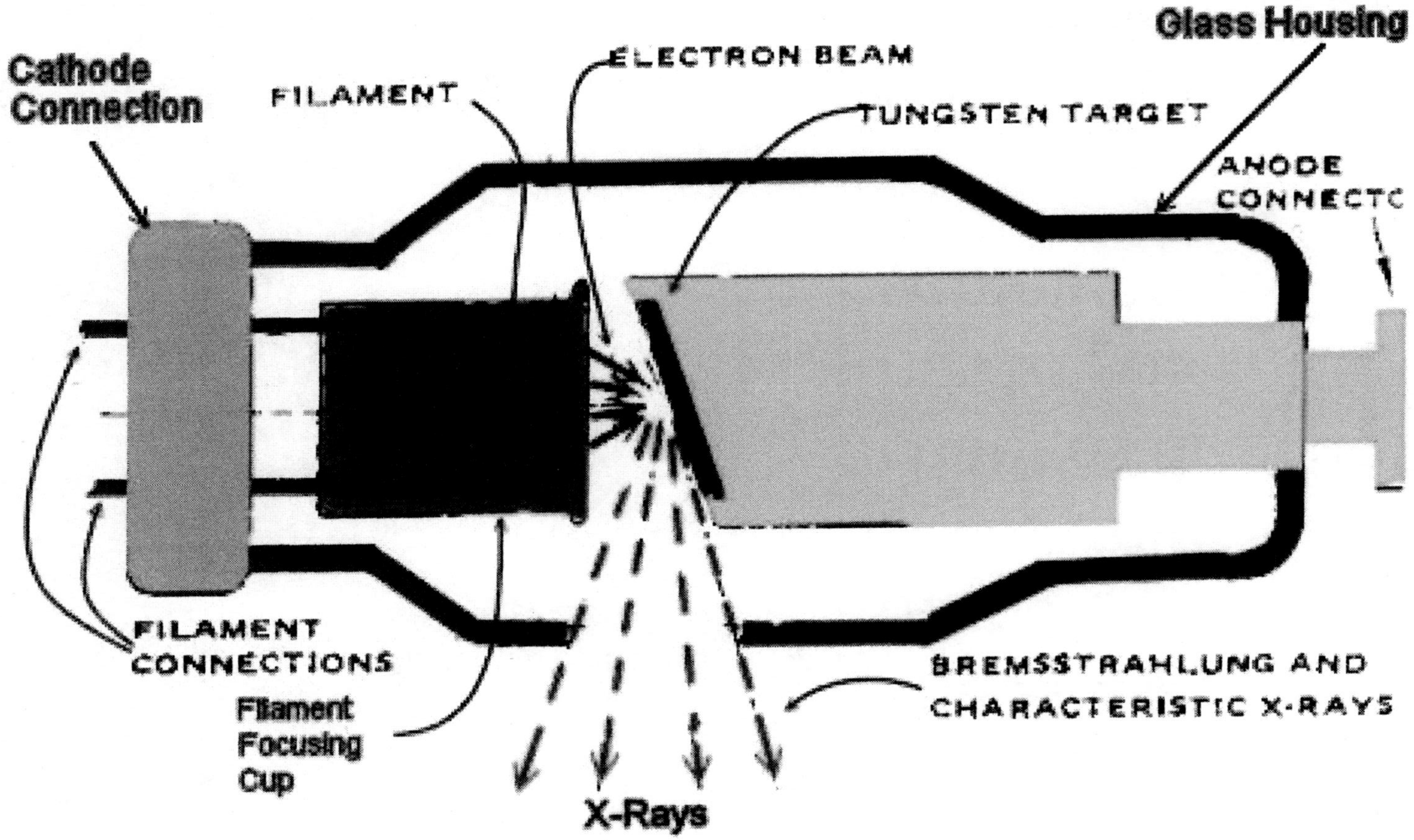

Radiative stopping power – bremsstrahlung

when a charge undergoes acceleration it emits electromagnetic radiation

when a particle of mass m, charge ze enters field of nucleus of charge Ze it undergoes acceleration $\propto zZ/m$

radiation intensity $\propto z^2Z^2/m^2$

for a thin target intensity nearly constant with energy

after Dyson, fig 2.2, p 10

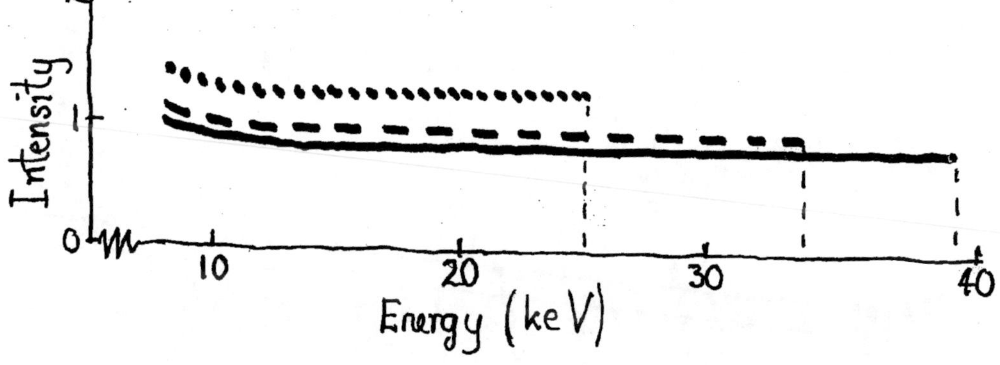

electrons of energies 25, 34, 40 keV on

thin aluminum target

intensity from thick target is superposition of successive thin targets

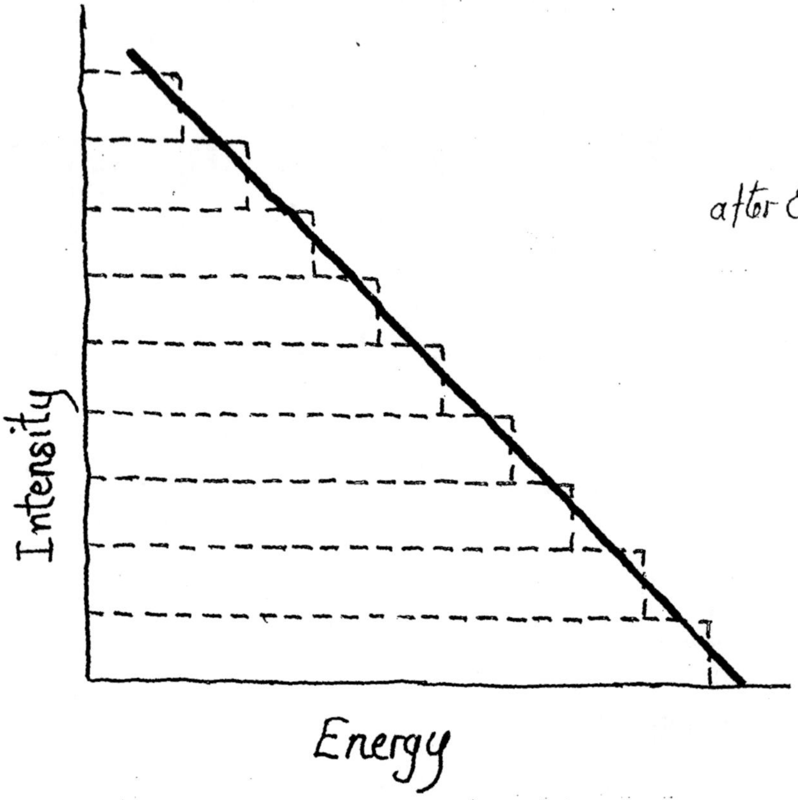

both 'base' and 'height' are proportional to energy, so total intensity proportional to energy^2

any practical bremsstrahlung source, such as an x-ray set, has filtration

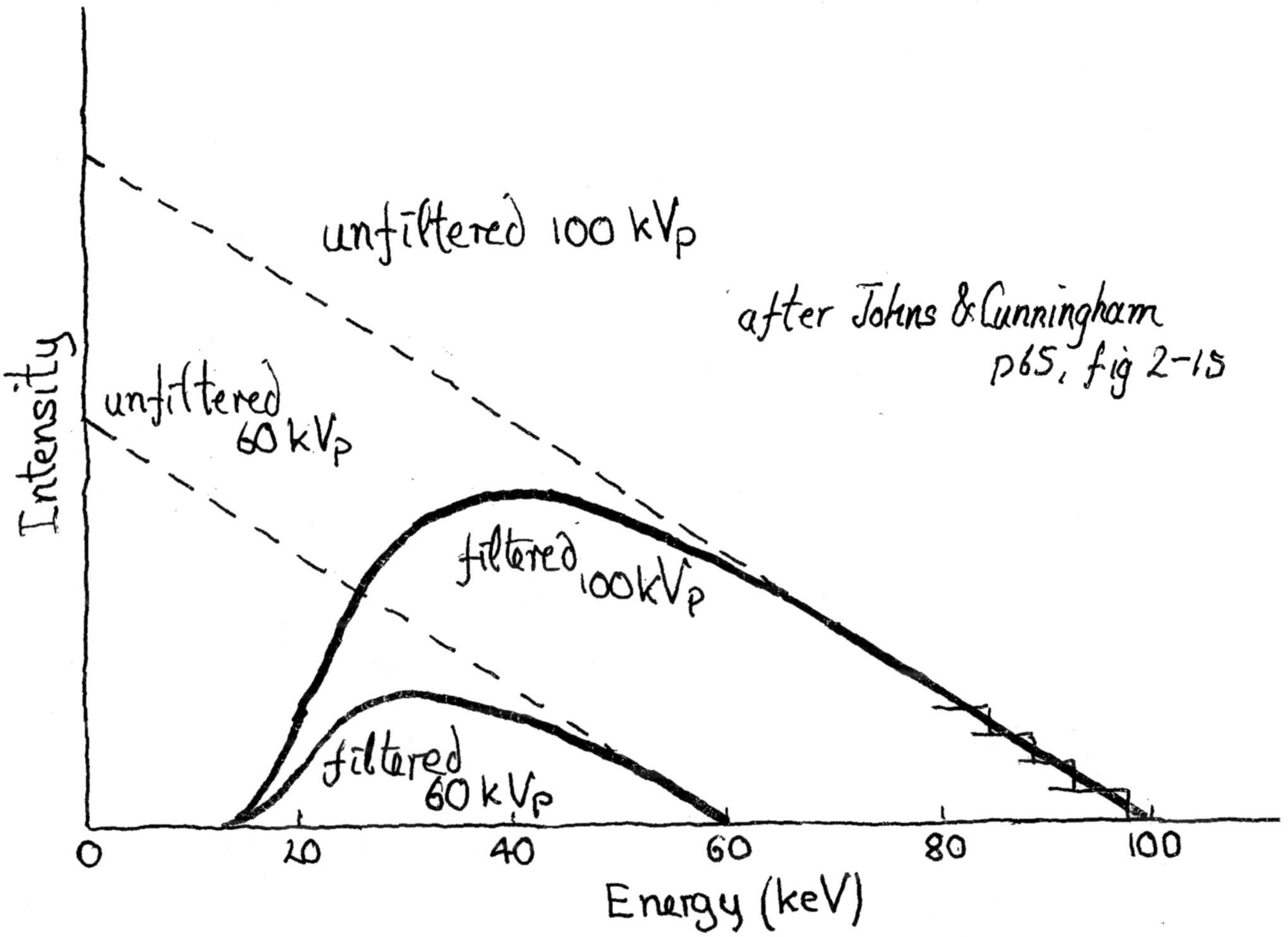

filtration tends to remove lower energies preferentially

in addition, there will be characteristic x-rays from the target, if the incident electron energy is high enough to excite them

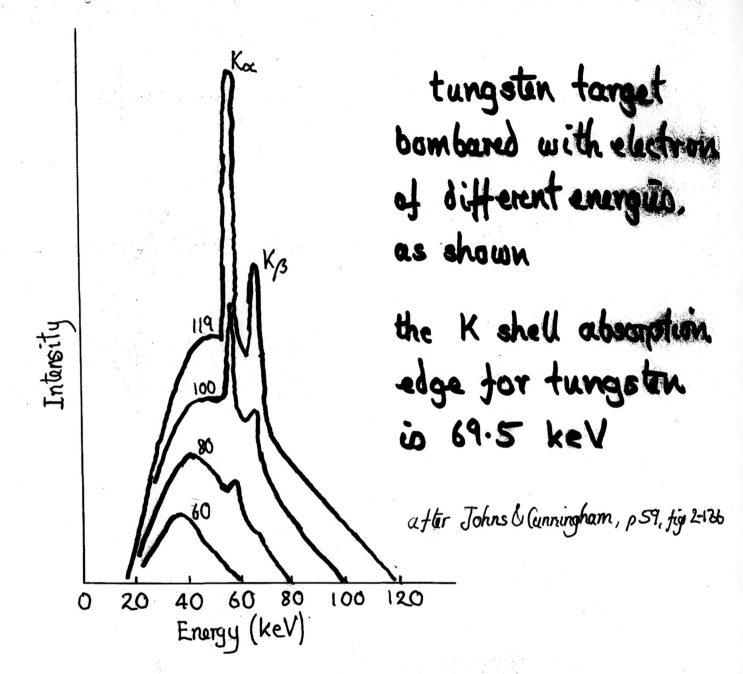

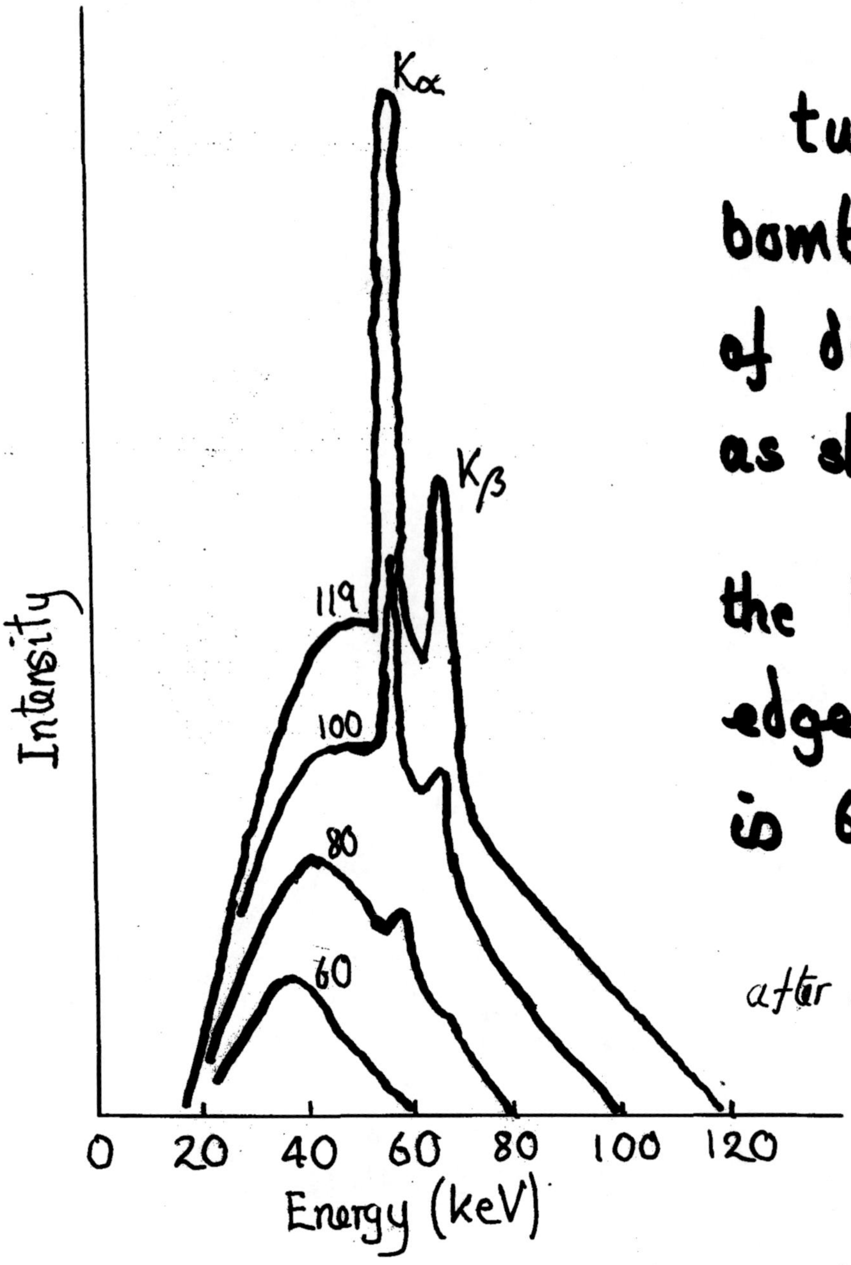

tungsten target bombared with electrons of different energies, as shown

the K shell absorption edge for tungsten is 69.5 keV

after Johns & Cunningham, p59, fig 2-13b

the intensity, I, depends on the initial kinetic energy of the electron, T, the target atomic number, Z and the current, A

$I = kZT^2A$, where k is a constant

the proportion of the total electron energy that is emitted as bremsstrahlung (as opposed to collision loss) is given by:

radiation yield, $Y = \dfrac{6 \times 10^{-4} ZT}{1 + 6 \times 10^{-4} ZT}$

for decay βs, $Y \simeq 3.5 \times 10^{-4} Z T_{\beta max}$

this means that high atomic number materials are not the best shield for $\beta^{\pm}$, because of a relatively high yield of e-m radiation, which is more penetrating than βs

a good combination would be Al $(Z = 13)$ to absorb βs surrounded by Pb $(Z = 82)$ to absorb bremsstrahlung (+ any γ rays)

consider medical linear accelerator

20 MeV electrons onto tungsten (W) target

$Y = 0.47$

proton induced x-ray emission analysis (pixe)

2.5 MeV p^+ on tissue ($\bar{Z} \sim 7.4$)

Y_p for protons will be $\left(\frac{m_e}{m_p}\right)^2 \times Y_e$ for electrons

$= 2.97 \times 10^{-7} Y_e$

ie x-rays on much smaller background when protons used instead of electrons

- This is the core of the McMaster Nuclear Reactor;
- While the reactor is operating the Cerenkov Radiation makes the core glow blue;
- When the reactor is shut down each night, the glow goes away.

D.F. Moscu

Cerenkov radiation

electron (charged particle) passing through medium produces polarization

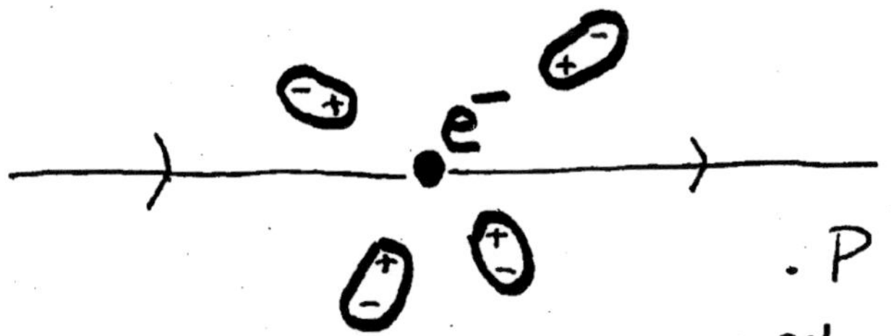

polarization varies with time and, being a time varying charge distribution, can produce a radiation field at a distant point, P

for slowly moving particles field vectors at P have no definite phase relationship and radiation field self-cancels

if particle velocity exceeds velocity of light in medium of refractive index, n

$$v = \beta c > c/n$$

can get coherence between the contributions at P from polarization at different points along path of particle

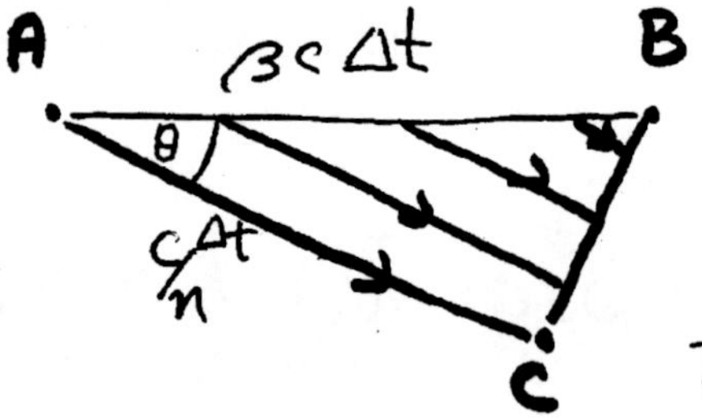

$$\cos\theta = \frac{c/n}{\beta c} = \frac{1}{\beta n}$$

this is only defined if $\beta n \geq 1$

so threshold for Čerenkov radiation

$$T_{th} = Mc^2\left(\sqrt{1+\frac{1}{n^2-1}} - 1\right)$$

for water $n = 1{\cdot}33$

$T_{th} = 0{\cdot}264$ MeV for electrons

481·4 MeV for protons

it has been shown that number of photons at a given wavelength, λ, is proportional to $1/\lambda^2$

so bias towards blue-violet end of spectrum

in water, absorption structure results in characteristic bright blue in swimming pool reactor

range

in low Z materials (like tissue)

$$R = 0.412\,T^{(1.27 - 0.0954 \ln T)}\ g\,cm^{-2}$$
or
$$\ln T = 6.63 - 3.24(3.29 - \ln R)^{1/2}$$
$\Big\}\ 0.01 \leq T \leq 2.5\ MeV$

$$R = 0.530\,T - 0.106 \quad g\,cm^{-2}$$
$$T = 1.89\,R + 0.200$$
$\Big\}\ T > 2.5\ MeV$

consider ^{32}P, $E_{\beta max} = 1.71$ MeV, $\bar{E}_{\beta} = 0.695$ MeV

range in tissue	R	0.792 cm	0.256 cm
	^{3}H	0.0186 MeV	
		5.75 μm	

nearly all $\beta^{\pm}$ energy is absorbed in tissue, close to where the $\beta^{\pm}$ emitter is located

except: bremsstrahlung

annihilation photons

Interaction of photons with matter

several quite distinct types of interaction

photo-electric
Compton
pair production

} principal processes for energy transfer to medium

photo nuclear - can produce specific shielding problems

elastic, Thompson and Rayleigh scattering

Photo-electric effect

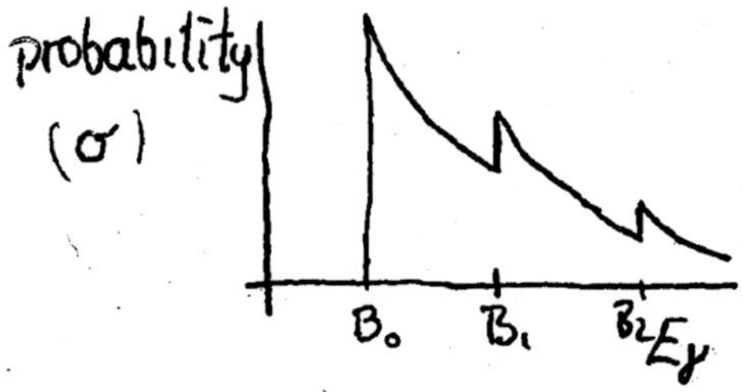

if E_γ > electron binding energy (ϕ)

then can get photo-electric effect

photon is entirely absorbed

photo-electron has kinetic energy E_{pe} given by

$$E_{pe} = E_\gamma - \phi$$

probability (σ) is maximum when photo-electric effect is only just energetically possible

get different peaks in σ vs E_γ as different electron energy levels become involved

probability increases with atomic number and decreases with photon energy

$$\sigma \propto \frac{Z^4}{E_\gamma^3} \quad \text{(approximately)}$$

ϕ, electron binding energy released as characteristic x-rays or Auger electrons

gives rise to x-ray fluorescence

in most cases all the energy remains in the absorbing medium

Compton scattering (in many cases the predominant energy loss mechanism in tissue)

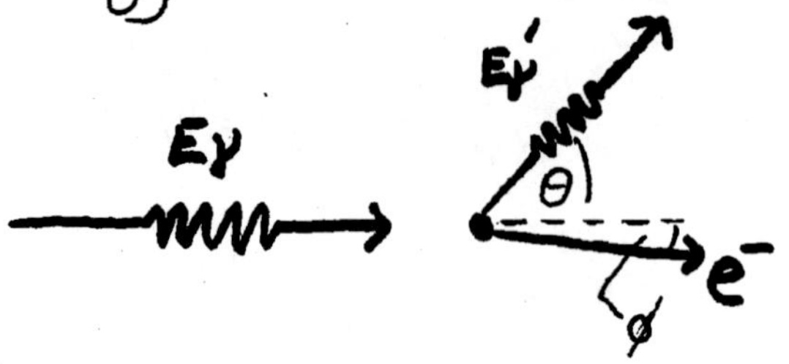

energy: $E_\gamma = E_\gamma' + T_e$, where T_e is the kinetic energy of the target electron

total electron energy, $E_e = m_e c^2$, where m_e is the relativistic electron mass

$$m_e = \frac{m_0}{(1 - v^2/c^2)^{1/2}}$$

momentum, $p_e = m_e v$

$$m_0^2 = m_e^2 (1 - v^2/c^2)$$

$$m_0^2 c^4 = m_e^2 c^4 - m_e^2 v^2 c^2$$

$$m_0^2 c^4 = E_e^2 - p_e^2 c^2, \quad E_e^2 - m_0^2 c^4 = p_e^2 c^2$$

but $E_e^2 = (m_0 c^2 + T_e)^2 = m_0^2 c^4 + T_e^2 + 2 m_0 c^2 T_e$

so $P_e^2 c^2 = T_e(T_e + 2m_0c^2)$

$$= (E_\gamma - E_\gamma')\{(E_\gamma - E_\gamma') + 2m_0c^2\}$$

$$P_e^2c^2 = E_\gamma^2 + E_\gamma'^2 - 2E_\gamma E_\gamma' + (E_\gamma - E_\gamma')2m_0c^2$$

conservation of momentum

$$\rightarrow \quad E_\gamma/c = E_\gamma'/c \cos\theta + P_e \cos\phi$$

$$\uparrow \quad 0 = \frac{E_\gamma'}{c}\sin\theta - P_e \sin\phi$$

from $\rightarrow$ $\quad P_e^2c^2\cos^2\phi = (E_\gamma - E_\gamma'\cos\theta)^2 = E_\gamma^2 + E_\gamma'^2\cos^2\theta - 2E_\gamma E_\gamma'\cos\theta$

from $\uparrow$ $\quad P_e^2c^2\sin^2\phi = E_\gamma'^2\sin^2\theta$

add $\quad P_e^2c^2 = E_\gamma^2 + E_\gamma'^2 - 2E_\gamma E_\gamma'\cos\theta$

from energy: $\quad P_e^2c^2 = E_\gamma^2 + E_\gamma'^2 - 2E_\gamma E_\gamma' + (E_\gamma - E_\gamma')2m_0c^2$

$$E_\gamma E_\gamma'(1-\cos\theta) = (E_\gamma - E_\gamma')m_0c^2$$

$$E_\gamma - E_\gamma' = E_\gamma'\frac{E_\gamma}{m_0c^2}(1-\cos\theta)$$

$$E_\gamma = E_\gamma'\left(1 + \frac{E_\gamma}{m_0c^2}(1-\cos\theta)\right)$$

$$\boxed{E_\gamma' = \frac{E_\gamma}{1 + \frac{E_\gamma}{m_0c^2}(1-\cos\theta)}}$$

spectrum from ^{137}Cs (^{137m}Ba) $E_\gamma = 661$ keV

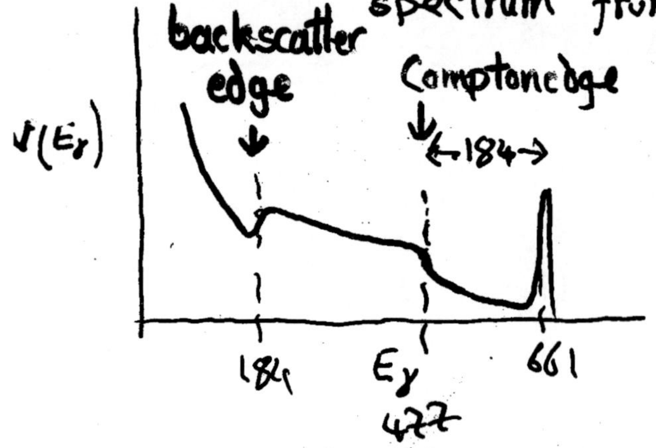

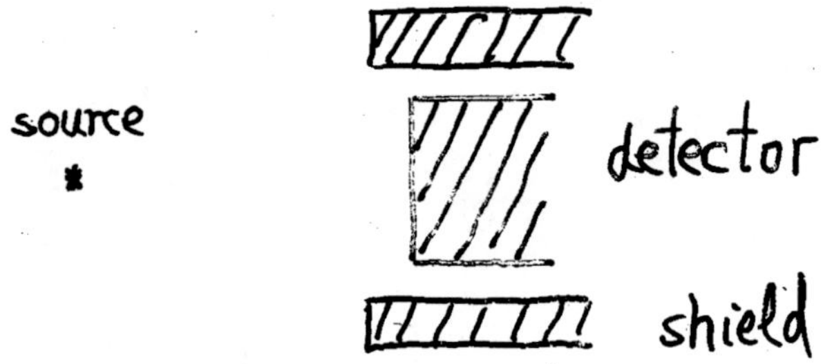

661 keV photon Compton scatter in detector

$$E_\gamma' = \frac{E_\gamma}{1 + \frac{E_\gamma}{511}(1 - \cos\theta)}$$

$$E'_{\gamma\,min} = \frac{E_\gamma}{1 + \frac{2E_\gamma}{511}}$$

for $E_\gamma = 661$ keV $\quad E'_{\gamma\,min} = 184$ keV

If γ-ray undergoes Compton scatter in detector, scattered γ-ray might escape. Energy of Compton electron remains in detector and equals full energy minus scattered γ-ray energy. Compton electron energy has maximum when scattered γ-ray has minimum energy, producing Compton edge, in this case at 477 keV.

If γ-ray undergoes Compton scatter in shielding, scattered γ-ray might enter detector. This has a minimum energy, producing the back scatter edge, in this case at 184 keV.

kinetic energy of electron is likely to be absorbed by medium

scattered photon may undergo another interaction or it may escape

energy of scattered photon varies with angle of scatter; it is a minimum for $\theta = 180°$ (backscatter)

in this case: $E'_{\gamma(min)} = \dfrac{E_\gamma}{1 + \dfrac{2E_\gamma}{m_0 c^2}}$

and $T_{e\,(max)} = \dfrac{2E_\gamma}{\dfrac{m_0 c^2}{E_\gamma} + 2}$

probability for Compton scattering depends largely on electron density

given that Compton scatter takes place, probability varies with angle of scatter and energy, in general high angle scatter => large energy transfer most probable

pair production

photon with $E_\gamma \geq 2m_0c^2$ can be converted to an electron-positron pair in field of nucleus (can also occur in atomic electron field [triplet production], but much less probable and require $E_\gamma \geq 4m_0c^2$)

probability increases $\sim Z^2$ and (fairly slowly) with increasing E_γ

full photon energy converted to electron plus positron, each with kinetic energy (T)

$$E_\gamma = m_0c^2(\beta^+) + T_{\beta^+} + m_0c^2(\beta^-) + T_{\beta^-}$$

β^+ and β^- both slow down in usual way depositing energy $T_{\beta^+} + T_{\beta^-} = E_\gamma - 2m_0c^2$

positron then annihilates with an electron releasing further energy $2m_0c^2$ as photons which may or may not interact in medium

photo-nuclear reactions

eg $^{206}_{82}Pb + \gamma \rightarrow ^{205}_{82}Pb + ^{1}_{0}n + Q$

Δ (MeV) $-23.79 + 0 = -23.77 + 8.07 + Q$

$Q = -8.09$ MeV

this particular reaction has a threshold of ~8 MeV

in general, photonuclear reactions require high energy photons

(γ, n) is usually more probable and often has lower threshold than (γ, p) because proton has to escape nucleus through Coulomb barrier

exceptions to needing high energy photons:

$^{2}_{1}H + \gamma \rightarrow ^{1}_{1}H + ^{1}_{0}n + Q$

Δ (MeV) $13.136 + 0 = 7.289 + 8.071 + Q$

$Q = -2.224$

natural ^{2}H in body can lead to neutron production

$$^{9}_{4}Be + \gamma \rightarrow {}^{8}_{4}Be + {}^{1}_{0}n + Q$$

$$\Delta\,(MeV) \quad 11.348 + 0 = 4.942 + 8.071 + Q$$

$$Q = -1.665 \text{ MeV}$$

γ-rays from an ^{124}Sb source (1.691 MeV) used with Be to form a photo neutron source

photo nuclear is never a major interaction process

however, it can produce secondary radiation of a different type (neutrons from photons) which requires different types of shielding material

elastic scattering

photon scatters off electron (Thompson) or nucleus (nuclear Thompson), low probability, affecting low energy photons

photon can scatter off atom as a whole (Rayleigh), no significant loss in energy, most probable for high Z, low E_γ and small angle

in those limits it can be a significant interaction process, but energy loss remains very small, so it does not matter dosimetrically

an application:

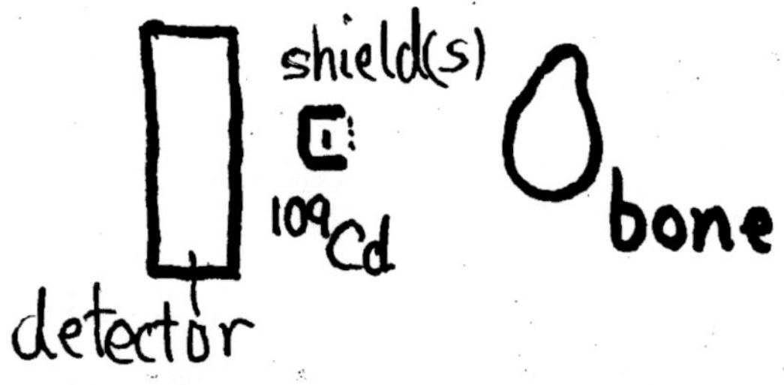

^{109}Cd emits Ag x-rays (~1 per decay), 88 keV γ-rays (.036 per decay)

thin Cu shield absorbs most Ag x-rays, but few 88 keV γ-rays

thicker shield (~2mm W) prevents x-rays or γ-rays reaching detector directly

88 keV γ-rays interact with bone (in leg)

some photoelectric with C, H, O, N, Ca, P, but not much, because low Z

major interaction is Compton, median angle of scatter ~ 160°, so median

$$E_\gamma' = \frac{88}{1+\frac{88}{511}(1-\cos 160°)} = 66 \text{ keV}$$

(pair production is not possible energetically)

Rayleigh scattering is a minor interaction, but it does occur, even at this large angle of scatter

at this angle & energy, probability increases approximately Z^5, so what Rayleigh scattering is observed takes place with Ca and P in bone rather than H, C, O, N in soft tissue what is photon energy loss in Rayleigh scattering?

consider 180° scatter (maximum loss, cf nuclear recoil) off ^{40}Ca.

momentum: $E_\gamma/c = P_{Ca} - E_\gamma'/c$

since $E_\gamma' \simeq E_\gamma$, $P_{Ca} \simeq 2E_\gamma/c$

energy: $E_\gamma = \frac{P_{Ca}^2}{2M_{Ca}} + E_\gamma'$

$$E_\gamma - E_\gamma' = \frac{P_{Ca}^2}{2M_{Ca}} \simeq \frac{2E_\gamma^2}{M_{Ca}c^2} = 4.16 \times 10^{-7}\ \text{MeV}$$

(0.416 eV)

if there is Pb present, most of it will be in bone

^{109}Cd 88 keV γ-ray is just above (greater in energy) the K shell absorption edge in Pb

so γ-rays interacting with any Pb there are likely to undergo photoelectric absorption, leaving electron vacancy in K shell => Pb x-rays

what the detector sees

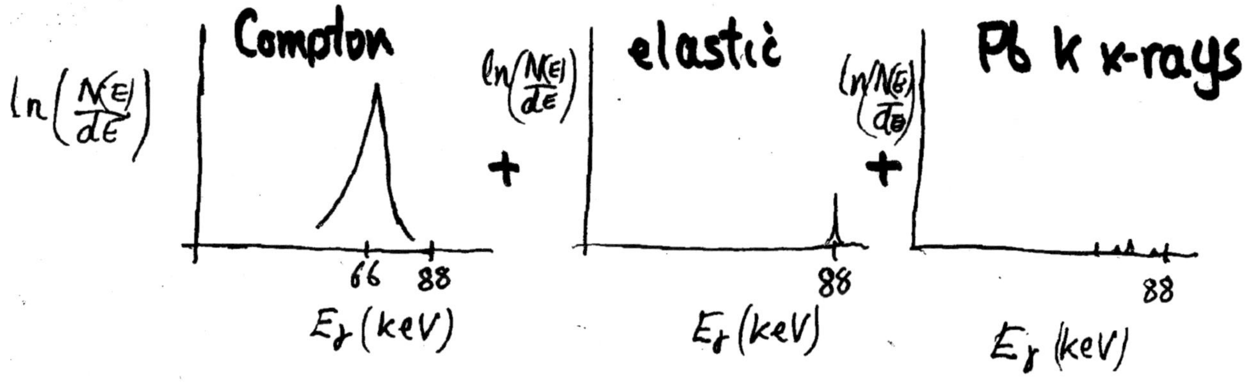

together & expanded

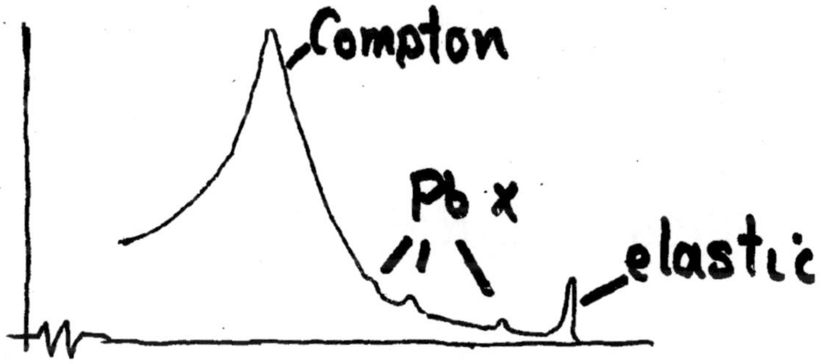

elastic comes from bone (Ca, P)

Pb is stored in bone

both elastic and Pb x require full energy (88 keV)

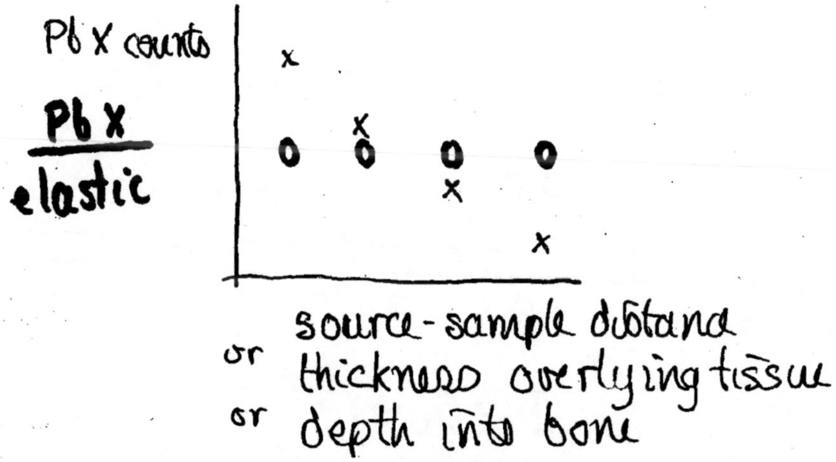

normalisation produces robust, accurate measurement

interaction probability - cross section - attenuation coefficient

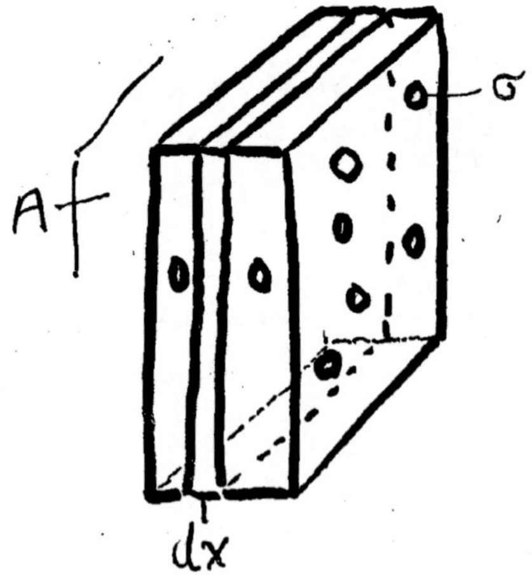

consider beam incident on a target of total area A

assume n scattering centres per unit volume

number of scatterers between x and x + dx = n A dx

if each scattering centre presents a cross section σ, chance of collision per scatterer relative to total intersection probability = σ/A

and total interaction probability = nσdx / particle incident

if number of incident particles per unit time per unit area is ø (flux) or beam intensity, I

total collision probability = ø nσdx   I nσdx

$d\phi = -\phi n\sigma\, dx$ $dI = -I n\sigma\, dx$

$\phi = \phi_0 e^{-n\sigma x}$ $I = I_0 e^{-n\sigma x}$

for $\phi = \phi_0$ at $x = 0$ for $I = I_0$ at $x = 0$

can re-express this several ways

$$I = I_0 e^{-\mu x}$$ $\mu = n\sigma$ is linear attenuation coefficient

or $$I = I_0 e^{-\frac{\mu}{\rho} t}$$ μ/ρ is mass attenuation coeff't
t is 'thickness' in ML^{-2}, eg $g\,cm^{-2}$

or $$I = I_0 e^{-x/\lambda}$$ λ is mean free path

μ is L^{-1} eg cm^{-1}, m^{-1}

μ/ρ is $L^2 M^{-1}$ eg $cm^2 g^{-1}$, $m^2 kg^{-1}$

λ is L eg cm, m

number of particles interacting given by

$$I_{int} = I_0 - I = I_0 (1 - e^{-\mu x})$$

if μx is small $\ll 1$

$$I_{int} = \mu x I_0$$

half value layer: $I = I_0 e^{-\mu x}$

when $I = 0.5 I_0 = I_0 e^{-\mu x_h}$ $\ln 2 = \mu x_h$

$$x_h = \frac{\ln 2}{\mu} \qquad \left(\text{cf } t_{1/2} = \frac{\ln 2}{\lambda}\right)$$

4 Oct.

consider attenuation of photons of 2 different energies through the same material

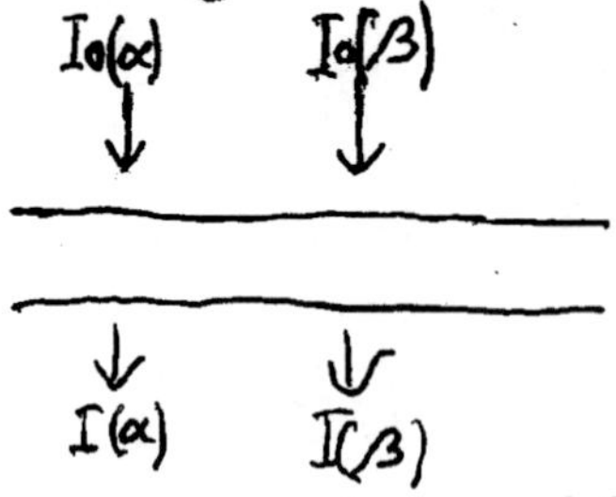

Mn x-rays, from ^{55}Fe passing through soft tissue

K_α x-rays: 5.895 keV, intensity 150.5

K_β x-rays: 6.49 keV, intensity 20.3

$$I(\alpha) = I_0(\alpha)\, e^{-\frac{\mu}{\rho}(\alpha) \cdot t}$$

$$\frac{\mu}{\rho}(\alpha) = 2.585 \ m^2 kg^{-1}$$

vs.

$$I(\beta) = I_0(\beta)\, e^{-\frac{\mu}{\rho}(\beta) \cdot t}$$

$$\frac{\mu}{\rho}(\beta) = 1.942 \ m^2 kg^{-1}$$

↑ E = less likely to interact

$$I_0(\alpha) = \frac{150.5}{20.3} I_0(\beta)$$

(# α = # β)

if $I(\alpha) = I(\beta)$, how thick is t ?

$$\frac{150.5}{20.3} e^{-\frac{\mu}{\rho}(\alpha) \cdot t} = e^{-\frac{\mu}{\rho}(\beta) \cdot t}$$

$$\ln\left(\frac{150.5}{20.3}\right) = t\left(\frac{\mu}{\rho}(\alpha) - \frac{\mu}{\rho}(\beta)\right)$$

$$t = \frac{\ln\left(\frac{150.5}{20.3}\right)}{2.585 - 1.942} = 3.116 \ kg\,m^{-2}, \text{ for } \rho = 1.03 \times 10^{3} \ kg\,m^{-3}$$

3.025×10^{-3} m (~3mm)

↑ something like this will prob be on assign. or test

what about 2 materials and 2 energies?

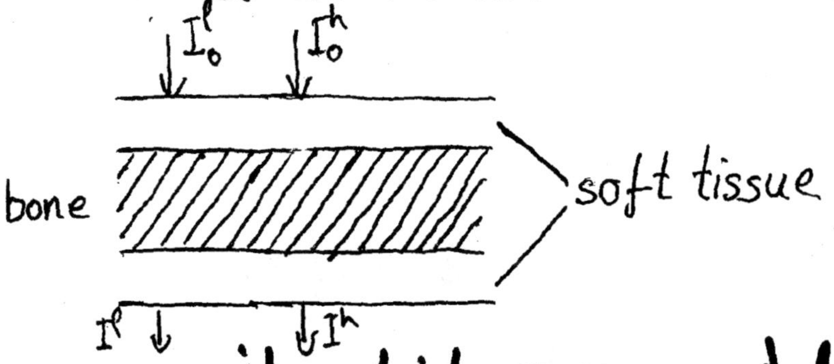

consider high energy and low energy photons

$$I^l = I_0^l \, e^{-\underbrace{\left(\left(\frac{\mu}{\rho}\right)_s^l \cdot t_s + \left(\frac{\mu}{\rho}\right)_b^l \cdot t_b\right)}_{\text{sum}}}$$

$$I^h = I_0^h \, e^{-\left(\left(\frac{\mu}{\rho}\right)_s^h \cdot t_s + \left(\frac{\mu}{\rho}\right)_b^h \cdot t_b\right)}$$

where superscripts h, l refer to high and low energy photons and subscripts s, b refer to soft tissue and bone

$$\ln\left(\frac{I_0}{I^l}\right)^l = \left(\frac{\mu}{\rho}\right)_s^l \cdot t_s + \left(\frac{\mu}{\rho}\right)_b^l \cdot t_b$$

$$t_s = \frac{\ln\left(\frac{I_0}{I^l}\right)^l - \left(\frac{\mu}{\rho}\right)_b^l \cdot t_b}{\left(\frac{\mu}{\rho}\right)_s^l}$$

$$\ln\left(\frac{I_0}{I^h}\right)^h = \left(\frac{\mu}{\rho}\right)_s^h \cdot t_s + \left(\frac{\mu}{\rho}\right)_b^h \cdot t_b$$

$$\ln\left(\frac{I_0}{I^h}\right) = \frac{\left(\frac{\mu}{\rho}\right)_s^h}{\left(\frac{\mu}{\rho}\right)_s^l}\left(\ln\left(\frac{I_0}{I^l}\right) - \left(\frac{\mu}{\rho}\right)_b^l \cdot t_b\right) + \left(\frac{\mu}{\rho}\right)_b^h \cdot t_b$$

$$t_b\left(\frac{\left(\frac{\mu}{\rho}\right)_s^h}{\left(\frac{\mu}{\rho}\right)_s^l}\cdot\left(\frac{\mu}{\rho}\right)_b^l - \left(\frac{\mu}{\rho}\right)_b^h\right) = \frac{\left(\frac{\mu}{\rho}\right)_s^h}{\left(\frac{\mu}{\rho}\right)_s^l}\ln\left(\frac{I_0}{I^l}\right) - \ln\left(\frac{I_0}{I^h}\right)$$

$$t_b\left(\left(\frac{\mu}{\rho}\right)_s^h\cdot\left(\frac{\mu}{\rho}\right)_b^l - \left(\frac{\mu}{\rho}\right)_b^h\cdot\left(\frac{\mu}{\rho}\right)_s^l\right) = \left(\frac{\mu}{\rho}\right)_s^h\ln\left(\frac{I_0}{I^l}\right) - \left(\frac{\mu}{\rho}\right)_s^l\ln\left(\frac{I_0}{I^h}\right)$$

similarly $t_s\left(\left(\frac{\mu}{\rho}\right)_s^h\cdot\left(\frac{\mu}{\rho}\right)_b^l - \left(\frac{\mu}{\rho}\right)_b^h\cdot\left(\frac{\mu}{\rho}\right)_s^l\right) = \left(\frac{\mu}{\rho}\right)_b^l\ln\left(\frac{I_0}{I^h}\right) - \left(\frac{\mu}{\rho}\right)_b^h\ln\left(\frac{I_0}{I^l}\right)$

consider ^{109}Cd photons incident on bone plus soft tissue, photon energies 22.61keV, 88.03keV

	soft tissue	vs	bone
low energy	$\left(\frac{\mu}{\rho}\right)_s^l = .07144\ m^2kg^{-1}$		$\left(\frac{\mu}{\rho}\right)_b^l = .2945\ m^2kg^{-1}$
vs			
high energy	$\left(\frac{\mu}{\rho}\right)_s^h = .01770\ m^2kg^{-1}$		$\left(\frac{\mu}{\rho}\right)_b^h = .02082\ m^2kg^{-1}$

if $I_0^l = 8\times10^4\ s^{-1}$ $\quad I^l = 0.5\ s^{-1}$ } he's looked up these #'s

$I_0^h = 2.9\times10^3 s^{-1}$ $\quad I^h = 950\ s^{-1}$

what are t_b and t_s ?

$$t_b = \frac{.01770 \ln\left(\frac{8\times10^4}{0.5}\right) - .07144 \ln\left(\frac{2.9\times10^3}{950}\right)}{.01770\times.2945 - .02082\times.07144}$$

$$= \frac{.212098 - .079727}{5.21265\times10^{-3} - 1.48738\times10^{-3}} = 35.66\ kg\,m^{-2}$$

$$t_s = \frac{.2945 \ln\left(\frac{2.9\times10^3}{950}\right) - .02082 \ln\left(\frac{8\times10^4}{0.5}\right)}{.01770\times.2945 - .02082\times.07144}$$

$$= 21.25\ kg\,m^{-2}$$

this forms the basis of dual energy absorptiometry, commonly used for bone density measurements (although not using ^{109}Cd as a source)

for photons have different probabilities for different types of interactions and these probabilities vary in different ways with E_γ and atomic number of medium

therefore have different microscopic and corresponding macroscopic cross section

photoelectric,	σ_{pe}	τ
Compton,	σ_c	s (Turner uses σ)
pair production	σ_{pp}	κ
elastic	σ_{el}	
photo nuclear	σ_{pn}	

big 3 (photoelectric, Compton, pair production)

don't matter on real-life scale (elastic, photo nuclear)

total, $\sigma_{tot} = \sigma_{pe} + \sigma_c + \sigma_{pp} + \sigma_{el} + \sigma_{pn}$

in practice $\mu = \tau + s + \kappa$

all of these vary with E_γ and Z

energy transfer and energy absorption coefficients

need to define fluence, energy fluence, fluence rate

fluence is the number of particles per unit area that cross a plane perpendicular to the beam (Φ_0)

energy fluence is the energy that passes per unit area $\Psi_0 = \Phi_0 h\nu$ (fluence × E per particle)

fluence rate is number of particles crossing unit area per unit time

$$\dot{\Phi}_0 = d\Phi_0/dt = \phi_0$$ sometimes referred to as (flux density)

energy fluence rate $\dot{\Psi}_0 = \dot{\Phi}_0 h\nu$ (intensity)

consider each major energy loss process, first energy transfer, then energy absorption

<u>photoelectric effect</u> photoelectron has kinetic energy $T = h\nu - B$, where B is the binding energy of ejected electron, binding energy released as Auger electrons or x-rays, if δ is the average energy emitted as x-rays (fluorescence radiation) so

$$\frac{\tau_{tr}}{\rho} = \frac{\tau}{\rho}\left(1 - \frac{\delta}{h\nu}\right)$$ is then the mass energy transfer coefficient for the photoelectric effect

<u>Compton scattering</u>

$$\frac{s_{tr}}{\rho} = \frac{s}{\rho}\frac{T_{avg}}{h\nu}$$ where $T_{avg}/h\nu$ is the average fraction of incident photon energy converted into initial kinetic energy of Compton electron

pair production · total initial kinetic energy of electron-positron pair is $h\nu - 2mc^2$, so

$$\frac{\kappa_{tr}}{\rho} = \frac{\kappa}{\rho}\left(1 - \frac{2mc^2}{h\nu}\right)$$

total mass energy transfer coefficient μ_{tr}/ρ given by

probability of ħ being absorbed →

$$\mu_{tr}/\rho = \tau_{tr}/\rho + s_{tr}/\rho + \kappa_{tr}/\rho$$

$$= \frac{\tau}{\rho}\left(1 - \frac{\delta}{h\nu}\right) + \frac{s}{\rho}\frac{T_{avg}}{h\nu} + \frac{\kappa}{\rho}\left(1 - \frac{2mc^2}{h\nu}\right)$$

~ energy transferred to electrons ↓ some will be released as bremstralung, depends on material, so need correction factor = g

energy transferred is not the same as energy absorbed because the electrons to which energy has been transferred will emit some energy as bremsstrahlung, can put fraction of electron energy thus emitted = g, then mass energy absorption coefficient

probability of interaction →

$$\frac{\mu_{en}}{\rho} = \frac{\mu_{tr}}{\rho}(1 - g)$$

this coefficient remains a probability, it doesn't give the amount of energy absorbed

energy absorption and energy transfer

energy fluence is Ψ per unit area

energy fluence transmitted through a slab width x

$$\Psi = \Psi_0 e^{-\mu_{en} x}$$

(i.e. energy lost in medium)

energy fluence lost, ie energy absorbed in slab

$$\Psi_0 - \Psi = \Psi_0 (1 - e^{-\mu_{en} x})$$

if $\mu_{en} x << 1$ then

$$\Psi_0 - \Psi = \Psi_0 \mu_{en} x$$

if slab has area A, energy absorbed in whole slab $= \Psi_0 \mu_{en} x A$

mass of slab is $\rho A x$, so energy absorbed per unit mass is $\frac{\Psi_0 \mu_{en} x A}{\rho A x} = \Psi_0 \frac{\mu_{en}}{\rho} = D$

(volume) very important

similarly $\dot{\Psi}_0 \frac{\mu_{en}}{\rho} = \dot{D}$

where D and $\dot{D}$ are dose and dose rate respectively

recall $\Psi_0 = \Phi_0 h\nu$, so $D = \Phi_0 h\nu \frac{\mu_{en}}{\rho}$

fluence energy

aside (not used regularly in practice)

can use mass energy transfer coefficient similarly

$$K = \Psi_0 \frac{\mu_{tr}}{\rho} \quad K \text{ is kerma}$$

(**k**inetic **e**nergy **r**eleased per unit **ma**ss)

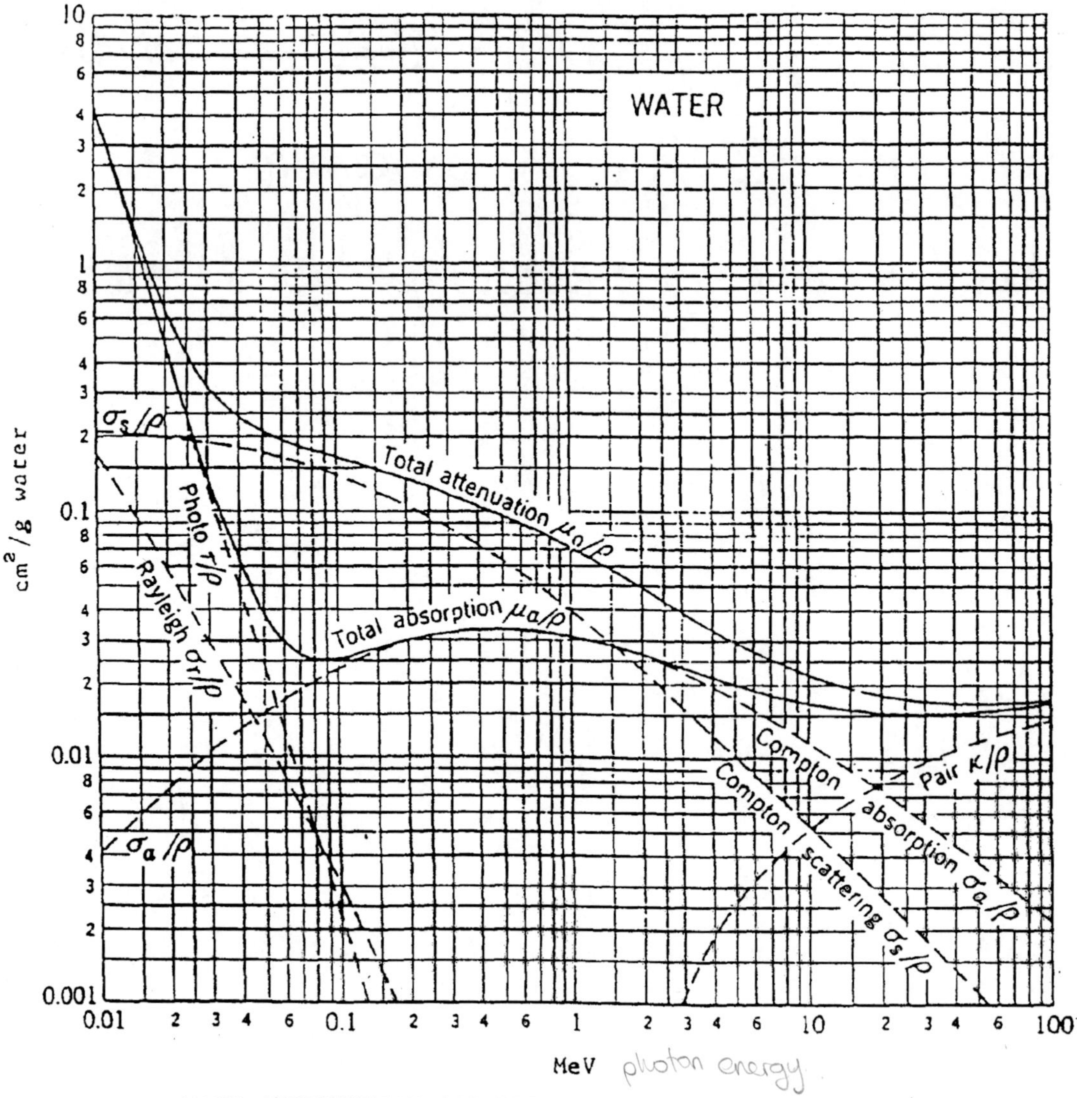

MASS ATTENUATION COEFFICIENTS FOR GAMMA RAYS IN WATER

trend

- photoelectric dominant at low energy
- ↑E - pair production
- mid range - compton.

trend

- photoelectric + pair production depend on Z^n
- compton depends on Z

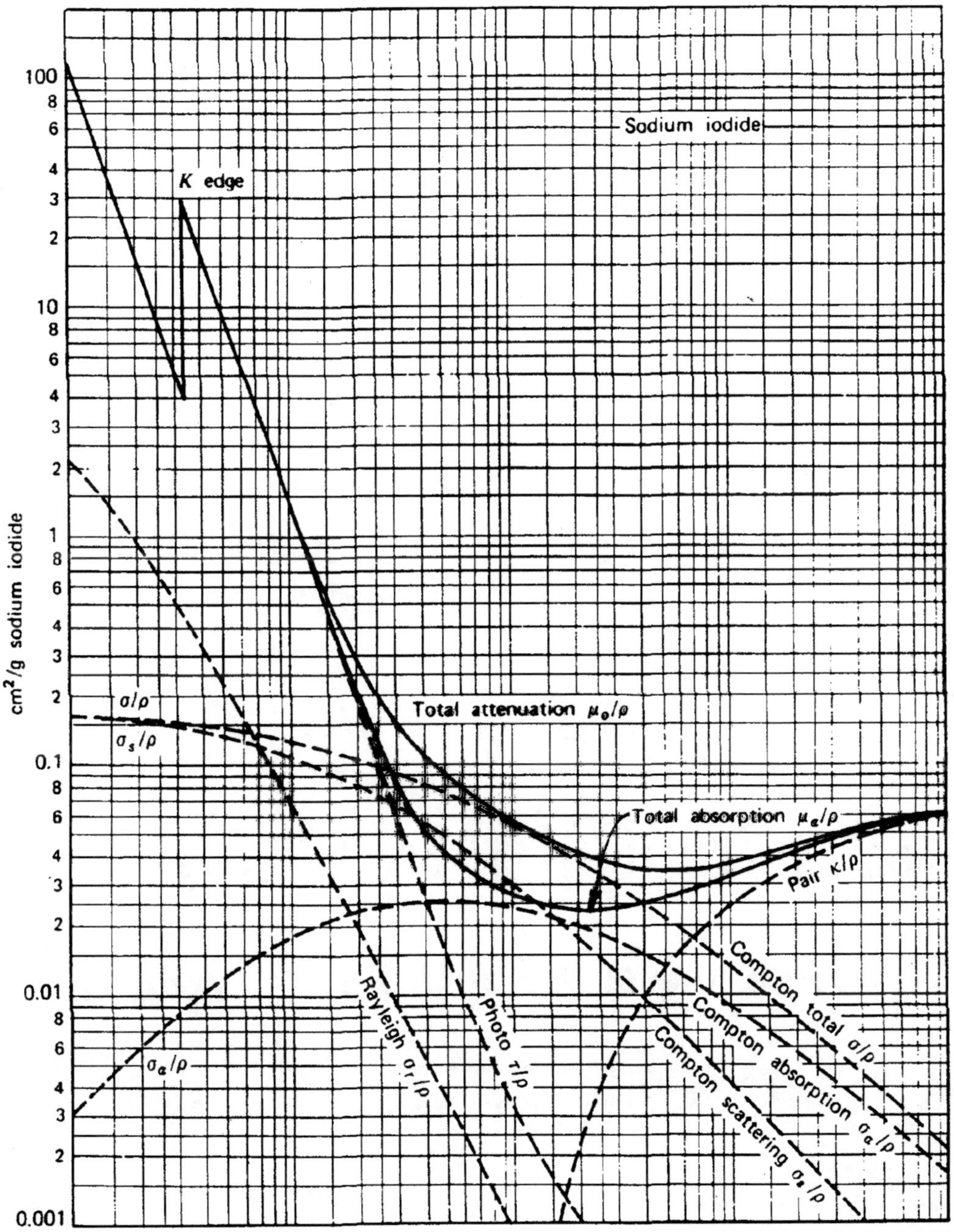

Figure 2-18 Energy dependence of the various gamma-ray interaction processes in sodium iodide. (From *The Atomic Nucleus* by R. D. Evans. Copyright 1955 by the McGraw-Hill Book Company. Used with permission.)

From G F Knoll 'Radiation Detection and Measurement' 2nd ed Wiley 1989

Oct 4.

Oct 5

dose to tissue from 88 keV photons

assume soft tissue is:

H	·1	
O	·716	by mass
C	·149	
N	·035	

tabulated mass energy absorption coefficient

} these values from NIST site (Xcom)

σ_a/ρ	E(keV)	70	80	90	100	88
H		·0335	·0362	·0385	·0406	·0380
C		·0169	·0182	·0194	·0204	·0191
N		·0168	·0182	·0194	·0204	·0191
O		·0168	·0182	·0194	·0204	·0191

factor of 2 diff for H.

very similar b/c e:m is the same

interpolated

} ·02099 cm²/g

(·002099 m²/kg)

b/c we're talking Compton.

$$D = \Phi E_\gamma \frac{\mu_{en}}{\rho}$$

this is kind of a preview; more on dose later

consider 1 GBq of ^{109}Cd (^{109m}Ag), 10^9 decays s^{-1}

but only ·036 of decays give 88 keV γ-ray; measurement takes 30 min; solid angle $\frac{1}{4\pi . 2.5^2}$

(silver x-rays don't figure into calc)

~1 cm² area on surface of sphere

so $\Phi = \dfrac{10^9 \times 1800 \times .036}{4\pi \times 2.5^2}$

and $D = \dfrac{10^9 \times 1800 \times .036}{4\pi \times 2.5^2} \times 88 \times 1.6 \times 10^{-16} \times .02099$ J/g

(keV → J)

$= 2.44 \times 10^{-7}$ J/g

$= 2.44 \times 10^{-4}$ J/kg $= 2.44 \times 10^{-4}$ Gy

end test 1

Neutrons - sources and interactions

neutron discovered by Chadwick, using α-particles from ^{226}Ra interacting with beryllium

$$^{9}_{4}Be + \overset{\alpha}{^{4}_{2}He} \rightarrow {}^{12}_{6}C + {}^{1}_{0}n$$

$$\Delta\ (MeV) \quad 11.348 + 2.425 = 0 + 8.071 + Q$$

$$Q = 5.702\ MeV$$ ← quite significant

but α-particles emitted with appreciable energy

consider $^{238}_{94}Pu$, preferable to ^{226}Ra because few γ-rays emitted

not pure α emitter but relatively small γ emission

$$^{238}_{94}Pu \rightarrow {}^{234}_{92}U + {}^{4}_{2}He + Q$$

$$\Delta\ (MeV) \quad 46.161 = 38.143 + 2.425 + 0$$

$$Q = 5.593\ MeV.$$

$$E_\alpha = Q\left(1 - \frac{4}{238}\right) = 5.499\ MeV$$

so maximum energy available to $^{12}C + n = 11.201$ MeV

so $E_{n\ max} = 10.34$ MeV

doesn't go to ground often, usually γ

but 1st excited state of ^{12}C at 4.43 MeV is frequently populated

& deexcited & give γ → not pure n source

also varying amount of α energy lost in Be powder before producing reaction

emitter mixed with Be.

result is broad band neutron spectrum

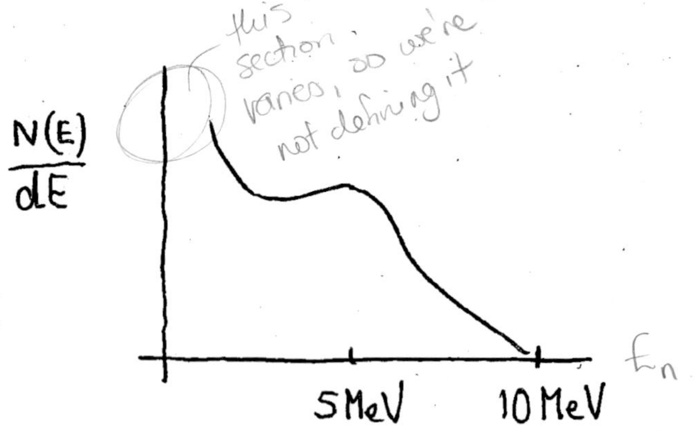

other sources

downsides

also, photo-nuclear, eg ^{124}Sb, Be ← ½ life of year, high γ : n ratio

reactor - fission ← most intense source also photons (not pure).

spontaneous fission - eg ^{252}Cf ← small, ↑ n source → plus.

branching ratio for α-emission = 0.9691, fission is 0.0309

downsides

$t_{1/2}$ for ^{252}Cf = 2.64 y & Cf is mostly α emitter

activity = $N\lambda$ and $\lambda_\alpha + \lambda_{sf} = \lambda$

$$\lambda_\alpha + \lambda_{sf} = \frac{\ln 2}{2.64} \; y^{-1}$$

$$\lambda_\alpha = 0.9691 \left(\frac{\ln 2}{2.64}\right) = 0.254 \; y^{-1} \; (\text{partial } t_{1/2} = 2.72 y)$$

(prob.)

$$\lambda_{sf} = 0.0309 \left(\frac{\ln 2}{2.64}\right) = 0.00811 \; y^{-1} \; (\text{partial } t_{1/2} = 85.4 y)$$

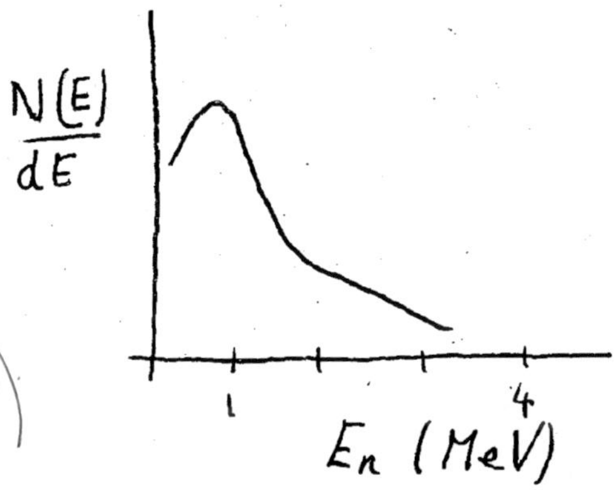

(Cf not f_i → 20 MeV)

	^{235}U fission	^{252}Cf
E_{mode} (MeV)	0.7	1.0
$\bar{E}$ (MeV)	2.0	2.3

(E_{mode}: more useful than mean in this case.)

(most typical E vs. avg of spread)

(Cf: spectrum shifted up in E compared to $U^{235}+n$ (makes sense, larger mass))

other sources.

accelerator sources eg $^3H(p,n)^3He$, $^3H(d,n)^4He$ etc

$$^7_3Li + ^1_1H \longrightarrow ^7_4Be + ^1_0n$$

$$\Delta\,(\text{MeV}) \; 14.907 + 7.289 = 15.769 + 8.071 + Q$$

$$Q = -1.644$$ must supply energy, hence accelerator

on collision $P_p^2 = P_{Li}^2$

so threshold $= \frac{8}{7} \times 1.644 = 1.879$ MeV

(generally use between ex. 1.9 - 2.5 MeV)

if bounces, just as likely to give energy as to receive energy

neutron energy classification

thermal - in thermal equilibrium with surroundings

most probable (modal) energy given by $E = k_B T$

Boltzmann's constant, $k_B = 1.38 \times 10^{-23}$ J K^{-1}

$= 8.62 \times 10^{-5}$ eV K^{-1}

for room temperature (290 K)

$E = 0.025$ eV

modal energy describing distribution of energies

neutron velocity given by

$\frac{1}{2} m v^2 = k_B T$

$v = 2200$ m/s

below - ↑ prob
above - dramatic fall in prob of orders of magnitude

upper end of thermal often taken as 0.5 eV, where ^{113}Cd neutron absorption cross section falls $T = 5{,}800$ K, $v = 9{,}800$ m/s

below thermal energies, cold neutrons, used in neutron scattering, materials analysis

eg $E_n = 1$ meV, $T = 11.6$ K, $v = 437$ m/s

also "epithermal"

at higher energies have "intermediate" or "resonance"
inconsistant terminology
(sometimes called slow) neutrons

range is ill-defined 0.5 eV → 10 keV } blurry

or 0.5 eV → 100 keV

above this fast neutrons
when encountering these things, context matters.

Oct 5

Fri Oct 19 neutron interactions – note neutral

elastic scattering

inelastic scattering

neutron absorption

nuclear reactions

(energy always conserved)

elastic scattering (kinetic energy conserved)

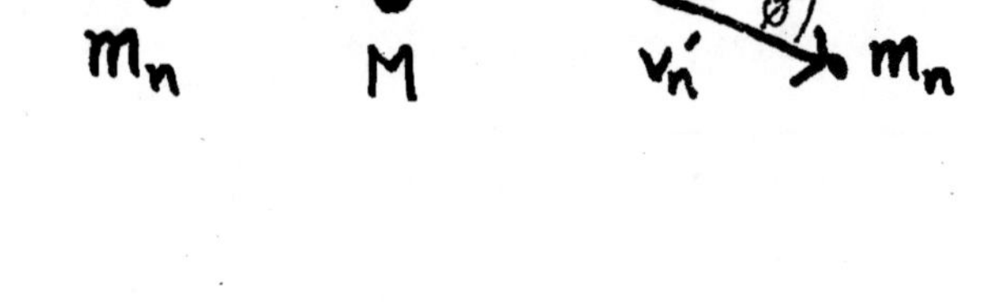

from KE: $\frac{1}{2} m_n V_n^2 = \frac{1}{2} m_n V_n'^2 + \frac{1}{2} M V_M'^2$

$$m_n^2 V_n'^2 = m_n (m_n V_n^2 - M V_M'^2)$$

from momentum: → $m_n V_n = m_n V_n' \cos\phi + M V_M' \cos\theta$

$$(m_n V_n' \cos\phi)^2 = (m_n V_n - M V_M' \cos\theta)^2$$

↑ $0 = m_n V_n' \sin\phi - M V_M' \sin\theta$

$$(m_n V_n' \sin\phi)^2 = (M V_M' \sin\theta)^2$$

$$m_n^2 V_n^2 - m_n M V_M'^2 = m_n^2 V_n^2 + M^2 V_M'^2 - 2 m_n V_n M V_M' \cos\theta$$

$$(M + m_n) V_M' = 2 m_n V_n \cos\theta$$

KE of target mass $= \frac{1}{2} M V_M'^2$

$$= \frac{1}{2} M . \frac{4 m_n^2 V_n^2 \cos^2\theta}{(M + m_n)^2}$$

$$= \left(\frac{1}{2} m_n V_n^2\right) \frac{4 m_n M \cos^2\theta}{(M + m_n)^2}$$

$$\boxed{= \frac{4 m_n M \cos^2\theta}{(M + m_n)^2} . E_n}$$

for $\theta = 0$ (head on collision) $\cos\theta = 1$

so max energy transferred = $\boxed{\frac{4 m_n M}{(m_n + M)^2} E_n}$

for neutron - proton scattering $m_p \simeq m_n$ nearly equal.

so energy transferred = $E_n \cos^2\theta$

and max energy transfer = E_n

(actually H atom has mass 1·0078 AMU

n has mass 1·0087 AMU) how good of an approx. is it?

max energy transfer = $\frac{4 \times 1{\cdot}0078 \times 1{\cdot}0087}{(1{\cdot}0078 + 1{\cdot}0087)^2} E_n$

= 0·999 999 8 E_n pretty good! unlikely that will affect exp. results ....

in practice median fraction of energy transferred to target (f) is close to ½ maximum (Q_{max})

	(^{1}H)	(^{2}H)	(^{12}C)	(^{14}N)	(^{16}O)	(^{31}P)	(^{40}Ca)	(^{56}Fe)	(^{208}Pb)
A	1	2	12	14	16	31	40	56	208
Q_{max}/E_n	1 (max.)	0·889	·284	·249	·221	·121	·0952	·0689	·0190
f	0·632	0·516	·146	·127	·113	·061	·0480	·0347	·00954

so note lead is useless for elastic scattering
want to use something 1H to shield a neutron source (i.e. water, wax, etc..)

inelastic scattering (kinetic energy not conserved)

eg $n + {}^{56}Fe \rightarrow n' + {}^{56}Fe^{*}$ ← nuclear excited state, will decay promptly + emit a gamma.

$${}^{56}Fe^{*} \rightarrow {}^{56}Fe + \gamma$$

1st excited state of ${}^{56}Fe$ is 0.847 MeV

$$E_n \text{ threshold} = \frac{57}{56} \times 0.847 = 0.862 \text{ MeV}$$

a minimum of 0.847 MeV is lost from neutron energy (so n looses ~1MeV)

⇒ Fe is an important shield for fast neutrons

because energy loss per collision is reasonably high

ie ~1 MeV for E_n 1 – 10 MeV

cross section ~ 1 b from ~1 – 10 MeV

(1 barn ≡ 1×10^{-28} m^2 [1×10^{-24} cm^2])

will often see concrete (↑H) mixed with Fe @ nuclear facilities

mostly only one that matters for thermal neutrons

neutron absorption (neutron capture)

eg $n + {}^{1}_{1}H \rightarrow {}^{2}_{1}H + \gamma$

$n + {}^{113}_{48}Cd \rightarrow {}^{114}_{48}Cd + \gamma$

? technically 1 kind of "nuclear reaction" which we'll talk about next time

for many target nuclei and for thermal neutrons this is the only reaction that is energetically allowed

binding energy of last neutron typically ~ 6-8 MeV

this energy released as γ-rays

often cross section varies inversely as neutron speed ($1/v$ relationship), so if σ_0 at E_0 and σ at E

then $$\sigma = \sigma_0 \sqrt{\frac{E_0}{E}}$$

estimate cross section at higher E

crosssection @ thermal

^{113}Cd unusual in that it has sharp cut off at 0.5 eV, below this Cd filtering

^{113}Cd has a 20,000 b cross section for thermal neutron absorption, it is 12.22% abundant, natural cadmium has a density of 8.65 g cm^{-3} and an atomic weight of 112.4

really big!

what thickness of natural cadmium is required to reduce

so thermal neutrons can't get through

$E > 0.5$ MeV get through with no trouble

the intensity of a thermal neutron beam to 50% ? for 99.99% ?

$\sigma = 2 \times 10^{4} \times 10^{-28}$ m^2/ atom ^{113}Cd. (× 12.22% for natural Cd)

natural Cd has $\frac{6.02 \times 10^{23}}{112.4} \times 10^{3} \times 8.65 \times 10^{3}$ atoms / m^3

so $\mu = 2 \times 10^{4} \times 10^{-28} \times \frac{6.02 \times 10^{23}}{112.4} \times 10^{3} \times 8.65 \times 10^{3} \times 0.1222$ m^{-1}, for natural Cd

$= 1.13 \times 10^{4}$ m^{-1}

for 50% absorption: $\frac{I}{I_0} = 0.5 = e^{-\mu x}$

$\mu x = \ln 2$

$x = \frac{\ln 2}{1.13 \times 10^{4}}$ m

$= 61.2\ \mu m$

for 99.99% absorption: $\frac{I}{I_0} = 10^{-4} = e^{-\mu x}$

$\mu x = \ln 10^{4}$

$x = \frac{\ln 10^{4}}{1.13 \times 10^{4}}$ m

$= 0.813$ mm

∴ very useful

normally burn up isn't an issue (for say 1b) but since Cd has 20,000 b, burnup becomes significant.

what about 'burn up' in a thermal neutron fluence rate of $\dot{\Phi} = 10^{12}\ cm^{-2} s^{-1}$, how long does it take to use up 10% of the ^{113}Cd?

$$\frac{dN}{dt} = -N\dot{\phi}\sigma$$

for $N = N_0$ at $t = 0$

$$N = N_0 e^{-\dot{\phi}\sigma t}$$

$$\ln\left(\frac{N}{N_0}\right) = \ln(0.9) = -\dot{\phi}\sigma t$$

$\dot{\phi} = 10^{12}\ cm^{-2} s^{-1}$, $\sigma = 2\times10^{4}\times10^{-24}\ cm^2$, $\dot{\phi}\sigma = 2\times10^{-8}\ s^{-1}$

$$t = -\frac{\ln(0.9)}{2\times10^{-8}}\ s$$

$$= 5.27\times10^{6} s$$ ~ couple of months

$$= 61\ d$$

★ note pertains to control rods made of Cd
how often might you need to replace them?
(though they are usually not in the reactor)

→ also similar to Gadolinium.
→ Xe dead time effect

Oct. 19 end.

Oct. 23 start

nuclear reactions

eg $^{14}N(n,p)^{14}C$ $\sigma_{th} = 1.70$ b

$^{10}B(n,\alpha)^{7}Li$ $\sigma_{th} = 4000$ b

these two are unusual in that they take place with thermal neutrons, both are important $^{14}N(n,p$ is one of two major reactions by which thermal neutrons deliver dose, the other is $^{1}H(n,\gamma)^{2}H$, also basis of ^{14}C dating

$^{10}B(n,\alpha$ is used in many neutron detectors, also provides basis for boron neutron capture therapy

more usually these kinds of reactions take place with fast neutrons

$^{19}F(n,\alpha)^{16}N$

$^{56}Fe(n,p)^{56}Mn$

$^{14}N(n,2n)^{13}N$

most common

neutron absorption and (fast) neutron reactions can be used for activation analysis

eg $^{23}Na(n,\gamma)^{24}Na$; $\sigma = 0.53\ b$; $t_{1/2} = 15.0\ h$

consider 100g Na irradiated for 10 min in $10^4\ n\ cm^{-2}s^{-1}$

let target area $= A$. total neutron fluence rate $= A \times 10^4\ n\ s^{-1}$

no. of target atoms per unit area $\dfrac{100 \times 6.02 \times 10^{23}}{23 \times A}$

using build up and decay of activity (previously derived)

no. of ^{24}N nuclei at time t, N given by

$$N = \frac{100 \times 6.02 \times 10^{23}}{23 \times A} \times A \times 10^4 \times 0.53 \times 10^{-24} \times \frac{15.0 \times 3600}{\ln 2}\left(1 - e^{-\frac{\ln(2) \times 10}{15.0 \times 60}}\right)$$

$= 8.29 \times 10^6$

suppose ½ hour count, starting 1 hour after end of irradiation

1hr — 1.5hr

no. decaying in interval $= N\left(e^{-\frac{\ln 2 \times 1}{15.0}} - e^{-\frac{\ln 2 \times 1.5}{15.0}}\right)$

$= 181,000$

if radiation counter 3% efficient ⟹ 5425 counts

energy consequences of neutron interactions

elastic median energy transferred/absorbed

$= f \times E_n$ $\left(f \simeq \frac{Q_{max}}{E_n} \times \frac{1}{2} \text{, except } {}^1H, {}^2H \right)$

inelastic energy available for scatter $= E_n - h\nu$

γ-ray may later interact

absorption no immediate charged particle

γ-ray may later interact

product nucleus may be radioactive

reactions charged particle energies, p, α, recoil nucleus

will be absorbed

neutrons, γ's may later interact

product nucleus may be radioactive

cross sections for neutron interactions

σ_{el}, $\sigma_{nn'}$, $\sigma_{n\gamma}$, σ_{np} etc

$\sigma = \sum \sigma_i$

then, in principle, consider energy consequence of each interaction type (as with photons)

BUT

for fast neutrons in tissue, elastic scattering with ^1H predominates

for thermal neutrons in tissue two reactions are important $^1H(n,\gamma)^2H$

$^{14}N(n,p)^{14}C$

kind of a summary

Comparison of decay and interactions

decay	interactions
$\lambda \equiv$ probability per unit time for decay through any mode	$\mu \equiv$ probability per unit path length for interaction through any mode
λ_i = prob./unit time for decay through mode i $\lambda = \sum \lambda_i$	μ_i = prob./unit path length for interaction through mode i $\mu = \Sigma \mu_i$
$e^{-\lambda t}$ = prob. of survival for time t	$e^{-\mu x}$ = prob. of survival for path length x
$1-e^{-\lambda t}$ = prob. of decay through any mode for time interval t	$1-e^{-\mu x}$ = prob. of interaction of any type for path length x

$P_i = \frac{\lambda_i}{\lambda}(1 - e^{-\lambda t})$ = prob. of decay through mode i for time interval t

$P_i = \frac{\mu_i}{\mu}(1 - e^{-\mu x})$ = prob. of interaction of type i for path length x

other relationships

$(100)\frac{\lambda_i}{\lambda}$ = branching ratio

$\mu_i = n\sigma_i$ where σ_i is the cross section for interaction type i and n is the target density

Radiation dosimetry

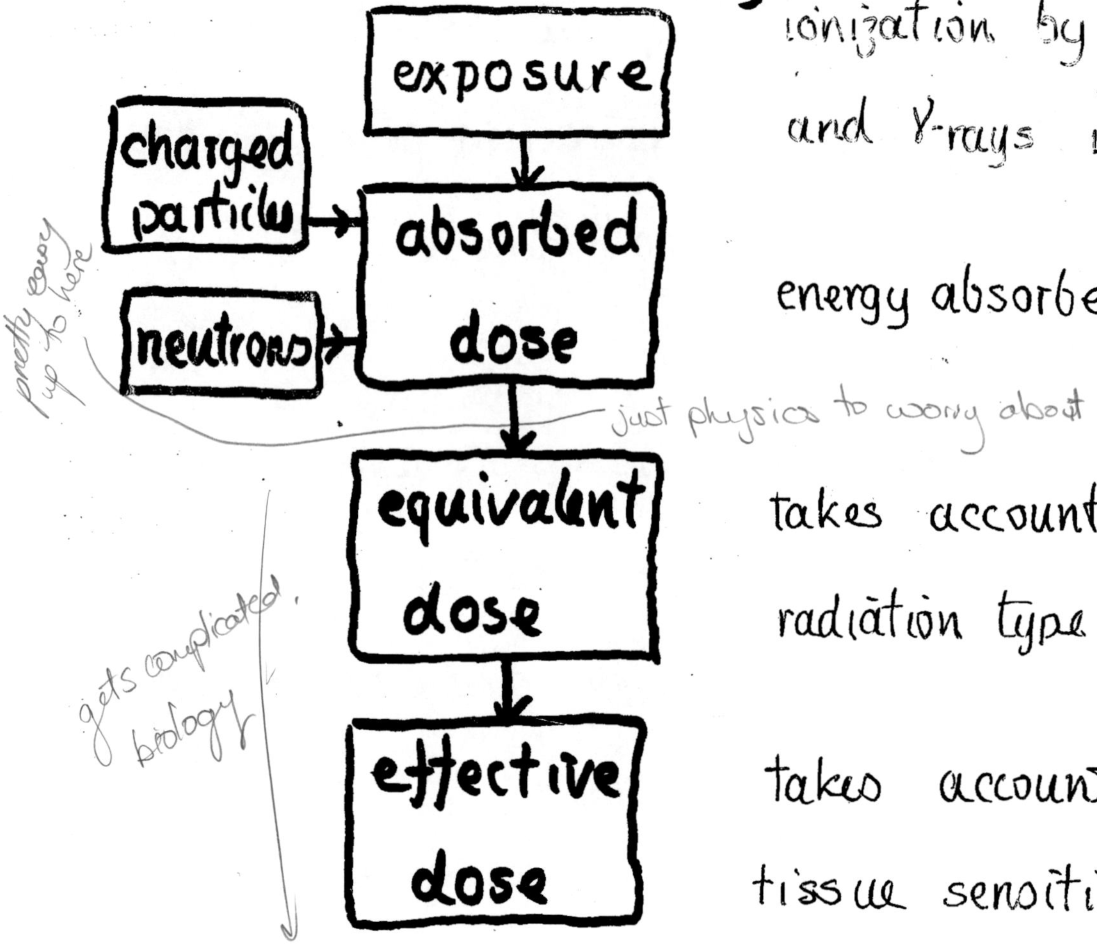

ionization by x-rays and γ-rays in air

energy absorbed

takes account of radiation type

takes account of tissue sensitivity

Oct 23 end (Tues)

Oct. 25 start (thurs)

directly measurable!

exposure

applies to x-rays and γ-rays and is defined in terms of ionization produced in air, unit is roentgen

$$1\,R \equiv 2{\cdot}58 \times 10^{-4}\ C\ kg^{-1}$$

the charge involved (coulombs) is the total charge (ie primary + secondary + ... events) of one sign

exposure is useful because it provides a measurable standard

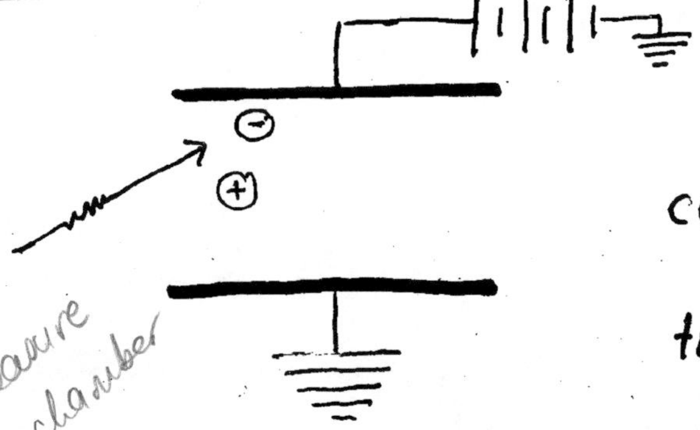

highly simplified

collect charge per unit time as current (or individual current pulses, relating to each initial photon

we want
- to only measure charges in chamber
- to not let charges in chamber escape

require electron equilibrium (more generally, charged particle equilibrium)

Compton scattering most likely (not only option)

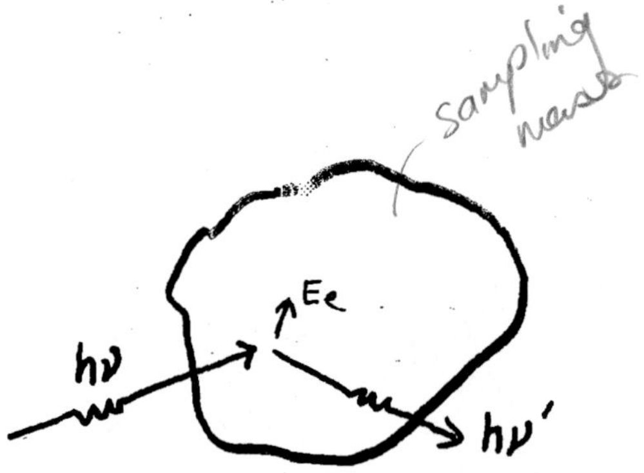

in this example, scattered photon escapes, but that is allowed for in mass energy absorption coefficient. Compton electron has short range and is absorbed; however, if interaction is within electron range of medium boundary, may lose more electrons than gain from surrounding medium (or vice versa)

consider 1.332 MeV γ-ray from ^{60}Co, maximum energy of Compton electron, E_e

$$E_{e(max)} = E_\gamma - E'_{\gamma(min)} = E_\gamma - \frac{E_\gamma}{1 + \frac{2E_\gamma}{0.511}}$$

$$= 1.118 \text{ MeV}$$

for electrons range, $R = 0.412\,T^{1.27 - 0.0954 \ln T}$

where range is in $g\,cm^{-2}$ and T is electron kinetic energy MeV (for $T \leq 2.5$ MeV)

$$R = 0.474 \text{ g cm}^{-2}$$

$\Rightarrow$ 3.67 m in air → could improve this by pressurizing, but most are not

(though chamber would need to be size of room...

so use plastic 'build up' cap, 4·74 mm (for $\rho = 1 g cm^{-3}$)

would ensure electron equilibrium

but $\mu \simeq 0{\cdot}06$ for 1·3 MeV photon in plastic

so lose ~3% of photons to attenuation

in practice, compromise & calibrate

(adjust thickness, etc

absorbed dose

energy absorbed per unit mass from any kind of ionizing radiation in any target

note 1 Gy is a serious dose.

$$1 \text{ gray (Gy)} \equiv 1 \text{ J kg}^{-1}$$

in context: annual natural background ~ 2-3 mGy

(short compared to cell cycle time ~1 hr.

an acute dose of 4 Gy would probably kill half of adults so exposed

how does exposure relate to dose?

$$1 \text{ R} \equiv 2{\cdot}58 \times 10^{-4} \text{ C kg}^{-1}$$

because each electron (or +ve ion) carries

a charge of 1.6×10^{-19} C, can determine number of ion pairs

$$1\,R \Rightarrow \frac{2.58 \times 10^{-4}}{1.6 \times 10^{-19}} \text{ ion pairs kg}^{-1}$$

how much energy per ion pair? (not just the ionization energy, best you can do is find average)

W is average energy needed to produce an ion pair

W varies with radiation type, energy and medium, but it is relatively constant for electrons, for air,

$$W_{air} = 34\,eV \text{ per ion pair}$$

$$34\,eV \equiv 34 \times 1.6 \times 10^{-19}\,J$$

so
$$1\,R = \frac{2.58 \times 10^{-4}}{1.6 \times 10^{-19}} \times 34 \times 1.6 \times 10^{-19}\ J\,kg^{-1}$$

$$= 8.8\ mGy \quad \text{(dose to air)}$$

what about tissue?

for photons in tissue main energy loss mechanism is Compton scattering, which depends on electron density

$$n_{air} = 3.01 \times 10^{26}\,kg^{-1},\quad n_{muscle} = 3.28 \times 10^{26}\,kg^{-1}$$

$$\Rightarrow 1\,R \Rightarrow 9.6\,mGy$$ (often rounded to 10mGy)

old units

previously used unit for absorbed dose was rad

still used

totally gone

$$1 \text{ rad} \equiv 100 \text{ erg g}^{-1} = 10^{-2} \text{ J kg}^{-1}$$
$$= 10^{-2} \text{ Gy}$$

so annual natural bg ~ 200-300 m rad

LD_{50} for an acute dose of 400 rad

$1 \text{ rad} \equiv 1 \text{ cGy}$

Total Body Irradiation

Mass = 70 kgm
LD/50/60 = 4 Gy
Energy absorbed =

$$70 \times 4 = 280 \text{ Joules}$$
$$= \frac{280}{4.18} = 67 \text{ calories}$$

A

Drinking Hot Coffee

Excess temperature (°C) = 60° − 37° = 23°
Volume of coffee consumed to
equal the energy in the LD/50/60 = $\frac{67}{23}$

$$= 3 \text{ ml}$$
$$= 1 \text{ sip}$$

B

Mechanical Energy: Lifting a Person

Mass = 70 kgm
Height lifted to equal
the energy in the

$$\text{LD/50/60} = \frac{280}{70 \times 9.81}$$
$$= 0.4\text{m (16 inches)}$$

C

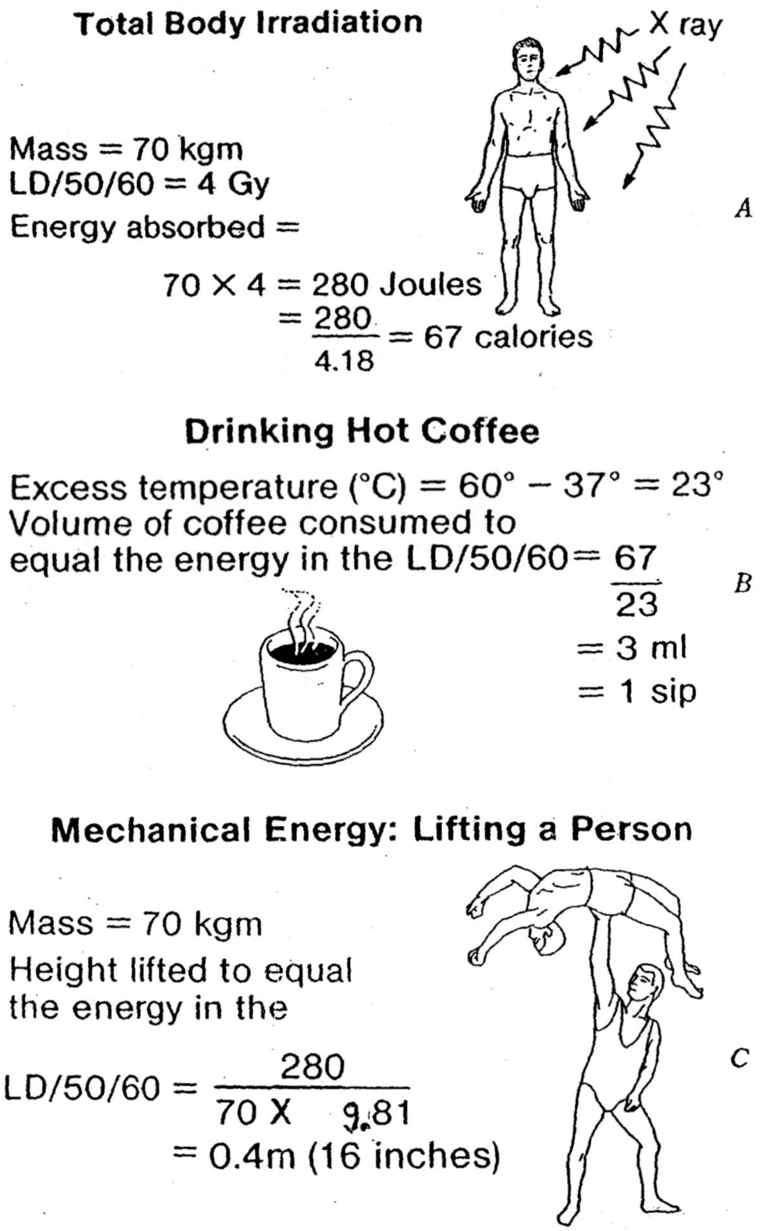

FIGURE 2.3. Illustrating that the biological effect of radiation it *NOT* due to the *amount* of the energy absorbed, but due to the photon size or "packet" size of the energy. (a) The total amount of energy absorbed in a 70 Kilogram (154 lb) human exposed to a lethal dose of 4 Gray is only 67 calories. (b) This is equal to the energy absorbed when drinking 1 sip of hot coffee. (c) It also equals the potential energy imparted by lifting a person about 16 inches.

short term

dose ranges - whole body, acute exposure

(central nervous system)

10 → 20 + Gy CN damage → death

(gastrointestinal) — like burst appendix.

6 - 10 Gy GI damage → death (3 days)

intervention possible

3 - 6 Gy bone marrow, hemopoietic damage LD_{50} (2 months)

can detect in blood, but ok unless other issue

1 - 3 Gy hematologic damage, survival likely

0.25 - 1 Gy measurable decrease in blood cell popn

~.01 Gy (10 mGy) maximum diagnostic doses

2-3 mGy annual natural background

50 - 500 μGy 'low dose' diagnostic procedures

1-5 μGy bone mineral by DEXA

50 nGy bone Pb by xrf

long term

contencious, unclear if it has any basis in reality, data seems to disagree (just keep that in mind)

delayed - cancer risk 8×10^{-2}/person Gy

⇒ 1 person receives 1 Gy, 8% additional chance of getting cancer (~ 4% of dying) cf 20% of deaths are cancer 'naturally'

Oct 25 end (Thurs)

Oct 26 start (Fri)

note for A3 - use Cr in place of Gy

(kinetic energy released per unit mass)

kerma and boundaries between media

at an air-tissue interface, there will be many more interactions in the tissue than in the air so more electrons are likely to 'leak' out of the tissue than 'leak' in from the air

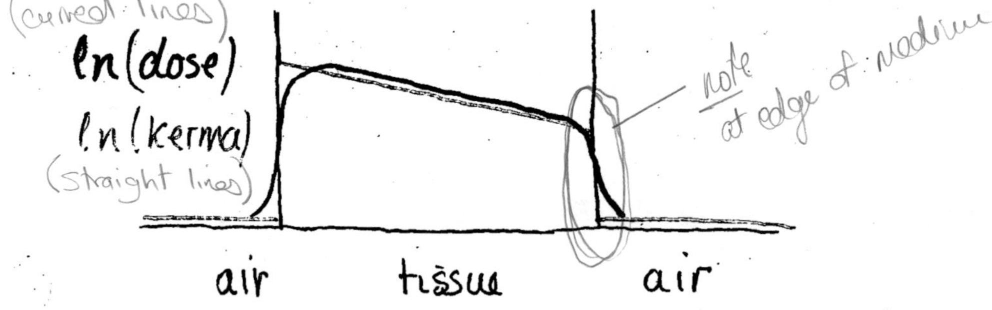

medium boundary can be between different types of tissue

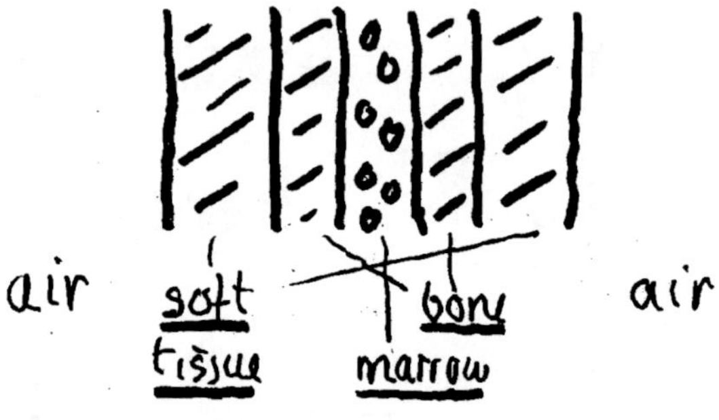

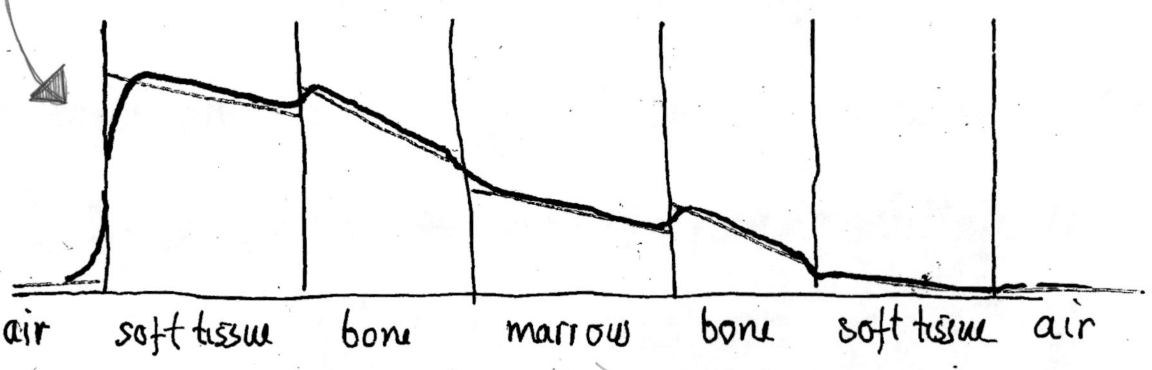

(this would be like an arm/leg)

Bragg-Gray theory and microdosimetry

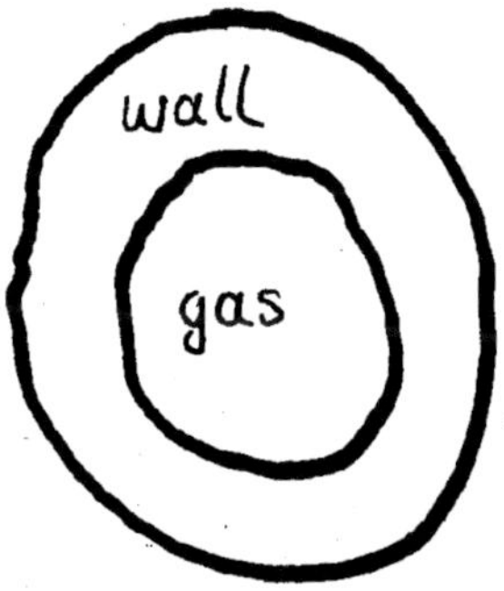

1. if wall and gas are of the same atomic composition and if the gas volume is relatively small, in particular if it is small enough not to alter charged particle velocity distributions then the gas effectively samples the dose distribution in the walls

so make walls (and gas) of tissue equivalent material

$$\text{so} \quad D_W = D_g = \frac{N_g W}{m}$$

where D_w is dose in wall, D_g is dose in gas, N_g is number of ions in gas and m is the mass of the gas

2. if walls are tissue equivalent, but gas is not can still find D_w providing we know mass stopping powers, S_w and S_g, of wall and gas

$$D_w = \frac{D_g S_w}{S_g} = \frac{N_g W S_w}{m S_g}$$

in practice, N_g will be measured as charge or current, W will be known for a particular gas, m will be known from the counter construction S_w/S_g will be very similar (if not identical) to the ratio of mass energy absorption coefficients

microdosimetry

actual energy deposition is a small scale event for electrons, and therefore for γ-rays, range and mean free path are relatively long, so 'dose' where there is an actual ionisation, but there can be a relatively long 'dose-free' gap in between

dose is a macroscopic, average quantity, but it is delivered as a series of specific, localised events - asking the question - is dose a valid measure with the average assumption?

the contrast between dose and the specific energy deposition is even more extreme for types of radiation with large stopping power (high LET) ~ typically expr as keV/μm

(LET is linear energy transfer, it is stopping power looked at from the point of view of the medium, rather than the particle, ie energy transferred to to the medium per unit path length on average)

(photons < 10 < protons/alphas)

a uniform whole body dose of low LET radiation of 1mGy results in 2/3 of cell nuclei receiving no dose at all, whereas 1/3 of nuclei receive an average dose of ~3 mGy

a uniform whole body dose of high LET radiation (fission neutrons) results in 99.8% of cell nuclei receiving no dose, whereas 0.2% of nuclei receive an average dose of 500 mGy - not lethal but notable

sometimes want to know actual distribution of 'microscopic doses' or 'specific energies'. these can be determined by microdosimetry

following Bragg-Gray cavity measured dose is

$$\frac{\text{number of ions in gas} \times \text{W value of gas}}{\text{mass of gas}}$$

reduce pressure in gas, so reduce mass

eventually linear path length is $1 \mu m$ equivalent in tissue

eg 5 cm diameter spherical counter filled with gas at ~ 0.03 atmospheres has thickness

$$\sim 2.5 \times 1.293 \times 10^{-3} \times 0.03 \simeq 1 \times 10^{-4} \text{ g cm}^{-2}$$

mass of $1 \mu m$ radius volume of tissue

$$= \frac{4}{3}\pi (10^{-4})^3 = 4.2 \times 10^{-12} \text{ g}$$

but cross sectional area $= \pi \times (10^{-4})^2 \text{ cm}^2$

so thickness is $\sim 1.3 \times 10^{-4} \text{ g cm}^{-2}$

compare ^3H with ^{32}P

	$\bar{E}_{\beta^-}$ (MeV)	med range (cm)	mass of sphere (kg)	local dose per decay (Gy)
^3H	.0062	5.34×10^{-5}	6.57×10^{-16}	1.51 — issue
^{32}P	.570	.190	2.97×10^{-5}	3.07×10^{-9} ? no issue

exposure from point source of γ-rays

specific gamma-ray constant ($\dot{\Gamma}$)

~ • = time varying

also known as specific gamm-ray emission or specific gamma constant (Γ)

define specific gamma-ray constant as exposure rate resulting from a unit of activity at a unit distance from a point source

assume source is sphere emitting uniformly

if $S(E)$ is the source strength (activity) which emits photons of energy E, then $\dot{\Phi}(E,r) = \frac{S(E)}{4\pi r^2}$ per unit area per unit time

but source strength is more generally the product of activity and probability of emission (branching ratio)

$$\dot{\Phi}(E,r) = \frac{p(E)N\lambda}{4\pi r^2}$$

energy fluence rate, $\dot{\Psi}(E,r) = \frac{E\,p(E)N\lambda}{4\pi r^2}$

rate of energy absorption in air

$$\dot{D} = \dot{\Psi}(E,r)\cdot\frac{\mu_{en}}{\rho} = \frac{E\,p(E)N\lambda}{4\pi r^2}\left(\mu_{en}/\rho\right)_{air}$$

back calc from dose to

to get exposure rate, use W value as energy required to produce ion pair

so exposure rate, $\dot{X} = \frac{e}{W_{air}} \frac{E\, p(E)\, N\lambda}{4\pi r^2} \left(\frac{\mu_{en}}{\rho}\right)_{air}$

why X? No official SI unit for exposure, but people have attempted to use this X.

but this only applies to one energy, in practice many radioactive sources emit γ-rays of more than one energy

then $$\dot{X} = \frac{e}{4\pi W_{air}} \cdot \frac{N\lambda}{r^2} \sum_{i=1}^{n} P_i(E)\, E_i \left(\frac{\mu_{en}(E_i)}{\rho}\right)_{air}$$ ← sum over different emissions

now define $\dot{\Gamma}$ such that $\dot{X} = \dot{\Gamma}\left(\frac{N\lambda}{r^2}\right)$

so $$\dot{\Gamma} = \frac{e}{4\pi W_{air}} \sum_{i=1}^{n} P_i(E)\, E_i \left(\frac{\mu_{en}(E_i)}{\rho}\right)_{air}$$

$e = 1.6 \times 10^{-19}$ C

we'll be flipping back & forth

$W_{air} = 34 \times 1.6 \times 10^{-19}$ J

E_i depends on decay scheme, can be measured in J (or eV)

$P_i(E)$ depends on decay scheme

$\left(\frac{\mu_{en}(E_i)}{\rho}\right)_{air}$ measured in $m^2\, kg^{-1}$ (or $\mu_{en}(E_i)$ in m^{-1} and ρ in $kg\, m^{-3}$)

for ^{24}Na, 2 γ rays of significance

E (MeV)	$P(E)$	$\left(\frac{\mu_{en}(E)}{\rho}\right)_{air}$ ($m^2 kg^{-1}$)
1·37	1·0	·00254
2·75	1·0	·00205

MeV → eV

$$\dot{\Gamma} = \frac{1.6\times10^{-19}}{4\pi\times34\times1.6\times10^{-19}}\left(\underbrace{1.0\times1.37\times2.54\times10^{-3}}_{1^{st}\ \gamma}+\underbrace{1.0\times2.75\times2.05\times10^{-3}}_{2^{nd}\ \gamma}\right)\times10^{6}\times1.6\times10^{-19}$$

$$= 3.4\times10^{-18}\ (C\ kg^{-1})\ m^2 (Bq^{-1}\ s^{-1})$$ (per disintegration)

end Oct 26 (Fri)

more practical (if slightly peculiar) units $R\ m^2\ Ci^{-1}\ h^{-1}$

$$\dot{\Gamma}_{^{24}Na} = 1.76\ R\ m^2\ Ci^{-1}\ h^{-1}$$

Turner gives approximate formula

$$\dot{\Gamma} = 0.5\ \Sigma E_i p \qquad \text{with } E \text{ in MeV}$$

this would give $0.5(1.37+2.75) = 2.06$

it is based on treating $\left(\frac{\mu_{en}}{\rho}\right)_{air}$ as constant over energy range of interest at $2.7\times10^{-3}\ m^2 kg^{-1}$

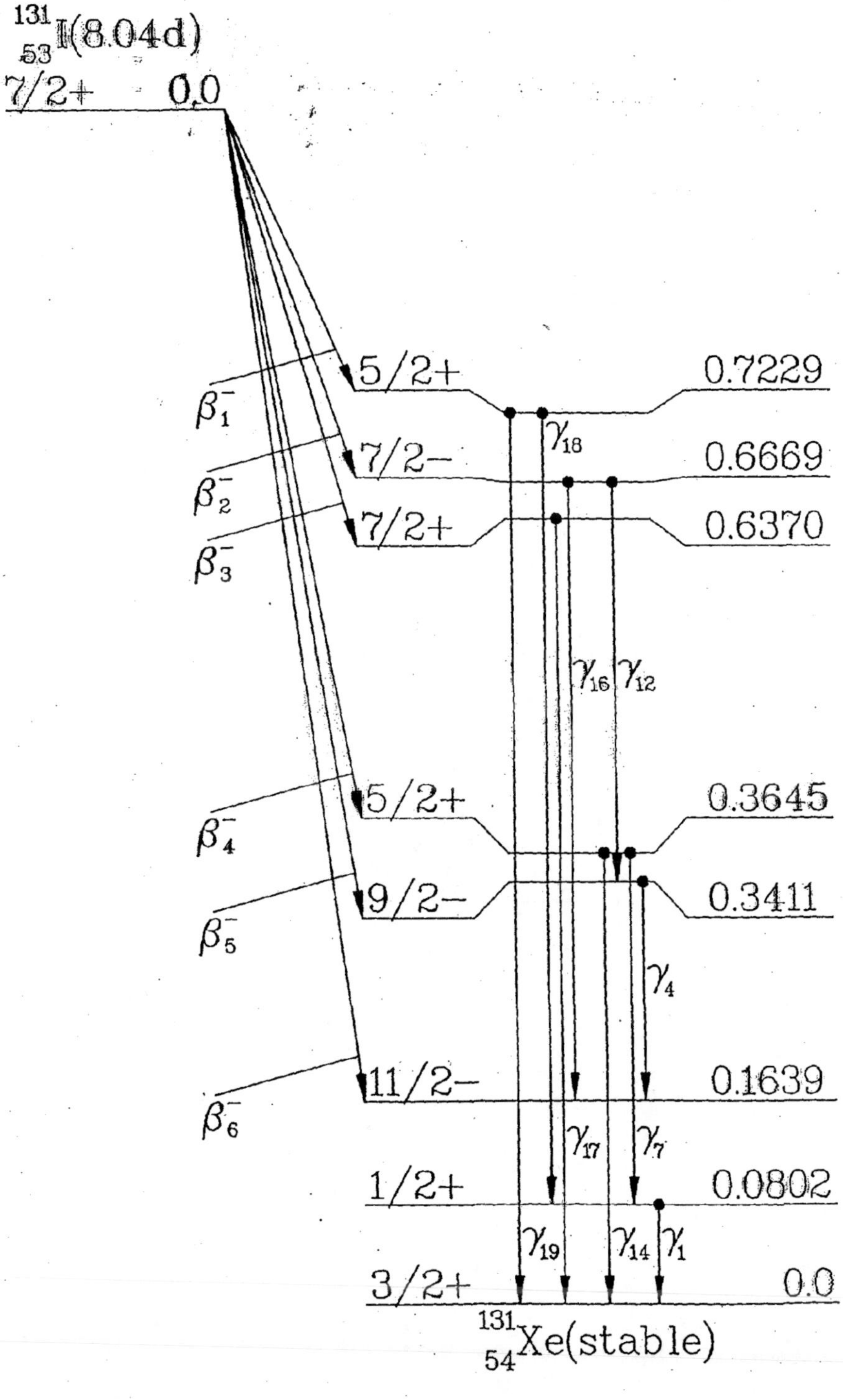

$^{131}_{53}$I(8.04d)
7/2+ 0.0
β_1^-
β_2^-
β_3^-
β_4^-
β_5^-
β_6^-
5/2+ 0.7229
7/2− 0.6669
7/2+ 0.6370
5/2+ 0.3645
9/2− 0.3411
11/2− 0.1639
1/2+ 0.0802
3/2+ 0.0
γ_{18}
γ_{16}
γ_{12}
γ_4
γ_{17}
γ_7
γ_{19}
γ_{14}
γ_1
$^{131}_{54}$Xe(stable)

IODINE

53–IODINE–131

HALFLIFE = 8.04 DAYS 21–JAN–76
DECAY MODE(S): β^-

RADIATION	y(i) $(Bq-s)^{-1}$	E(i) (MeV)	y(i)×E(i)
β^- 1	2.13E–02	6.935E–02*	1.48E–03
β^- 2	6.20E–03	8.693E–02*	5.39E–04
β^- 3	7.36E–02	9.660E–02*	7.11E–03
β^- 4	8.94E–01	1.915E–01*	1.71E–01
β^- 6	4.20E–03	2.832E–01*	1.19E–03
γ 1	2.62E–02	8.018E–02	2.10E–03
ce–K, γ 1	3.63E–02	4.562E–02	1.66E–03
ce–L_1, γ 1	4.30E–03	7.473E–02	3.21E–04
γ 4	2.65E–03	1.772E–01	4.70E–04
γ 7	6.06E–02	2.843E–01	1.72E–02
ce–K, γ 7	2.48E–03	2.497E–01	6.20E–04
γ 12	2.51E–03	3.258E–01	8.18E–04
γ 14	8.12E–01	3.645E–01	2.96E–01
ce–K, γ 14	1.55E–02	3.299E–01	5.10E–03
ce–L_1, γ 14	1.71E–03	3.590E–01	6.13E–04
γ 16	3.61E–03	5.030E–01	1.82E–03
γ 17	7.27E–02	6.370E–01	4.63E–02
γ 18	2.20E–03	6.427E–01	1.41E–03
γ 19	1.80E–02	7.229E–01	1.30E–02
$K\alpha_1$ X–ray	2.59E–02	2.978E–02	7.72E–04
$K\alpha_2$ X–ray	1.40E–02	2.946E–02	4.12E–04

LISTED X, γ AND $\gamma\pm$ RADIATIONS	3.80E–01
OMITTED X, γ AND $\gamma\pm$ RADIATIONS**	1.09E–03
LISTED β, ce AND Auger RADIATIONS	1.90E–01
OMITTED β, ce AND Auger RADIATIONS**	1.86E–03
LISTED RADIATIONS	5.70E–01
OMITTED RADIATIONS**	2.95E–03

* AVERAGE ENERGY (MeV)
** EACH OMITTED TRANSITION CONTRIBUTES <0.100% TO $\Sigma y(i)\times E(i)$ IN ITS CATEGORY.
XENON–131M DAUGHTER, YIELD 1.11E–02, IS RADIOACTIVE.
XENON–131 DAUGHTER, YIELD 9.889E–01, IS STABLE.

#3 on assignment

branching ratio = $\frac{\lambda_i}{\lambda}$

nuud.

if have 5 mCi of ^{24}Na at 0.3 m

$$\text{exposure rate} = \dot{\Gamma} \times 5\times10^{-3} \times \frac{1}{0.3^2} \ \text{R h}^{-1}$$

$$= 0.098 \ \text{R h}^{-1}$$

values of $\dot{\Gamma}$ (Γ) are tabulated

calculation of $\dot{\Gamma}$ was straight forward for ^{24}Na

but consider ^{131}I, 8 most prominent γ-rays are

E (MeV)	branching ratio (P)	$(\mu_{en}/\rho)_{air}$ $m^2\,kg^{-1}$	$\dot{\Gamma}_i$ $R\,m^2\,Ci^{-1}\,h^{-1}$
0.080	0.0261	2.393×10^{-3}	1.18×10^{-3}
0.177	2.64×10^{-3}	2.578×10^{-3}	2.33×10^{-4}
0.284	0.0604	2.844×10^{-3}	9.43×10^{-3}
0.326	2.50×10^{-3}	2.894×10^{-3}	4.56×10^{-4}
0.365	0.81	2.93×10^{-3}	0.167
0.503	3.60×10^{-3}	2.966×10^{-3}	1.038×10^{-3}
0.637	0.0724	2.938×10^{-3}	0.0262
0.723	0.018	2.907×10^{-3}	7.31×10^{-3}

$$\sum_{i=1}^{8} \dot{\Gamma}_i = 0.213$$

there are at least another 12 γ-rays, bringing

$\dot{\Gamma}$ to 0.216 $R\,m^2\,Ci^{-1}\,h^{-1}$ (a tabulated value is 0.22)

photon energy (MeV)	mass energy absorption coefficient (μ_{en}/ρ) $m^2 kg^{-1}$ water	air	compact bone	muscle
0·010	0·489	0·466	1·90	0·496
0·015	0·132	0·129	0·589	0·136
0·020	0·0523	0·0516	0·251	0·0544
0·030	0·0147	0·0147	0·0743	0·0154
0·040	6.47×10^{-3}	6.40×10^{-3}	0·0305	6.77×10^{-3}
0·050	3.94×10^{-3}	3.84×10^{-3}	0·0158	4.09×10^{-3}
0·060	3.04×10^{-3}	2.92×10^{-3}	9.79×10^{-3}	3.12×10^{-3}
0·080	2.53×10^{-3}	2.36×10^{-3}	5.20×10^{-3}	2.55×10^{-3}
0·10	2.52×10^{-3}	2.31×10^{-3}	3.86×10^{-3}	2.52×10^{-3}
0·15	2.78×10^{-3}	2.51×10^{-3}	3.04×10^{-3}	2.76×10^{-3}
0·20	3.00×10^{-3}	2.68×10^{-3}	3.02×10^{-3}	2.97×10^{-3}
0·30	3.20×10^{-3}	2.88×10^{-3}	3.11×10^{-3}	3.17×10^{-3}
0·40	3.29×10^{-3}	2.96×10^{-3}	3.16×10^{-3}	3.25×10^{-3}
0·50	3.30×10^{-3}	2.97×10^{-3}	3.16×10^{-3}	3.27×10^{-3}
0·60	3.29×10^{-3}	2.96×10^{-3}	3.15×10^{-3}	3.26×10^{-3}
0·80	3.21×10^{-3}	2.89×10^{-3}	3.06×10^{-3}	3.18×10^{-3}
1·0	3.11×10^{-3}	2.80×10^{-3}	2.97×10^{-3}	3.08×10^{-3}
1·5	2.83×10^{-3}	2.55×10^{-3}	2.70×10^{-3}	2.81×10^{-3}
2·0	2.60×10^{-3}	2.34×10^{-3}	2.48×10^{-3}	2.57×10^{-3}
3·0	2.27×10^{-3}	2.05×10^{-3}	2.19×10^{-3}	2.25×10^{-3}
4·0	2.05×10^{-3}	1.86×10^{-3}	1.99×10^{-3}	2.03×10^{-3}
5·0	1.90×10^{-3}	1.73×10^{-3}	1.86×10^{-3}	1.88×10^{-3}
6·0	1.80×10^{-3}	1.63×10^{-3}	1.78×10^{-3}	1.78×10^{-3}
8·0	1.65×10^{-3}	1.50×10^{-3}	1.65×10^{-3}	1.63×10^{-3}
10·0	1.55×10^{-3}	1.44×10^{-3}	1.59×10^{-3}	1.54×10^{-3}

what about dose calculation?

consider a fluence rate of $10^7\ m^{-2}\ s^{-1}$ of 0.3 MeV photons incident on soft tissue (muscle)

$$\dot{D} = \dot{\Phi} . E . (\mu_{en}/\rho)_{muscle} = \underbrace{10^7}_{m^{-2}s^{-1}} \times \underbrace{0.3 \times 1.6 \times 10^{-13}}_{J} \times \underbrace{3.17 \times 10^{-3}}_{m^2\,kg^{-1}}$$

$$= 1.52 \times 10^{-9}\ Gy\ s^{-1}$$

what about bone? photoelectric effect in Calcium

$$(\mu_{en}/\rho)_{bone} = 3.11 \times 10^{-3}\ m^2\ kg^{-1}$$

$$\dot{D} = 10^7 \times 0.3 \times 1.6 \times 10^{-13} \times 3.11 \times 10^{-3}$$

$$= 1.49 \times 10^{-9}\ Gy\ s^{-1}$$

same fluence rate of 30 keV photons (cf ^{125}I)

$$\dot{D}_{muscle} = 10^7 \times 30 \times 1.6 \times 10^{-16} \times 1.54 \times 10^{-2}$$

$$= 7.39 \times 10^{-10}\ Gy\ s^{-1}$$

$$\dot{D}_{bone} = 10^7 \times 30 \times 1.6 \times 10^{-16} \times 7.43 \times 10^{-2}$$

$$= 3.57 \times 10^{-9}\ Gy\ s^{-1}$$

- have so far considered exposure → dose
this applies to external dosimetry for photons
- external dosimetry for heavy charged particles
is either trivial (they don't get in) or rarely needed
(eg high energy protons)
- external dosimetry for $\beta^{\pm}$ often not important
$\bar{E}_\beta$ usually < 1 MeV, so range in tissue ≤ 4 mm
also β fluence often significantly attenuated in
escaping source
- external dosimetry for high energy electrons
significant in therapy

$-\left(\frac{dE}{dx}\right)_{collision}$ falls with increasing energy

$-\left(\frac{dE}{dx}\right)_{radiation}$ increases with increasing energy

resulting in broad minimum for total stopping
power between 0.3 MeV and 20 MeV

below 0.3 MeV stopping power rises so dose rate rises as electron energy falls as its nears the end of its range

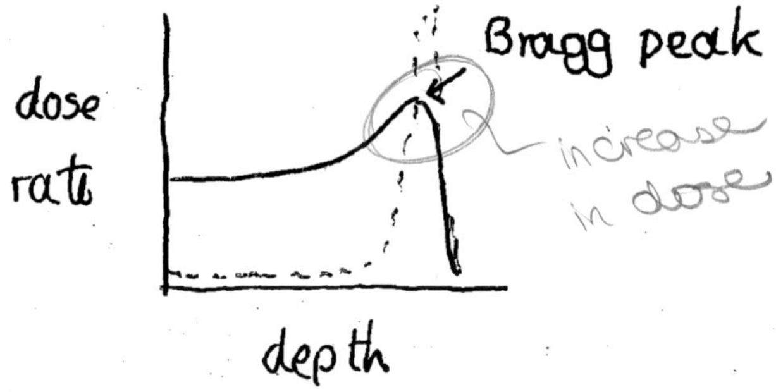

Bragg peak tends to be sharper for heavier, higher energy particles

- external dosimetry for neutrons different for fast neutrons and thermal neutrons, thermal neutron dosimetry includes $^1H(n,\gamma)^2H$ reaction, so need to consider γ-ray emitter internal to the body

  so postpone neutron dosimetry until after internal dosimetry

Oct. 30 end

Nov. 1 start

Internal dosimetry

different approach depending on whether all of energy is absorbed in tissue or not

in practice, all energy absorbed for α's and nearly all for β's, even for a relatively small organ

consider ^{35}S in testis, organ mass 18g, 7 kBq uniformly distributed, ^{35}S is pure β emitter

$\bar{E}_\beta = 0.0488$ MeV

dose rate from β's $\quad \dot{D}(\beta) = \dfrac{\overset{s^{-1}}{7\times10^{3}} \times \overset{J}{48.8\times1.6\times10^{-16}}}{\underset{kg}{18\times10^{-3}}} \text{ J kg}^{-1}\text{s}^{-1}$

$= 3.04\times10^{-9}$ Gy s^{-1}

that's not much, but what if it stays there?

$= 2.62\times10^{-4}$ Gy d^{-1}

(natural bg ~ $5 \rightarrow 9\times10^{-6}$ Gy d^{-1})

how long does this dose last for?

activity is decaying, also biological transport is likely to be removing activity (could consider gradual incorporation to steady state)

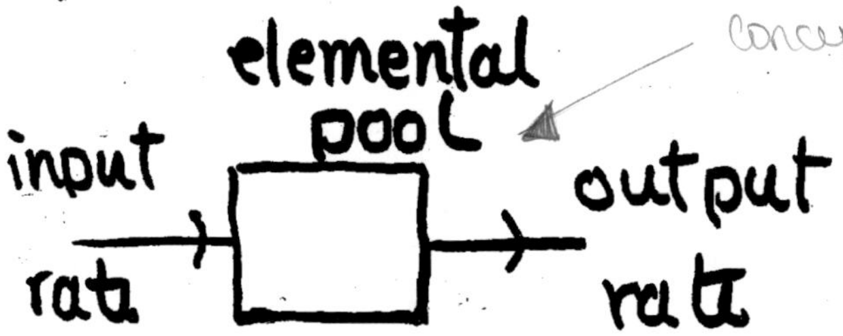

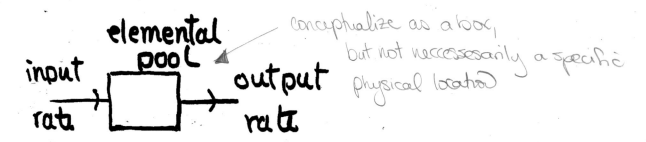

conceptualize as a box, but not neccessesarily a specific physical location

for adults in steady state, input rate = output rate

if have N_o radioactive nuclei of an element amongst a much larger number, M, of stable nuclei of that element, what is the probability of losing nuclei?

let output rate be R

can usually define k (specific to each pool) such that $R = kM$

ie k is a rate constant, or probability of transport out per atom (or could be defined per unit mass)

in example shown input rate = output rate

so $$\frac{dM}{dt} = +kM - kM = 0$$

but $$\frac{dN}{dt} = -kN$$ (if there is no continuing input of N) and, if there are N_0 active nuclei at $t = 0$, then

$$N = N_0 e^{-kt}$$

in the absence of any other loss (or gain) mechanisms

this would be approximately true for long lived radionuclides (eg ^{238}U) or stable nuclides of minor isotope (eg ^{204}Pb)

in general, for radioactive nuclei

$$\frac{dN}{dt} = \underset{\text{biological transport}}{-kN} \quad \underset{\text{physical decay}}{-\lambda N}$$

$$\frac{dN}{N} = -(k+\lambda)\,dt$$

$$N = N_0 e^{-(k+\lambda)t} \quad \text{with } N = N_0 \text{ at } t = 0$$

or $$N = N_0 e^{-(\lambda_M + \lambda_R)t}$$

where λ_M is the metabolic rate constant and λ_R is the radioactive (physical) decay constant

can define biological (or metabolic) half life like radioactive half life $t_M = \frac{\ln 2}{\lambda_M}$

cf $t_{1/2} = t_R = \frac{\ln 2}{\lambda_R}$

also, effective half life $T_{eff} = \frac{\ln 2}{(\lambda_M + \lambda_R)}$

$$\frac{1}{T_{eff}} = \frac{1}{T_M} + \frac{1}{T_R}$$

$$T_{eff} = \frac{T_M T_R}{T_M + T_R}$$

for ^{35}S in testis example

$T_R = 87.1$ d , $T_M = 623$ d

so $T_{Eff} = 76.4$ d (note: sanity check, is $T_{eff} < T_R + T_M$?)

note, T_M was quoted for sulphur in testis, sulphur in other organs or in body as a whole will, in general, be different

have used simplified single compartment model full reality often much more complex

initial dose rate was 2.62×10^{-4} Gy d^{-1} $= \dot{D}_0$

rate of change of dose rate

$$\frac{d\dot{D}}{dt} = -\lambda_{eff}\dot{D}$$

$$\dot{D} = \dot{D}_0 e^{-\lambda_{eff} t}$$

$$D = \int \dot{D}\, dt$$

total dose rate in interval 0 to τ

$$D = \int_0^{\tau} \dot{D}\, dt = \dot{D}_0 \int_0^{\tau} e^{-\lambda_{eff} t}\, dt$$

$$= \frac{\dot{D}_0}{\lambda_{eff}} (1 - e^{-\lambda_{eff}\tau})$$

for the special case of $\tau = 50y$, this is defined as the committed dose, for many examples, 50y is so long that it is effectively infinite – so don't really worry about it

and $$D = \frac{\dot{D}_0}{\lambda_{eff}} = \frac{\dot{D}_0 T_{eff}}{\ln 2}$$

$$D = \frac{2.62 \times 10^{-4} \times 76.4}{\ln 2} = 0.029 \text{ Gy}$$

now go back and work out the number of ^{35}S nuclei

activity at time zero $= N_0 \lambda_R = 7 \times 10^3$

$$N_0 = \frac{7\times10^3}{\lambda_R} = \frac{7\times10^3}{\ln 2/87.1\times24\times3600}$$

$$= 7.6\times10^{10} \text{ nuclei}$$

note: we had to use λ_R, the physical decay const.

if the number of nuclei, N_0, is known, then

$$\dot{D}_0 = \frac{(N_0\lambda_R)(\bar{E}_\beta)}{m}$$ still assuming all energy absorbed

and $$D = \frac{N_0 \lambda_R \bar{E}_\beta}{\lambda_E m}\left(1 - e^{-\lambda_E \tau}\right)$$

also activity, $A(t) = N_0 \lambda_R e^{-(\lambda_R + \lambda_H)t}$

we're not really going to do this – too complicated

have considered a single compartment, characterised by one elimination rate constant, sometimes need to consider two or more compartments

if q_0 is quantity administered at time $t=0$,

$q(t)$ is total quantity remaining at time t and

q_{10}, λ_{1E}; q_{20}, λ_{2E}; q_{n0}, λ_{nE}

are initial quantities and effective elimination rates for compartments 1 to n

then $q(t) = q_{10} e^{-\lambda_{1E} t} + q_{20} e^{-\lambda_{2E} t} + \cdots + q_{n0} e^{-\lambda_{nE} t}$

similarly, if the initial dose rates in compartments are

$\dot{D}_{10}$, $\dot{D}_{20}$, $\dot{D}_{n0}$

then $D = \frac{\dot{D}_{10}}{\lambda_{1E}}(1-e^{-\lambda_{1E}t}) + \frac{\dot{D}_{20}}{\lambda_{2E}}(1-e^{-\lambda_{2E}t}) + \cdots + \frac{\dot{D}_{n0}}{\lambda_{nE}}(1-e^{-\lambda_{nE}t})$

and, when all the isotope has been eliminated $t \gg T_{max\,E}$

$$D = \frac{\dot{D}_{10}}{\lambda_{1E}} + \frac{\dot{D}_{20}}{\lambda_{2E}} + \cdots + \frac{\dot{D}_{n0}}{\lambda_{nE}}$$

still a simplification, activity may increase in a compartment as a result of metabolic transport

internal dosimetry - γ emitters

there are two inter-related complications

(i) some, but not all, γ energy is absorbed in the organ of origin

(ii) γ's emitted from one organ can deposit energy in another (or 1 person to another)

the following factors need to be taken into consideration

a) distance from source to target (R) so $1/R^2$

b) attenuation $e^{-\mu R}$

c) generate secondary scattered fluence

d) not a point source, so integrate over volume

e) not a point target, so integrate over that volume

f) once arrived at target, consider mass-energy absorption $e^{-(\mu_{en}/\rho)}$

a) to f) can be collected into a single factor, the absorbed fraction AF this will apply to a particular energy of photon, a particular source organ and a particular target organ

so have $AF(T \leftarrow S)_R$ which is the absorbed fraction for radiation type R emanating from organ S and impinging on organ T

then specific absorbed fraction is $\frac{AF(T \leftarrow S)_R}{M_T}$

where M_T is the target organ

this is the fraction of the energy absorbed per unit mass of target organ, need to multiply by energy of the particular radiation, E_R

also, a particular radioisotope may emit a number of different types of radiation, each with its own branching ratio (or yield) Y_R

~~end Nov 1st~~
Nov 2nd start

for each type of radiation, then energy absorbed per unit mass of target organ is $\frac{AF(T \leftarrow S)_R \, Y_R E_R}{M_T}$

then, for each disintegration of radioisotope get

$$\sum_R \left(\frac{AF(T \leftarrow S)_R \, Y_R E_R}{M_T} \right)$$

for dose rate then just need to know number of disintegrations per unit time (activity)

saw earlier that $A(t) = N_0 \lambda_R e^{-(\lambda_R + \lambda_M)t}$

so $$\dot{D}(T \leftarrow S) = \frac{N_0(S) \lambda_R e^{-(\lambda_R + \lambda_M)t}}{M_T} \sum_R \left(AF(T \leftarrow S)_R \, Y_R E_R \right)$$

can then take this forward to committed dose, but wait until look at effect of radiation type and tissue type

the only complicated part of this is AF, which depends on radiation type/energy, source organ, and target organ – values are tabulated

analytical calculations are impractical for real geometries so use numerical technique – Monte Carlo simulation

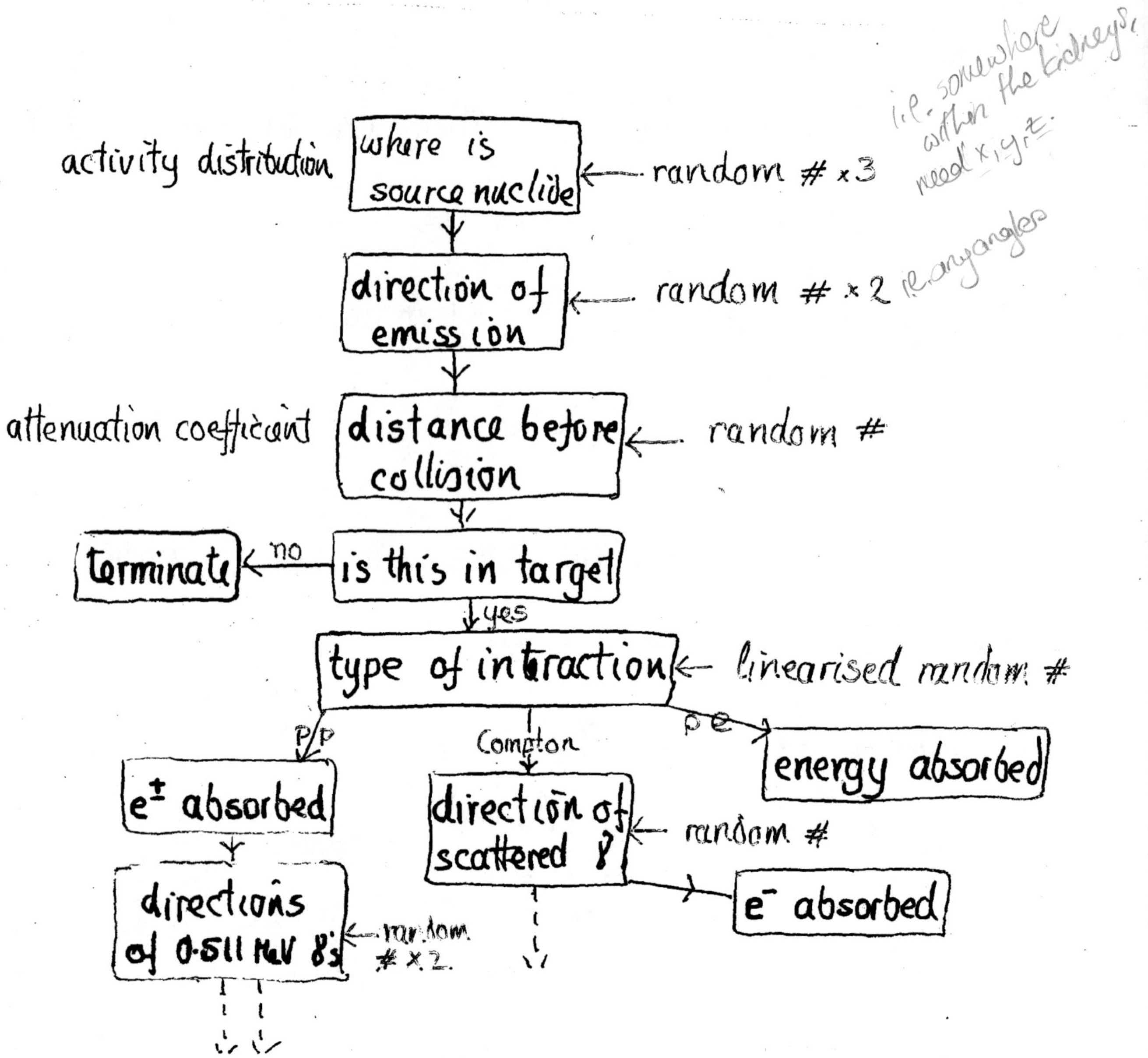

activity distribution
where is source nuclide
random # × 3
i.e. somewhere within the kidneys, need x, y, z
direction of emission
random # × 2
i.e. any angles
attenuation coefficient
distance before collision
random #
terminate
no
is this in target
yes
type of interaction
linearised random #
P/P
Compton
pe
energy absorbed
e± absorbed
direction of scattered γ
random #
e⁻ absorbed
directions of 0.511 MeV γ's
random # × 2.

$$\dot{D}(T \leftarrow S) = \frac{N_0(S)\,\lambda_R\, e^{-\lambda_E t}}{M_T} \sum_R \{AF(T \leftarrow S)_R\, Y_R\, E_R\}$$

committed dose, $D(50) = \frac{N_0(S)\,\lambda_R\,(1 - e^{-\lambda_E \tau})}{M_T\ \lambda_E} \sum \{AF(T \leftarrow S)_R\, Y_R\, E_R\}$

where τ is 50 years

if $T_E \ll 50y$, $\lambda_E \tau \gg 1$ and

$$D = D(50) = \frac{N_0(S)\ \lambda_R}{M_T\ \lambda_E} \sum \{AF(T \leftarrow S)_R\, Y_R\, E_R\}$$

consider total dose and initial dose rate to 70 kg, 1.8 m tall person given 1 MBq of $^{24}NaCl$ case 1

assume $^{24}NaCl$ rapidly becomes uniformly distributed

biological half life (T_M) of $^{24}NaCl$ = 11 days

$T_R = 15\ h$

$N_0(S)\lambda_R = 1\ MBq$; $M_T = 70\,kg$; $\lambda_E = \frac{\ln 2}{T_R} + \frac{\ln 2}{T_M}$

$$= \frac{\ln 2}{11 \times 24} + \frac{\ln 2}{15}\ h^{-1}$$

$$\doteq 0.0488\ h^{-1}$$

$$= 1.36 \times 10^{-5}\ s^{-1}$$

$$\frac{N_0(S)\,\lambda_R}{\lambda_E} = \frac{10^6}{1.36 \times 10^{-5}} = 7.37 \times 10^{10} \text{ disintegrations}$$

for ^{24}Na,

particle	Y_R	E_R (MeV)	$Y_R E_R$ (J/disint)	AF(body←body)
β_1	·999	0·555	$8{\cdot}87 \times 10^{-14}$	1
γ_1	·999	1·37	$2{\cdot}19 \times 10^{-13}$	0·306
γ_2	·999	2·75	$4{\cdot}402 \times 10^{-13}$	0·265

$$\sum AF(\text{body} \leftarrow \text{body})_R Y_R E_R = 2{\cdot}72 \times 10^{-13} \text{ J/decay}$$

$$D = \frac{7{\cdot}37 \times 10^{10} \times 2{\cdot}72 \times 10^{-13}}{70} \text{ J kg}^{-1}$$

$$= 0{\cdot}286 \text{ mGy}$$

initial dose rate, $\dot{D}_0 = \dfrac{N_0(S)\lambda_R \sum \{AF(T \leftarrow S)_R Y_R E_R\}}{M_T}$

$$\dot{D}_0 = D\lambda_E = 2{\cdot}86 \times 10^{-4} \times 1{\cdot}36 \times 10^{-5}$$

$$= 3{\cdot}89 \times 10^{-9} \text{ Gy s}^{-1}$$

where did the AF (body ← body) come from

table 6.8 in Cember gives absorbed fractions for γ-emitter uniformly distributed throughout the body for various target organs, including whole body

photon energy (MeV)	0·10	0·20	0·50	1·0	1·5	2·0	4·0
AF (body ← body)	0·370	0·338	0·340	0·321	0·302	0·284	0·240

interpolate, eg $\frac{\ln(\cdot 302) - \ln(\cdot 321)}{\ln(1\cdot 5) - \ln(1\cdot 0)} \times \ln\left(\frac{1\cdot 37}{1\cdot 0}\right) + \ln(\cdot 321) = -1\cdot 184$

$e^{-1\cdot 184} = 0\cdot 306$

or $\frac{\cdot 302 - \cdot 321}{1\cdot 5 - 1\cdot 0} \times 0\cdot 37 + 0\cdot 321 = 0\cdot 307$

for 2·75 MeV ln(AF) vs ln(E) fit gives 0·263

AF vs E fit gives 0·268

case 2

what would have happened if it had been $^{22}NaCl$ instead of $^{24}NaCl$?

$T_R = 2\cdot 6$ y, $T_M = 11$ d, $N_0(S)\lambda_R = 1$ MBq, $M_T = 70$ kg

$\lambda_E = \frac{\ln 2}{11} + \frac{\ln 2}{2\cdot 6 \times 365}$ d^{-1}

$= 0\cdot 0637\ d^{-1} = 7\cdot 38 \times 10^{-7}\ s^{-1}$ ($<Na^{24}$)

for ^{22}Na

particle	Y_R	E_R (MeV)	$Y_R E_R$ (J/disint)	AF(body ← body)
β^+	0·905	0·191	$2\cdot 77 \times 10^{-14}$	1
photon	1·81	0·511	$1\cdot 48 \times 10^{-13}$	0·339
γ	1	1·275	$2\cdot 04 \times 10^{-13}$	0·309

$\sum_R AF(\text{body} \leftarrow \text{body})_R Y_R E_R = 1\cdot 41 \times 10^{-13}$ J/disint cf $2\cdot 72 \times 10^{-13}$ for ^{24}Na

next class test — prob week of Nov12 (maybe Fri.)

$$\dot{D}_0 = \frac{N_0(S)\,\lambda_R}{M_T} \sum AF(body \leftarrow body)_R\, Y_R\, E_R$$

$$= \frac{10^6 \times 1.41 \times 10^{-13}}{70} = 2.01 \times 10^{-9}\ Gy\ s^{-1}$$

so the initial dose rate is nearly a factor of 2 lower than for ^{24}Na

$$D = \frac{\dot{D}_0}{\lambda_E} = \frac{2.0 \times 10^{-9}}{7.37 \times 10^{-7}}$$

$$= 2.73\ mGy$$

End Nov 2nd.

but the committed dose is nearly 10 times higher

Start Nov. 6th

a more complicated example, Comber example 6.10

accidental exposure to ^{203}Hg, found afterwards that there is 0.5 MBq in kidneys and that the effective turnover rate in kidneys is 2.6% d^{-1}. Assume 50% of total ^{203}Hg in kidneys (uniformly distributed), 20% in liver and 30% uniformly distributed through the rest of the body

$$D(kidney) = D(kidney \leftarrow kidney) + D(kidney \leftarrow liver) + D(kidney \leftarrow body)$$

kidney mass = 0.3 kg

need λ_E's for different organs

$$\lambda_E(\text{kidney}) = 0.026\ d^{-1} \quad (\text{given})$$

from tabulated data $\lambda_M(\text{liver}) = \frac{\ln(2)}{13.5}\ d^{-1}$

$$\lambda_M(\text{body}) = \frac{\ln(2)}{10}\ d^{-1}$$

$\lambda_R = \frac{\ln(2)}{46.9}\ d^{-1}$ so $\lambda_E(\text{liver}) = 0.0661\ d^{-1}$

$$\lambda_E(\text{body}) = 0.0841\ d^{-1}$$

$Y_R E_R AF_R$ values tabulated for ^{203}Hg, ie summing over all radiation

for ^{203}Hg $\sum_R AF(\text{kidney} \leftarrow \text{kidney})_R Y_R E_R = 1.82 \times 10^{-14}$ J disint^{-1}

$$\sum_R AF(\text{kidney} \leftarrow \text{liver})_R Y_R E_R = 1.55 \times 10^{-16} \text{ J disint}^{-1}$$

$$\sum_R AF(\text{kidney} \leftarrow \text{body})_R Y_R E_R = 1.37 \times 10^{-16} \text{ J disint}^{-1}$$

$$D(\text{kidney} \leftarrow \text{kidney}) = \frac{0.5 \times 10^6 \times 24 \times 3600}{0.026 \times 0.3} \times 1.82 \times 10^{-14}$$

$$= 0.1008\ Gy$$

$$D(\text{kidney} \leftarrow \text{liver}) = \frac{0.2 \times 10^6 \times 24 \times 3600}{0.0661 \times 0.3} \times 1.55 \times 10^{-16}$$

$$= 1.35 \times 10^{-4}\ Gy$$

$$D(\text{kidney} \leftarrow \text{body}) = \frac{0.3 \times 10^6 \times 24 \times 3600}{0.0841 \times 0.3} \times 1.37 \times 10^{-16}$$

$$= 1.41 \times 10^{-4}\ Gy$$

total kidney dose = 101·0 mGy

neutron dosimetry

for fast neutrons main energy transfer mechanism is elastic scattering

consider energy absorbed in the locality of the first collision, there will be subsequent collisions, but these will usually be some distance away from first collision

dose rate depends on neutron fluence rate, energy, target number density, scattering cross section and mean fraction of energy absorbed per collision

$$\dot{D}_n(E) = \dot{\Phi}(E)\, E \sum_i N_i \sigma_i(E) f_i$$

$$\text{or } D_n(E) = \Phi(E)\, E \sum_i N_i \sigma_i(E) f_i$$

$\dot{\Phi}(E)$ fluence rate of neutrons of energy E, in neutrons $cm^{-2}s^{-1}$ (or $m^{-2}s^{-1}$

E neutron energy in joules

N_i number of atoms of the ith element per kg target

$\sigma_i(E)$ cross section for elastic scattering of neutrons of energy E by the ith element, in cm^2 [barn × 10^{-24}] (or in m^2)

f_i mean fractional energy transferred in elastic collision with i^{th} element

consider 5 MeV neutrons and major elements (H, O, C, N...

of soft tissue

element	% mass	N (atom kg^{-1})	f	σ (m^2)	Nσf ($m^2 kg^{-1}$)	% total
H	10.0	5.98×10^{25}	0.632	1.61×10^{-28}	6.02×10^{-3}	90.4
O	71.27	2.69×10^{25}	0.113	1.55×10^{-28}	4.71×10^{-4}	7.00
C	14.89	6.41×10^{24}	0.146	1.65×10^{-28}	1.54×10^{-4}	2.29
N	3.47	1.49×10^{24}	0.127	1.00×10^{-28}	1.89×10^{-5}	0.28
Na	0.15	3.93×10^{22}	0.081	2.3×10^{-28}	7.3×10^{-7}	0.011
Cl	0.10	1.70×10^{22}	0.054	2.8×10^{-28}	2.6×10^{-7}	0.0038
					6.73×10^{-3}	

so, for 5 MeV neutrons dose given by

$$D_n(E) = \dot{\Phi}(E)\, E \sum_i N_i\, \sigma_i(E) f_i = 5 \times 1.6 \times 10^{-13} \times 6.73 \times 10^{-3}$$

$$= 5.38 \times 10^{-15}\ Gy\ m^2$$

Fred Noule

Start Nov 8:

thermal neutrons

2 reactions predominate $^{14}N(n,p)^{14}C$, $^{1}H(n,\gamma)^{2}H$

$^{14}N(n,p)^{14}C$

$$^{14}N + {}^{1}n \rightarrow {}^{14}C + {}^{1}H$$

$$\Delta\,(MeV) \quad 2.864 + 8.071 = 3.020 + 7.289 + Q$$

$$Q = 0.626 \text{ MeV}$$

proton takes 0.584 MeV, but all energy of ^{1}H plus ^{14}C likely to be absorbed in tissue

dose rate, $\dot{D}_{n,p} = \dot{\Phi} N \sigma Q$

where $\dot{\Phi}$ = thermal neutron fluence rate, $m^{-2} s^{-1}$

N = ^{14}N atoms, $(kg \text{ tissue})^{-1}$

σ = reaction cross section, m^2

Q = energy released by reaction, J

$\sigma = 1.75 \text{ b} = 1.75 \times 10^{-28} m^2$; $N = 1.49 \times 10^{24}$ atoms kg^{-1}

so $\dot{D}_{n,p} = \dot{\Phi} \times 1.49 \times 10^{24} \times 1.75 \times 10^{-28} \times 0.626 \times 1.6 \times 10^{-13}$

$= 2.61 \times 10^{-17}$ Gy s^{-1} [neutron $m^{-2} s^{-1}$]$^{-1}$

this considers dose from proton and recoiling ^{14}C, not ^{14}C decay

$^1H(n,\gamma)^2H$ get 2·223 MeV γ-ray for each reaction

$AF(\text{body} \leftarrow \text{body})_{2\cdot223\,MeV} = 0\cdot278$

$\dot{D}_{H(n,\gamma)} = \dot{\Phi}\, N\sigma\, AF(\text{body} \leftarrow \text{body})\, Y E$

$N = 5\cdot98 \times 10^{25}, \quad \sigma = 0\cdot33 \times 10^{-28}\ m^2$

$\dot{D}_{H(n,\gamma)} = \dot{\Phi} \times 5\cdot98 \times 10^{25} \times 0\cdot33 \times 10^{-28} \times 0\cdot278 \times 1 \times 2\cdot223 \times 1\cdot6 \times 10^{-13}$

$= 1\cdot95 \times 10^{-16}\ Gy\ s^{-1} [\text{neutron}\ m^{-2}\ s^{-1}]^{-1}$

next most prominent reaction

$^{35}Cl(n,\gamma)^{36}Cl$ get γ-rays of a number of different high energies ~ 6 MeV is typical $AF(\text{body} \leftarrow \text{body}) = 0\cdot22$

$N = 1\cdot7 \times 10^{22}; \quad \sigma = 43 \times 10^{-28}\ m^2$

$\dot{D}_{Cl(n,\gamma)} = \dot{\Phi} \times 1\cdot7 \times 10^{22} \times 43 \times 10^{-28} \times 0\cdot22 \times 1 \times 6 \times 1\cdot6 \times 10^{-13}$

$= 1\cdot54 \times 10^{-17}\ Gy\ s^{-1} [\text{neutron}\ m^{-2}\ s^{-1}]^{-1}$

what about the dose from induced activity?

- there isn't much induced activity

the most abundant nuclei in the body are ^{1}H, ^{16}O, ^{12}C, ^{14}N neutron absorption leads to ^{2}H, ^{17}O, ^{13}C, ^{15}N all of which are stable

consider ^{24}Na (from $^{23}Na(n,\gamma)$) and ^{14}C

activity, $N\lambda$ given by $N\lambda = \dot{\Phi} N_{^{23}Na} \sigma (1 - e^{-\lambda_R t})$

where t is time of irradiation, if $t \ll T_R$ (15h)

then $N\lambda = \dot{\Phi} N_{^{23}Na} \sigma \lambda_R t$

consider committed dose, rather than initial dose rate

$$D(50) = \frac{N_0 \lambda_R}{\lambda_E \times m} \times \sum AF(\text{body} \leftarrow \text{body}) Y E$$

previously calculated $\sum AF(\text{body} \leftarrow \text{body}) YE = 2.722 \times 10^{-13}$ J disint^{-1}

$\lambda_E = 0.0488\ h^{-1}$, $N_{^{23}Na} = 3.93 \times 10^{22}$ atoms kg^{-1} ; $m = 1$ kg

$\sigma = 0.53 \times 10^{-28}\ m^2$, $\lambda_R = \ln 2/15\ h^{-1}$

$$D_{^{24}Na} = \dot{\Phi} t \times \frac{3.93 \times 10^{22} \times 0.53 \times 10^{-28}}{0.0488} \times \frac{\ln 2}{15} \times 2.722 \times 10^{-13}$$

$D_{^{24}Na} = 5.37 \times 10^{-19}$ Gy [neutron $m^{-2}]^{-1}$

for ^{14}C $\quad D(50) = \dfrac{N_0 \lambda_R \times \sum AF(\text{body} \leftarrow \text{body})\, YE}{\lambda_E \times m} \left(1 - e^{-\lambda_E \tau}\right)$

$$N_0 \lambda_R = 1.49 \times 10^{24} \times 1.75 \times 10^{-28} \times \frac{\ln 2}{5730 \times 365} \;\dot{\Phi} t$$

where $T_R = 5730$ y so $\lambda_R = \dfrac{\ln 2}{5730 \times 365}$ d^{-1}

^{14}C decays emitting only a β^- with $\bar{E}_\beta = 0.0495$ MeV

so have $\sum AF(\text{body} \leftarrow \text{body}) YE = 7.92 \times 10^{-15}$ J disint^{-1}

what about λ_E? suppose a person consumes 1.4 kg food d^{-1} and this has same proportional carbon content as the body, if body mass is 70 kg

then $\lambda_M \simeq \dfrac{1.4}{70} = 0.02$ d^{-1}

and $\lambda_E = 0.02 + \dfrac{\ln 2}{5730 \times 365} = 0.02$

so $D(50)_{^{14}C} = \dfrac{\dot{\Phi} t \times 1.49 \times 10^{24} \times 1.75 \times 10^{-28} \times \frac{\ln 2}{5730 \times 365}}{0.02} \times 7.92 \times 10^{-15}$

$= 3.42 \times 10^{-23}$ Gy [neutron $m^{-2}]^{-1}$

dose from thermal neutron irradiation per unit fluence $[\text{neutron m}^{-2}]^{-1}$

reaction	radiation type	dose $(Gy\ [\text{neutron m}^{-2}]^{-1})$
$^{1}H(n,\gamma)^{2}H$	γ	1.95×10^{-16}
$^{14}N(n,p)^{14}C$	p, ^{14}C recoil	2.61×10^{-17}
$^{35}Cl(n,\gamma)^{36}Cl$	γ	1.54×10^{-17}
$^{23}Na(n,\gamma)^{24}Na$	^{24}Na decay	5.37×10^{-19}
$^{14}N(n,p)^{14}C$	^{14}C decay	3.42×10^{-23}

total $= 2.37 \times 10^{-16}$ Gy m^2

cf 5 MeV neutrons 5.38×10^{-15} Gy m^2

also, note that thermal neutron dose comes from a mixture of low LET (γ, β) and high LET (p, ^{14}C recoil) radiation types

Test #2 @ Canadian Martyrs

pg 113 - 186 Friday Nov. 16th

US may use different terminology, rest of the world uses this

Equivalent Dose and Effective Dose

equivalent dose takes into account the fact that different types of radiation produce different amounts of biological damage for the same physical absorbed dose

effective dose takes into account the fact that the same amount of the same type of radiation produces different amounts of damage in different tissues (and different amounts of different types of damage) ⇒ radiosensitivity varies from organ to organ

Equivalent Dose

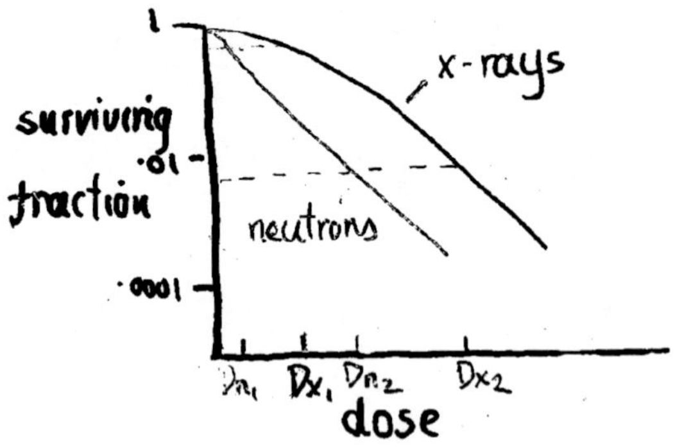

relative biological effectiveness (RBE) is ratio of x-ray dose to dose of radiation type R to produce same biological effect

$$RBE_1 = \frac{D_{x_1}}{D_{n_1}} \qquad RBE_2 = \frac{D_{x_2}}{D_{n_2}}$$

$$RBE_1 \neq RBE_2$$

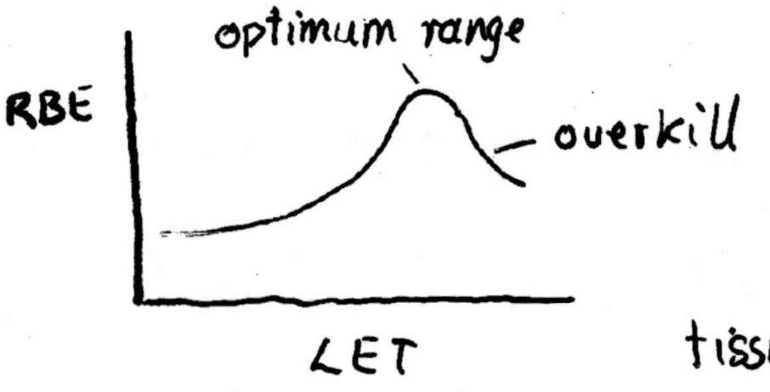

RBE varies with radiation type (LET), dose, dose rate, tissue type, biological effect ....

try to summarise variation of RBE with LET by using radiation weighting factor w_R (ICRP#60, 1990)

Radiation		w_R
X, γ, electrons, β^+, muons		1
neutrons	$E_n < 10$ keV	5
	10 keV $< E_n <$ 100 keV	10
	100 keV $< E_n <$ 2 MeV	20
	2 MeV $< E_n \nless$ 20 MeV	10
	$E_n >$ 20 MeV	5
protons (not recoil)	$E_p >$ 2 MeV	5
α, fission fragments, non-relativistic heavy nuclei		20 — essentially upper limit

for other radiation types or energies use

LET, L (keV μm^{-1} in water)	$Q(L)$
< 10	1
10 - 100	$0.32L - 2.2$
> 100	$300/\sqrt{L}$

and $$w_R \cong \bar{Q} = \frac{1}{D}\int_0^{\infty} Q(L)\, D(L)\, dL$$

End Nov 8th

return to neutron dosimetry

fast neutrons: for 5 MeV, 5.38×10^{-15} Gy [neutron m^{-2}]$^{-1}$

$w_R = 10$

equivalent dose, $H = w_R D$

$= 5.38 \times 10^{-14}$ Sv [neutron m^{-2}]$^{-1}$

for other energies both E_n and $\sigma(E)$ are different

for approximation, consider $\sigma(E)$ constant

then for $100\ keV < E_n < 2\ MeV$, $w_R = 20$

$H = 20 \times 1.076 \times 10^{-15} \times E_n$ Sv [neutron m^{-2}]$^{-1}$

where E_n is in MeV

an $^{241}Am/Be$ source gives spectrum of fast neutrons
total output $2.2 \times 10^6\ s^{-1}\ Ci^{-1}$

assume 25% have $100\ keV < E_n < 2\ MeV$ $w_R = 20$
(take typical $E_n = 0.5$ MeV)
75% have $2\ MeV < E_n < 20\ MeV$ $w_R = 10$
(take typical $E_n = 5$ MeV)

consider dose h^{-1} at 1 m

$$H = (0.25 \times 2.15 \times 10^{-14} \times 0.5 + .75 \times 5.38 \times 10^{-14}) \times \frac{2.2 \times 10^6 \times 3600}{4\pi \times 1^2}$$
$$= 1.69 \times 10^{-6} + 2.543 \times 10^{-5}\ Sv\ h^{-1}\ Ci^{-1}$$
$$= 27\ \mu Sv\ h^{-1}\ Ci^{-1}$$

alternatively

absorbed dose for 5 MeV neutrons

$$= 5{\cdot}38 \times 10^{-15}\ \text{Gy}\ [\text{neutron m}^{-2}]^{-1}$$

assume, as a first approximation, that

absorbed dose for fast neutrons of energy E_n

$$= \frac{5{\cdot}38 \times 10^{-15}}{5} \times E_n = 1{\cdot}076 \times 10^{-15} \times E_n\ \text{Gy}\ [\text{neutron m}^{-2}]^{-1}$$

where E_n is neutron energy in MeV

then equivalent dose, $H = w_R E_n \times 1{\cdot}076 \times 10^{-15}\ \text{Sv}\ [\text{neutron m}^{-2}]^{-1}$

given fluence at energy $E_n = \Phi_{E_n}$ neutron m^{-2}

$$H = w_R E_n \Phi_{E_n} \times 1{\cdot}076 \times 10^{-15}\ \text{Sv}$$

for different neutron energy groups

E_{n_i}, with fluences $\Phi_{E_{n_i}}$

$$H = 1{\cdot}076 \times 10^{-15} \sum (w_{R_i} E_{n_i} \Phi_{E_{n_i}})$$

or $$\dot{H} = 1{\cdot}076 \times 10^{-15} \sum (w_{R_i} E_{n_i} \dot{\Phi}_{E_{n_i}})$$

so $^{241}Am/Be$

$$\left.\begin{array}{l} 0.25 \times 2.2\times10^{6}, \quad E_n = 0.5\ \text{MeV}, \quad w_R = 20 \\ 0.75 \times 2.2\times10^{6}, \quad E_n = 5.0\ \text{MeV}, \quad w_R = 10 \end{array}\right\} s^{-1}\ Ci^{-1}$$

dose at 1m in 1 hr from 1 Ci

$$\dot{H} = \frac{2.2\times10^{6}\times1\times3600}{4\pi\times1^{2}}\times1.076\times10^{-15}\left(20\times0.5\times0.25+10\times5.0\times0.75\right)$$

$$= 6.78\times10^{-7}\times\left(2.5 + 37.5\right)\ \text{Sv hr}^{-1}$$

$$= 2.712\times10^{-5}\ \text{Sv hr}^{-1}$$

$$\approx 27\ \mu\text{Sv hr}^{-1}$$

thermal neutrons:

reaction	radiation type	w_R	equivalent dose, Sv [neutron m^{-2}]$^{-1}$
$^1H(n,\gamma)^2H$	γ	1	1.95×10^{-16}
$^{14}N(n,p)^{14}C$	p, ^{14}C recoil	20	5.22×10^{-16}
$^{35}Cl(n,\gamma)^{36}Cl$	γ	1	1.54×10^{-17}
			7.3×10^{-16}

a source of thermal neutrons with output $2.2 \times 10^6\ s^{-1}$ would produce $0.46\ \mu Sv\ h^{-1}$ at 1 m

more generally:

$$H_T = \sum_R (w_R D_{T,R})$$

where H_T is equivalent dose to a particular tissue

$D_{T,R}$ is (physical, Gy) dose to that tissue from radiation type R

w_R is radiation weighting factor for radiation type R

Effective Dose

try to summarise variation of RBE with type of tissue

Tissue Weighting Factors, w_T

Tissue or organ	w_T
gonads	0·20
bone marrow (red)	0·12
colon	0·12
lung	0·12
stomach	0·12
bladder	0·05
breast	0·05
liver	0·05
œsophagus	0·05
thyroid	0·05
skin	0·01
bone surface	0·01
remainder	0·05

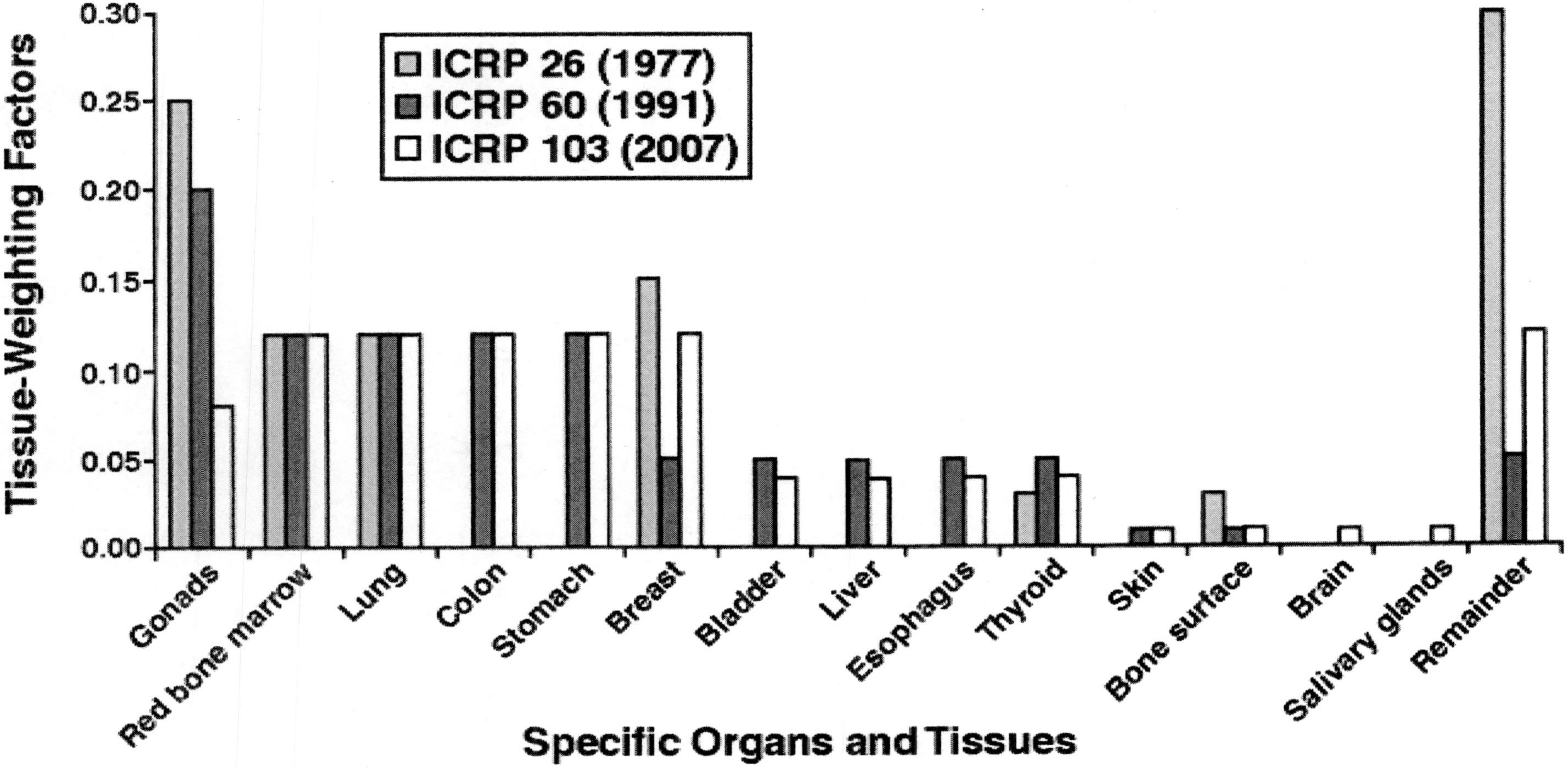
0.30
0.25
0.20
0.15
0.10
0.05
0.00
Tissue-Weighting Factors
ICRP 26 (1977)
ICRP 60 (1991)
ICRP 103 (2007)
Gonads
Red bone marrow
Lung
Colon
Stomach
Breast
Bladder
Liver
Esophagus
Thyroid
Skin
Bone surface
Brain
Salivary glands
Remainder
Specific Organs and Tissues

to measure Cd in liver use neutron activation

dose to liver = 25 μGy fast neutrons
+ 50 μGy γ-rays

in addition, 1% of these doses to whole body

to liver, $H_T = \sum_R w_R D_{T,R}$

$= 20 \times 25 + 1 \times 50 = 550\ \mu Sv$

to whole body, $H_T = \sum_R w_R D_{T,R}$

$= 20 \times 0{\cdot}25 + 1 \times 0{\cdot}5 = 5{\cdot}5\ \mu Sv$

effective dose, $E = \sum_T w_T H_T$

$= 0{\cdot}05 \times 550 + 1 \times 5{\cdot}5$

$= 33\ \mu Sv$

$$E = \sum_T w_T H_T = \sum_T w_T \sum_R w_R D_{T,R}$$

External Radiation Protection

build up factors

shielding x-ray installations

$$\text{dose} \propto \frac{\text{time}}{\text{distance}^2}$$

⇒ most obvious, simplest protection is minimise time, maximise distance

⇒ run away as fast as possible!

shielding

broad beam

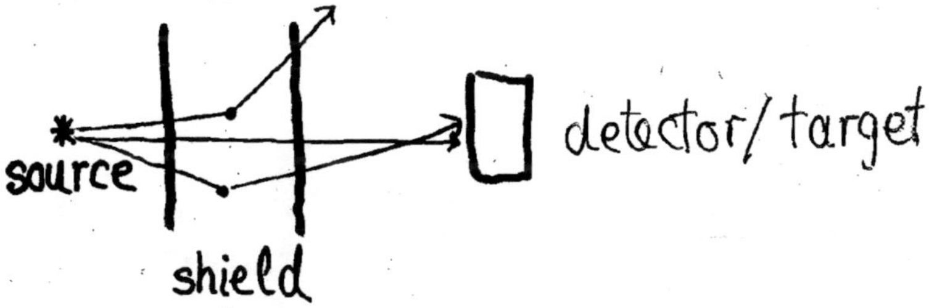

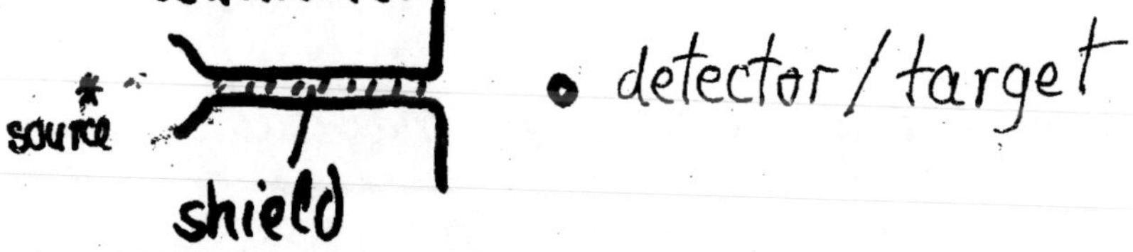

pencil beam

for 'pencil' beam geometry any interaction in shield results in loss of photon from beam, collima is so thick that effectively nothing gets through it in this case $I = I_0 e^{-\mu x}$ applies

'broad' beam is different, some interactions result in loss of photon from beam, other interaction can produce a scattered photon heading for the detect from an incident photon initially heading in a different direction

the total fluence reaching the detector is more than for pencil beam

put $I = B I_0 e^{-\mu x}$

$B \geq 1$ and is called the buildup factor

B varies with photon energy, shielding material (interaction medium) and shielding thickness and geometry

Start Nov. 13th.

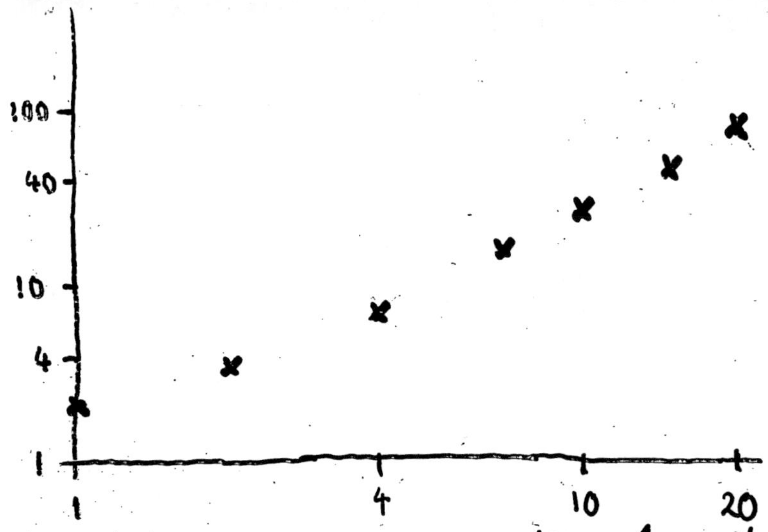

μx - relaxation lengths

medium water

photon energy 1 MeV

geometry isotropic point source

for $\mu x = 1$ $\quad e^{-\mu x} = 0.37$

4 $\quad 0.018$

20 $\quad 2.1 \times 10^{-9}$

For this particular case $\ln B = 1.23 \ln(\mu x) + 0.53$

R^2 for the fit $= 0.985$

for isotatropic source of 4 MeV photons in lead

$\ln(B) = 0.84 \ln(\mu x) - 0.08$

R^2 for the fit $= 0.924$

consider a lead shield to reduce exposure rate from 10 Ci point source of ^{42}K to 1.0 mR h^{-1} at 1 m

^{42}K emits 1.52 MeV γ-ray in 0.18 of decays

unshielded exposure rate

$$\frac{e}{4\pi r^2 \cdot W_{air}} \times E \times Y \times \left(\frac{\mu_{en}}{\rho}\right)_{air} \times N\lambda \quad C\,kg^{-1}\,s^{-1}$$

$$= \frac{1.6\times10^{-19} \times 0.18 \times 1.52 \times 1.6\times10^{-13} \times 2.52\times10^{-3}}{4\pi \times 1^2 \times 34 \times 1.6\times10^{-19}} \times \frac{3.7\times10^{10} \times 3600}{2.58\times10^{-4}} R$$

$$= 1.333\ R\,h^{-1}$$

required attenuation (without buildup)

$$\mu x = \ln\left(\frac{1.333}{1\times10^{-3}}\right) = 7.2$$

B(Pb) E(MeV)	μx	7	10
1		3.02	3.74
1.52		3.39	4.37
2		3.68	4.84

for $\mu x_1 = 7.2$, $B = 3.45$

need extra attenuation, so additional $\Delta\mu x = \ln$

new attenuation $\mu x_2 = \mu x_1 + \ln 3.45 = 7.2 + 1.24$

$\mu x_2 = 8.44$, new build up is 3.87

$\mu x_3 = \mu x_1 + \ln 3.87 = 7.2 + 1.35 = 8.55$

can continue to iterate

but try rounding μx up to 8·6

$\mu x_f = 8{\cdot}6$, $B_f = 3{\cdot}93$

will this be sufficient?

$$X = X_0 B e^{-\mu x_f} = 1{\cdot}333 \times 3{\cdot}93 e^{-8{\cdot}6}$$
$$= 0{\cdot}964 \ \mathrm{mR\,h^{-1}}$$

how thick is the lead?

μ_{Pb} at 1·52 MeV = 57·6 m^{-1}

so $x = \frac{8{\cdot}6}{57{\cdot}6} = 0{\cdot}149\ m \simeq 15\ cm$

a more complicated example

a 144 Ci point source of ^{24}Na is to be stored at the bottom of a pool of water. How deep must the water be to reduce the exposure rate at a point 2 m above the water to 2·5 $mR\,h^{-1}$?

first consider the 2.75 MeV γ-ray, because this will require more shielding than the 1.37 Me γ-ray

what would the exposure rate be with no shielding

$$\frac{N\lambda e}{4\pi r^2 W_{air}} \times E \times \left(\frac{\mu_{en}}{\rho}\right)_{air} = \frac{144 \times 3.7 \times 10^{10} \times 1.6 \times 10^{-19}}{4\pi . r^2 \times 34 \times 1.6 \times 10^{-19}} \times 2.75 \times 1.6 \times 10^{-13} \times 2.10$$

$$= \frac{1.15 \times 10^{-5}}{r^2} \; C\,kg^{-1}s^{-1}$$

$$= \frac{160.8}{r^2} \; R\,h^{-1}$$

or $40.2 \; R\,h^{-1}$ at 2 m

this would require a shield to attenuate

by $\frac{40.2}{2.5 \times 10^{-3}} = 16,080$ need to attenuate by factor of

what we want

linear attenuation coefficient for water

at 2.75 MeV is 4.3^{-1} m^{-1}

initial estimate is $e^{-\mu x} = \frac{1}{16,080}$ or $x = \frac{\ln 16080}{4.3}$

$x = 2.25$ m so need this much water

so actual distance from source is likely to be (at least) $2 + 2.25 = 4.25$ m at this distance, unshielded $\dot{X} = \frac{160.8}{4.25^2} = 8.90 \text{ R h}^{-1}$

make preliminary estimate of number of relaxation lengths and build up factor

attenuation factor $= \frac{8.9}{2.5 \times 10^{-3}} = 3560$

$\ln 3560 = 8.18$ relaxation lengths

B (water) E (MeV)	μx 7	10
1	16.2	27.1
2	8.46	12.4
2.75	6.79	9.57
3	6.23	8.63

interpolate to find figures for 2.75 MeV

then interpolate to estimate B for $\mu x = 8.18$

$B = 7.88$ so the exposure rate would be 7.88 times higher than for a pencil beam

=> require extra shielding

increase μx by $\ln 7.88 = 2.06$

so new $\mu x = 10.24$

B (water) E (MeV)	μx 10	15
1	27.1	50.4
2	12.4	19.5
2.75	9.57	14.48
3	8.63	12.8

estimate $B = 9.81$, $\ln 9.81 = 2.28$

so new $\mu x = 8.18 + 2.28 = 10.46$

next estimate of $B = 10.02$, $\ln 10.02 = 2.30$

new $\mu x = 8.18 + 2.30 = 10.48$, round up to 10.50

try $\mu x = 10.5$, $B = 10.06$

so $\dot{X} = 10.06 \times 8.9\, e^{-10.5} = 2.47 \times 10^{-3}\, R\, h^{-1}$

looks satisfactory. need to check distance

and check 1.37 MeV γ-ray

at 2·75 MeV, for $\mu x = 10{\cdot}5$ $\quad x_{water} = \frac{10{\cdot}5}{4{\cdot}3} = 2{\cdot}44\,m$

so actual exposure rate from 2·75 MeV γ-rays

is $\frac{160{\cdot}8}{4{\cdot}44^2} \times 10{\cdot}06\, e^{-10{\cdot}5} = 2{\cdot}26 \times 10^{-3}\ R\,h^{-1}$

for 1·37 MeV $\left(\frac{\mu_{en}}{\rho}\right)_{air} = 2{\cdot}59 \times 10^{-3}\ m^2\,kg^{-1}$

so $\quad \dot{X} = \frac{160{\cdot}8}{r^2} \times \frac{2{\cdot}59}{2{\cdot}10} \times \frac{1{\cdot}37}{2{\cdot}75}$

$$= \frac{98{\cdot}8}{r^2}\ R\,h^{-1}$$

linear attenuation coefficient for water at 1·37MeV is 6·1m

$x = 2{\cdot}44\,m$, so $\mu x = 14{\cdot}88$

B(water) E(MeV)	μx 10	15
1	27·1	50·4
1·37	21·7	39·0
2	12·4	19·5

estimate B = 38·6

$$\dot{X} = \frac{98{\cdot}8}{4{\cdot}44^2} \times 38{\cdot}6\, e^{-14{\cdot}88} = 6{\cdot}7 \times 10^{-5}\ R\,h^{-1}$$

total exposure rate = 2·26 + 0·07 = 2·33 $m R\,h^{-1}$

End Nov 13th

Shielding in X-ray Installations

need to consider primary radiation (in beam)

also secondary – leakage

– scatter

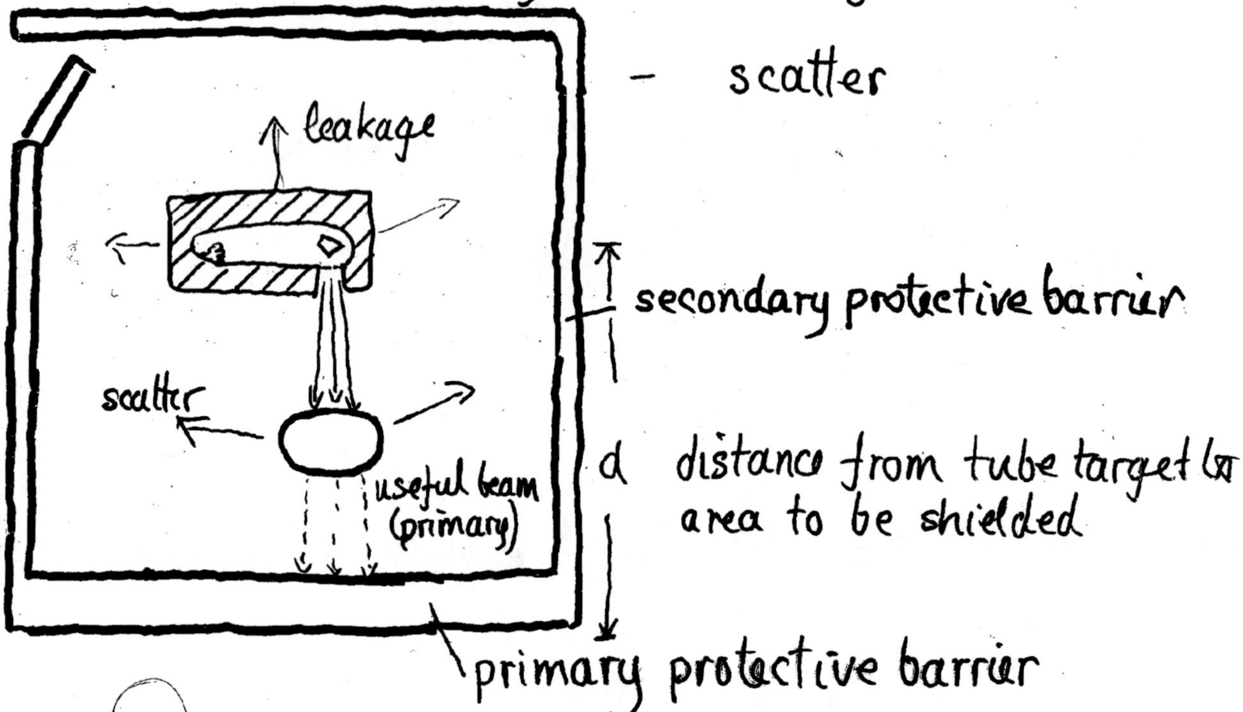

regulations ensure that leakage radiation is limited by the shielding effect of x-ray tube housing

for diagnostic tubes leakage produces exposure rate $\dot{X} \leqslant 0.1\,R\,h^{-1}$ at 1 m

for therapeutic tubes with accelerating potential $\leqslant 500$ kV

$\dot{X} \leqslant 1\,R\,h^{-1}$ at 1m

for therapeutic tubes with >500 kV

$\dot{X} \leq 1\,R\,h^{-1}$ or 0·1% in beam; at 1 m
whichever greater

dose limits ICRP # 26, (1977)

occupationally exposed workers $50\ mSv\ y^{-1}$

general public $5\ mSv\ y^{-1}$

w_R for photons = 1

exposure of 1 R leads to a dose in tissue ≃ 9·6 mGy

so exposure limits: occupational $5{\cdot}2\ R\ y^{-1}$

general public $0{\cdot}52\ R\ y^{-1}$

so use guideline: occupational $\leq 0{\cdot}1\ R\ wk^{-1}$

general public $\leq 0{\cdot}01\ R\ wk^{-1}$

an area to which access is controlled and which is normally occupied only by occupationally exposed workers is termed a 'controlled area'.

everywhere else is termed an 'uncontrolled area'

Primary Protective Barrier

consider a 'reference' situation which needs no shielding added to what it already has

suppose we have an x-ray set which is run for 1 minute at a current of 1mA and this produces an exposure of 0·1 R, this is the only use the x-ray set gets during the week

this 'reference' exposure ($R\ mA^{-1}\ min^{-1}$ at 1m) is given the symbol K

x-ray output per unit integrated current (current×time = charge) varies with accelerating voltage, so K is graphed for different voltages

in a practical situation the value of K depends on 5 factors

1. the maximum permissible exposure rate P

usually $P = 0.1\ R\ wk^{-1}$ for occupational exposure/controlled areas and $P = 0.01\ R\ wk^{-1}$ for general public/uncontrolled areas

the smaller P, the smaller K

2. the x-ray machine work load, W

W expressed in mA min wk^{-1}

the larger W, the smaller K

3. the use factor, U

the fraction of the work load during which the beam is pointed in the direction being considered

the larger U, the smaller K ($U \leq 1$)

4. the occupancy factor, T

the fraction of time that an area outside the protective is likely to be occupied by a given individual

the larger T, the smaller K ($T \leq 1$)

5. the distance, d, from the tube target to the area under consideration

d measured in meters, for comparison with the 'reference' distance of 1 m

the smaller d^2, the smaller K

so $$K = \frac{Pd^2}{WUT}$$

diagnostic x-ray machine operated at 125 kV_p and 220 mA for an average of 90 s wk^{-1}. Find thickness of either lead or concrete used as primary protective barrier for uncontrolled hallway 15 feet from tube target. The useful beam directed horizontally towards barrier 1/3 of time, rest of time into ground

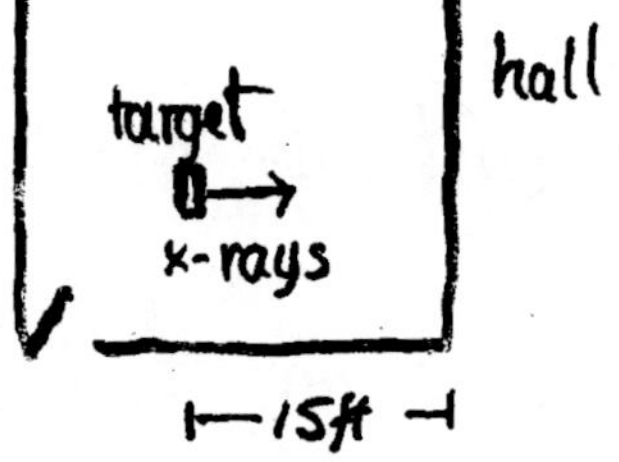

full occupancy $T = 1$	offices, laboratories, shops, wards nurses' stations, living quarters, play areas
partial occupancy $T = 1/4$	corridors, rest rooms, elevators using operators unattended parking lots
occasional occupancy $T = 1/16$	waiting rooms, toilets, stairways, unattended elevators, janitors' closets, outside areas used only for pedestrians or vehicular traffic

hall is uncontrolled so $P = 0.01\ R\ wk^{-1}$

$d = 15ft = 4.572\ m$

$W = 220\ mA \times 90s = 330\ mA\ min\ wk^{-1}$

$U = 1/3$

T, occupancy factor can be taken as $1/4$

so $$K = \frac{.01 \times 4.572^2}{330 \times 1/3 \times 1/4} = 7.6 \times 10^{-3}$$

from 125 kVp curve for lead (Turner fig 15.3)

require 1.1 mm Pb

from 125 kVp curve for concrete (Turner fig 15.6)

require 3.5 inch concrete (≡ 88.9 mm)

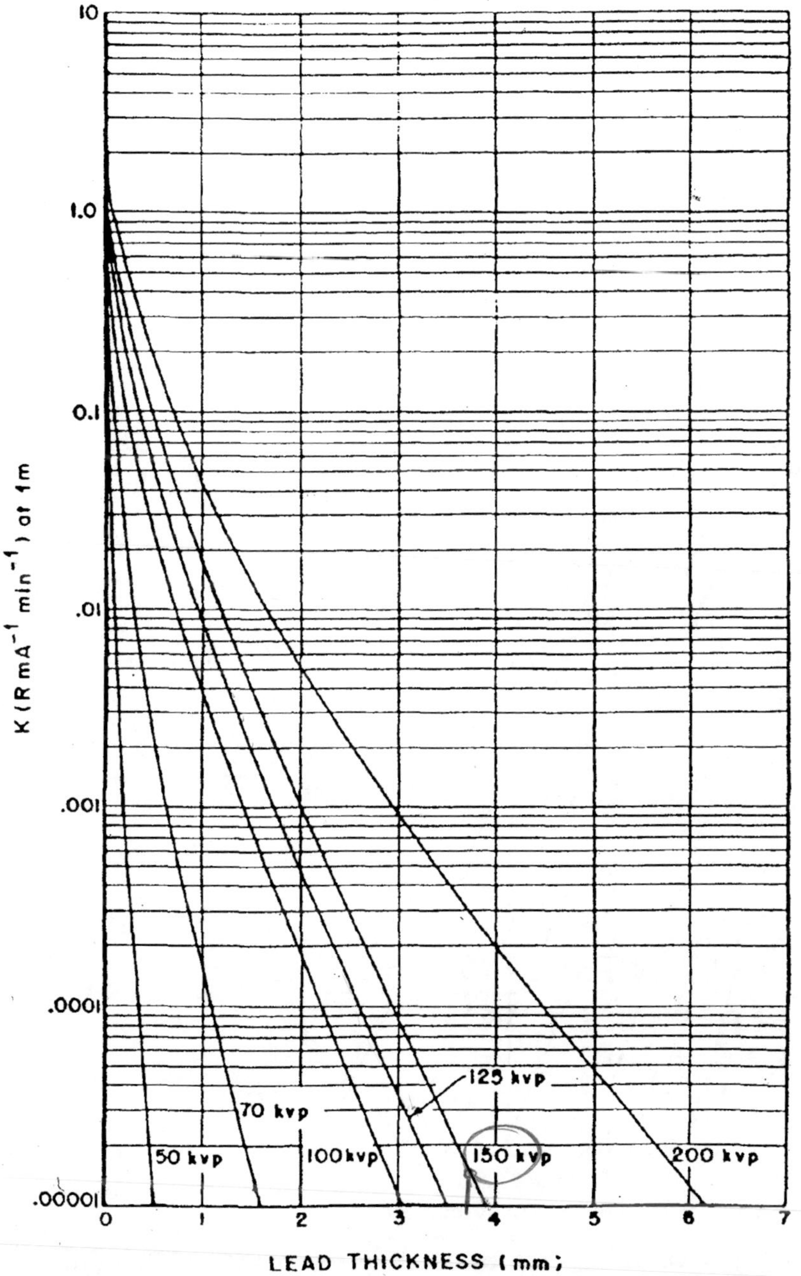

FIGURE 15.3. Attenuation in lead of X rays produced with (peak) potential differences from 50 kVp to 200 kVp. (*National Bureau of Standards Handbook 76*, 1961, Washington, DC)

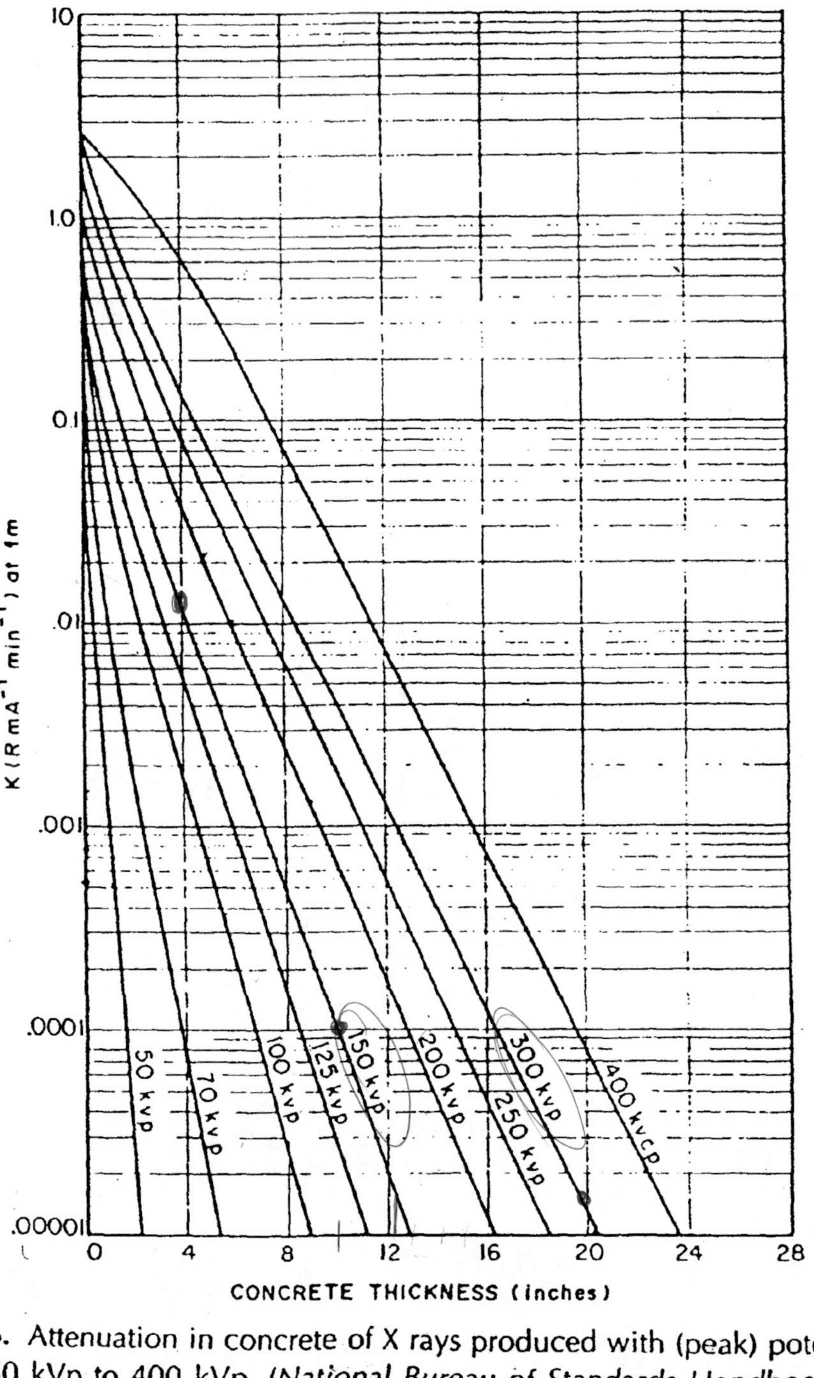

FIGURE 15.6. Attenuation in concrete of X rays produced with (peak) potential differences from 50 kVp to 400 kVp. (*National Bureau of Standards Handbook 76*, 1961, Washington, DC)

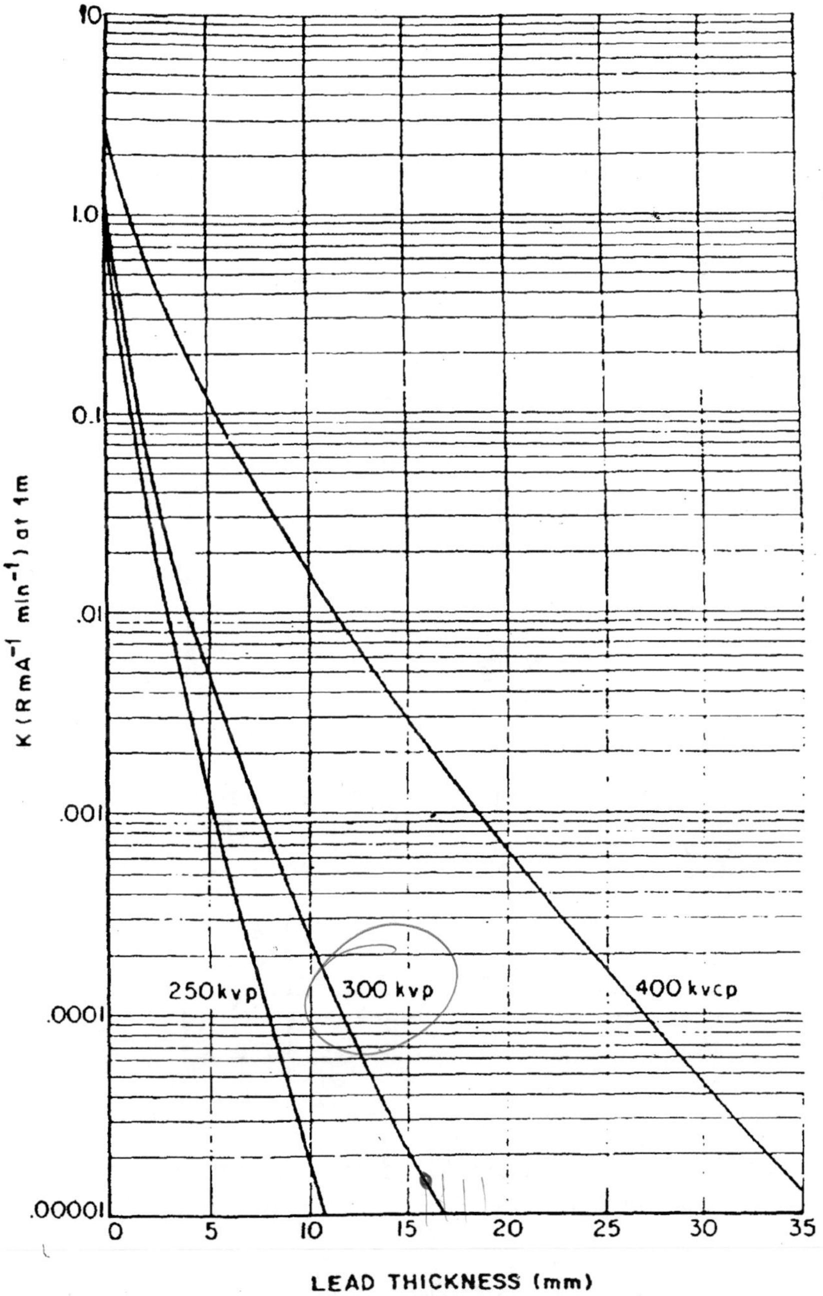

FIGURE 15.4. Attenuation in lead of X rays produced with (peak) potential differences from 250 kVp to 400 kVp. (*National Bureau of Standards Handbook 76*, 1961, Washington, DC)

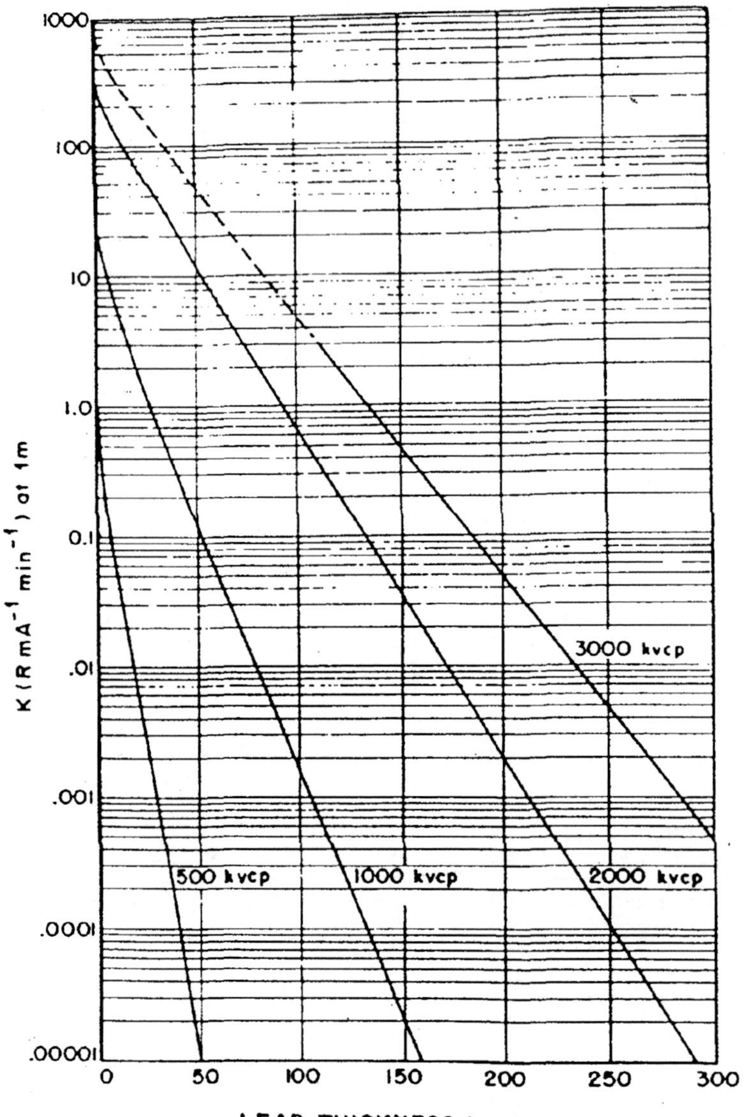

FIGURE 15.5. Attenuation in lead of X rays produced with (peak) potential differences from 500 kVp to 3000 kVp. (*National Bureau of Standards Handbook 76*, 1961, Washington, DC)

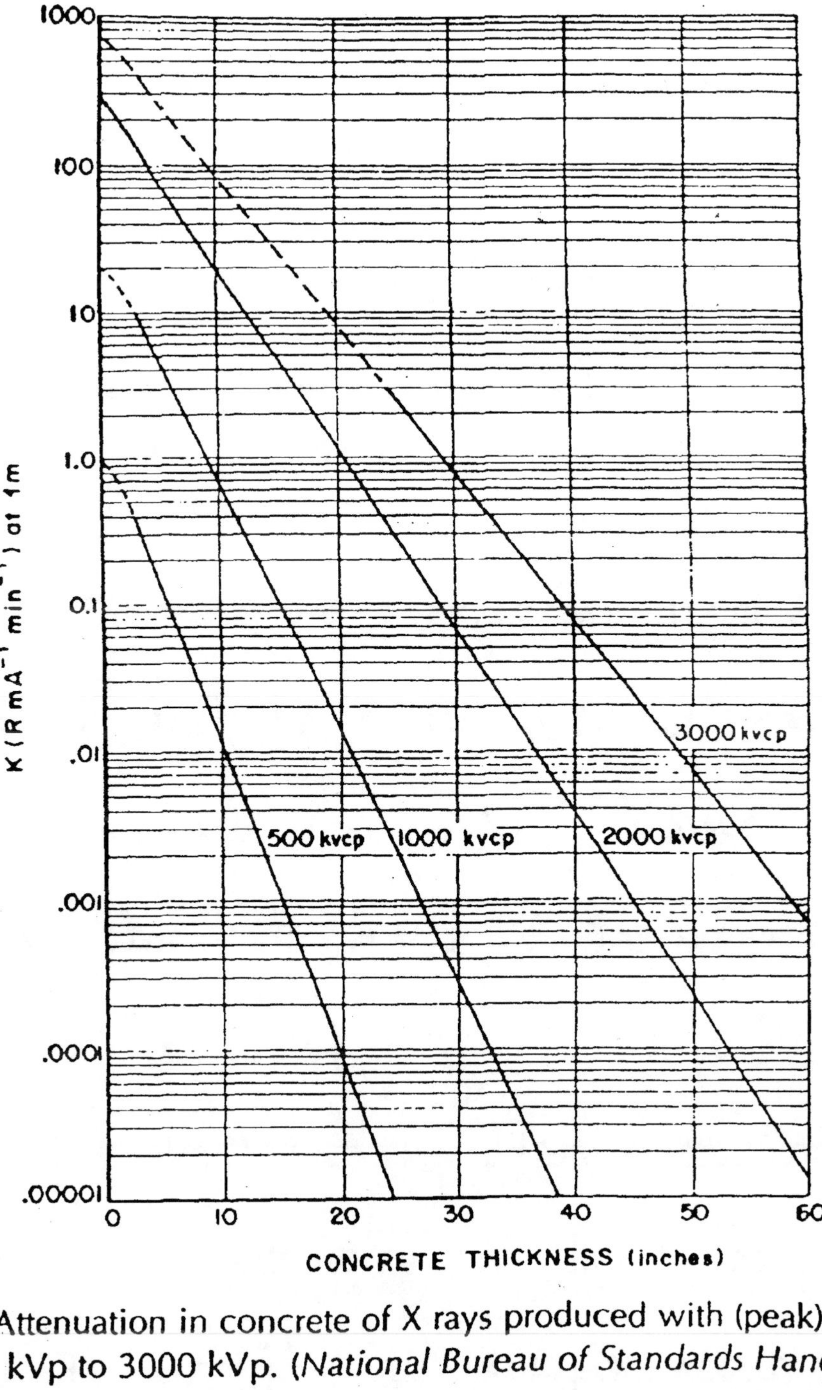

FIGURE 15.7. Attenuation in concrete of X rays produced with (peak) potential diffe ences from 500 kVp to 3000 kVp. (*National Bureau of Standards Handbook 76*, 196 Washington, DC)

Secondary Protective Barrier

need to consider both leakage and scattered radiation

Leakage

exposure rates: diagnostic $\leq 0{\cdot}1 \ \mathrm{R\,h^{-1}}$ at 1m

therapeutic, ≤ 500 kV, $\leq 1 \ \mathrm{R\,h^{-1}}$ at 1m

> 500 kV $\leq 1 \ \mathrm{R\,h^{-1}}$ or $\leq 0{\cdot}1\%$ in beam } at 1m

call this maximum allowed exposure rate Y, this is for machine when operating at full current

machine operates W mA min wk^{-1} $= \frac{W}{60}$ mA h wk^{-1}

if average current is I mA then machine operates the equivalent of $\frac{W}{60I}$ 'full current' h wk^{-1}

this produces a weekly exposure of $\frac{YW}{60I}$ R wk^{-1} at 1m

if distance is d m and occupancy factor is T then a person's exposure is $\frac{YWT}{60I\,d^2}$ R wk^{-1}

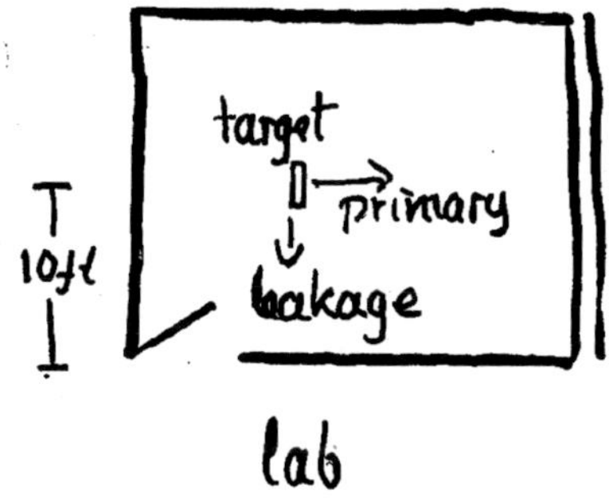

in machine for previous example, what about a lab (controlled area) occupancy factor, T = 1 10 feet from target

weekly exposure is $\dfrac{0.1 \times 330 \times 1}{60 \times 220 \times 3.048^2} = 2.69 \times 10^{-4}\ R\,wk^{-1}$

this is << $0.1\ R\,wk^{-1}$, so no extra shielding required

what if a therapy machine is installed (26 mA at 300 kVp)

$W = 24{,}000\ mA\ min\ wk^{-1}$

weekly exposure is $\dfrac{1 \times 24{,}000 \times 1}{60 \times 26 \times 3.048^2} = 1.656\ R\,wk^{-1}$

this is $\dfrac{1.656}{0.1} = 16.56 \times$ permitted limit

need to reduce exposure by a factor $B = \dfrac{1}{16.56} = 0.0604$

use tabulated values of half value layers for different materials $B = 2^{-N}$, $N = -\dfrac{\ln B}{\ln 2} = 4.05$

in general $B = \dfrac{60 I d^2 P}{Y W T}$

Scattered radiation

scattering object, often a person is now the secondary source

make rough approximations about energy

(i) primary beam ≤ 500 kV accelerating potential $\Rightarrow$ treat scattered fluence as same energy as primary beam.

(ii) primary beam > 500 kV $\Rightarrow$ treat scattered fluence as having 500 kV accelerating potential, this accounts reasonably for energy, but further adjustment will have to be made for the fact that intensity increases rapidly with accelerating voltage

the other factor is that the scattered beam is always much less intense than the primary beam, $\Rightarrow$ treat this as $\times$ 1000 reduction in intensity, then use formula for K again.

$$K_{sca} = \frac{1000\,Pd^2}{fWT}$$

where f is a factor applied when accelerating voltage > 500 kV to allow for increased intensity

kVp	f
≤ 500	1
1000	20
2000	300
3000	700

U (the use factor) is missing from the equation for K_{sca} because there will be scattered radiation in all directions, regardless of which way the primary beam is pointing

return to therapy x-ray set (26 mA at 300 kVp) with W = 24,000 mA min wk^{-1} and consider scattered radiation in controlled area 3·048 m from target with occupancy, $T = 1$

$$K_{sca} = \frac{1000\,Pd^2}{fWT} = \frac{1000 \times 0{\cdot}1 \times 3{\cdot}048^2}{1 \times 24{,}000 \times 1}$$

($f = 1$ because kV ≤ 500) $\qquad = 0{\cdot}0387$

from 300 kVp curve for lead (Turner fig 15.4)

require 2.5 mm Pb

from 300 kVp curve for concrete (Turner fig 15.6)

require 6 inch = 15.2 cm concrete

from tabulated data 2.5 mm Pb = 1.7 half value layer (HVL)

15.2 cm concrete = 4.9 half value layer

(in both cases for 300 kVp)

for leakage required 4.05 HVL

need to attenuate both leakage and scattered fluence

worst case is require same thickness for each of leakage and scattered, this is like 2× intensity, so add 1 HVL

in practice, if requirements for leakage and scatter differ by more than 3 HVL, just take larger value

if |leakage - scatter| < 3 HVL, use larger value + 1 HVL

Nov. Thurs 22nd start

fission reactor, ^{235}U

have seen before

$$^{235}_{92}U + ^{1}_{0}n \longrightarrow ^{236}_{92}U^{*} \longrightarrow ^{A_1}_{Z_1}X + ^{A_2}_{Z_2}Y + \nu\, ^{1}_{0}n$$

$\nu + A_1 + A_2 = 236$ $\qquad Z_1 + Z_2 = 92$

~ 200 MeV released of which

fission fragments kinetic energy	167
neutron kinetic energy	6
fission γ-rays	6
decay βs	5
decay γs	5
neutrinos	11
	200

energy budget

on average 2.5 neutrons per fission from ^{235}U

if each neutron were to cause fission then absorb 1 neutron and release $\nu = 2.5$ more

the change, Δ, is a factor of 1·5

if there are n neutrons in a generation (at one particular time), there are $n\Delta$ in the next generation

if mean lifetime of a neutron generation is ℓ

then $\frac{dn}{dt} = \frac{n\Delta}{\ell}$

$$\frac{dn}{n} = \frac{\Delta}{\ell} dt$$

$$\ln(n) = \frac{\Delta}{\ell} t + c$$

$$\frac{n}{n_0} = e^{\Delta t/\ell}, \text{ for } n = n_0 \text{ when } t = 0$$

unless Δ is negative, number of neutrons increases

if $t = \ell/\Delta$, then $n/n_0 = e^1$, that is an e-fold increase

ℓ/Δ is called the reactor period, T

mean neutron lifetime in pure ^{235}U, $\ell = 10^{-3}$ s

if $\Delta = 1.5$, then $T = \ell/\Delta = 6.67 \times 10^{-4}$ s ← very short

power increase in 1/100 s

$$n/n_0 = e^{\frac{\Delta t}{\ell}} = e^{t/T} = e^{.01/6.67\times10^{-4}}$$

$$n/n_0 = 3.27 \times 10^{6} \quad (\text{for } t = 0.01 \text{ s})$$

Δ has to be positive in order to achieve power production

if $\Delta = 0.5\%$ then $T = 10^{-3}/5\times10^{-3} = 0.2$ s

power increase in 1/100 s, $n/n_0 = e^{10^{-2}/.2} = 1.051$

but in 1 s $n/n_0 = e^5 = 148$

this would mean extremely fine balance and rapidly responding systems to control a reactor

however, not all neutrons are these "prompt" neutrons, there are also "delayed" neutrons, categorized into different groups

group	yield n_i (%)	mean generation time T_i (s)	yield x mean time $n_i \times T_i$
prompt	99.359	.001	.099359
1	.0267	.33	.008811
2	.0737	.88	.064856
3	.2526	3.31	.836106
4	.1255	8.97	1.125735
5	.1401	32.78	4.602312
6	.0211	80.39 ← up to 80k x as long	1.696229
			8.43 (/100)

(groups 1–6 bracketed: groups)

so the weighted mean generation time or mean neutron lifetime = .0843 (significantly larger)

provided Δ is small, control is feasible

for Δ = 0.5% $T = \frac{\ell}{\Delta} = \frac{.0843}{.005} = 16.86$ s

in 1 s $n/n_0 = e^{1/16.86} = 1.061$ (cf 148)

"prompt" neutrons come directly from fission

"delayed" neutrons are emitted as a possible decay mode of some radionuclides formed by fission

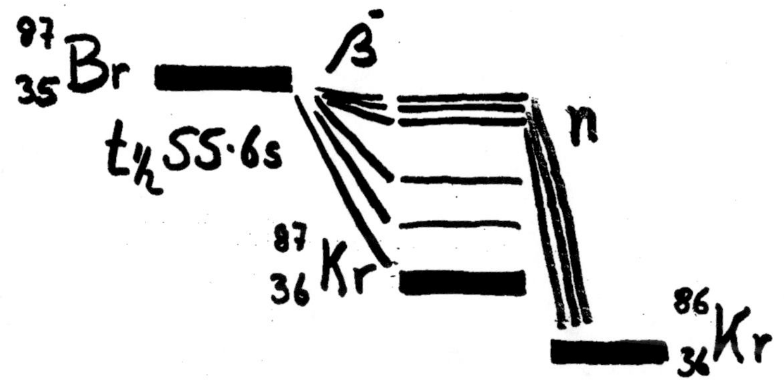

nuclide	Δ (MeV)
$^{87}_{35}Br$	−74·21
$^{87}_{36}Kr$	−80·707
$^{86}_{36}Kr$	− 83·263

for $^{87}_{35}Br + e^- \longrightarrow {}^{87}_{36}Kr + \beta^- + \bar{\nu}$

$\quad \hookrightarrow {}^{86}_{36}Kr + {}^{1}_{0}n$

Δ(MeV) $-74{\cdot}21 + 0{\cdot}511 \longrightarrow -80{\cdot}707 + 0{\cdot}511 + E_{ex}$

$\quad \hookrightarrow -83{\cdot}263 + 8{\cdot}071 + Q$

$$Q = 83{\cdot}263 - 74{\cdot}21 - 8{\cdot}071 = 0{\cdot}982 \text{ MeV}$$

this Q can be distributed amongst

$E_{\beta^- max}$, neutron kinetic energy, γ-ray(s), heavy ion recoil

- delayed neutron emission never dominant mode of decay (2·3% for ^{87}Br)
- follows β^- decay and is early in a succession of β^- decays
- can follow fission, because fission produces neutron rich isotopes

(proton decay can occur, but this is from neutron deficient nuclides)

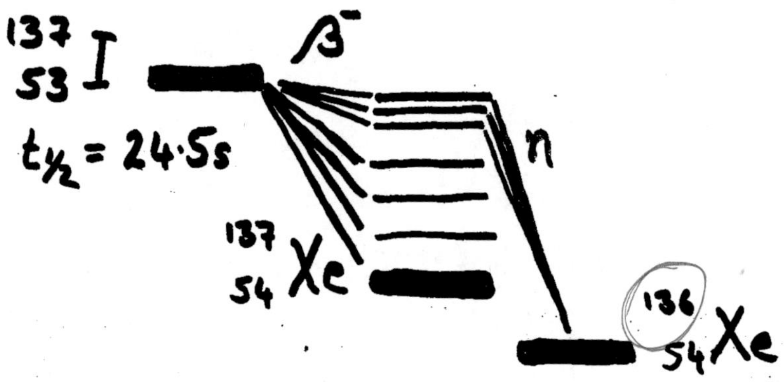

nuclide	Δ (MeV)
$^{137}_{53}I$	−76·72
$^{137}_{54}Xe$	−82·215
$^{136}_{54}Xe$	−86·425

$$Q = 86{\cdot}425 - 76{\cdot}72 - 8{\cdot}071 = 1{\cdot}634 \text{ MeV}$$

for ^{235}U ~ 0.64 % of neutrons are delayed

if $\Delta \geq .0064$ this is prompt critical

the reactor is in neutron multiplication

without waiting for delayed neutrons

if $.0064 \geq \Delta \geq 0$ this is delayed critical

⇒ control (when starting up, stay within this range while powering it up to desired power level, then try to keep it at ~0 (with slight fluctuations))

for $\Delta = .006$, $n/n_0 = e^{.006/.0843} = 1.074$ in 1 s

for $\Delta = .007$ get approximate idea by splitting

into .0064 delayed and .0006 prompt

$$n/n_0 = e^{.0064/.0843} \cdot e^{.0006/.001}$$

$$1.079 \times 1.822$$

End Nov. 22nd.

Start Nov 27th (final lecture)

need to ensure neutron multiplication

factor stays between 1.0 and 1.0064

while power is being increased and at 1.0

while running at steady power

if neutron multiplication is k, then the foregoing $\Delta = k - 1$

and $k_{eff} = \frac{n_{f+1}}{n_f}$ where n_{f+1} is the number of neutrons produced in generation $f+1$ by the number of neutrons, n_f, in the previous generation

if ν is the mean number of neutrons, including delayed neutrons, emitted per fission = 2.5 for ^{235}U then there are 5 further factors which affect the neutron balance or neutron multiplication or criticality

1. some neutrons are lost by leakage through the sides of the fuel/moderator assembly in an infinite assembly no neutrons are lost by leakage

$$k_{eff} = L k_{\infty}$$ where L is the non leakage probability

then $k_\infty = \eta \epsilon p f$

where η = mean number of neutrons emitted per absorption in uranium

ϵ = fast fission factor

p = resonance escape probability

f = thermal utilization factor

2. η. some neutrons are absorbed in ^{235}U without causing fission, also normally have ^{238}U as well

$\sigma_{a(235)}$ = 650 barn (total absorption)

$\sigma_{f(235)}$ = 549 barn (fission)

if have N_{235} atoms of ^{235}U per unit volume

and N_{238} atoms of ^{238}U per unit volume

and $\sigma_{a(238)}$ = 2·8 barn, is the absorption cross section in ^{238}U

then $$\eta = \frac{N_{235}\,\sigma_{f(235)}\,\nu}{N_{235}\,\sigma_{a(235)} + N_{238}\,\sigma_{a(238)}}$$

$$= \frac{\sigma_{f(235)}\,\nu}{\sigma_{a(235)} + \frac{N_{238}}{N_{235}}\sigma_{a(238)}}$$

3. ϵ some fissions caused by fast neutrons.

for unmoderated pure uranium metal

$\epsilon = 1{\cdot}29$ (maximum value) in practice close to 1

4. p resonance escape probability. fast neutrons slow down and can be absorbed (resonance absorption) before they are thermalized, so they never cause fission.

for highly moderated assembly p is quite large and approaches 1

for pure unmoderated natural uranium $p = 0$,

so ϵ and p maximise in opposite circumstances

5. f not all thermal neutrons are absorbed in uranium, some absorbed in moderator and other materials

$$f = \frac{\sigma_{a(235)} N_{235} + \sigma_{a(238)} N_{238}}{\sigma_{a(235)} N_{235} + \sigma_{a(238)} N_{238} + \sigma_{aM} N_M + \left(\sum \sigma_{ai} N_i\right)_p}$$

where σ_{aM}, N_M are absorption cross section and number of atoms per unit volume for the moderator

L depends on geometry of assembly, probably ranges $0.5 \rightarrow 1.0$

ϵ for moderated assemblies is close to 1, say $1 \rightarrow 1.0$

p for moderated assemblies is close to, but less than 1, say $0.8 \rightarrow 1.0$

$$\eta = \frac{\sigma_{f(235)}\,\nu}{\sigma_{a(235)} + \frac{N_{238}}{N_{235}}\sigma_{a(238)}}$$

for natural uranium $\frac{N_{238}}{N_{235}} = 139$

$$\text{so } \eta = \frac{549 \times 2.5}{650 + 139 \times 2.8} = 1.32$$

"highly enriched fuel" is 93% ^{235}U by mass

$$\eta = \frac{549 \times 2.5}{650 + \frac{.07/238}{.93/235} \times 2.8} = 2.11$$

"low enriched fuel" is 19.95% ^{235}U by mass

$$\eta = \frac{549 \times 2.5}{650 + \frac{.8005/238}{.1995/235} \times 2.8} = 2.08$$

$$f = \frac{\sigma_{a(235)} N_{235} + \sigma_{f(238)} N_{238}}{\sigma_{a(235)} N_{235} + \sigma_{a(238)} N_{238} + \sigma_{aH} N_H + (\Sigma \sigma_{ai} N_i)_P}$$

consider 925 g of uranium as uranyl sulphate, UO_2SO_4, in 14 litre water (H_2O, moderator)

^{235}U is enriched to 93% by weight (HEU)

$$^{235}U = \frac{.93 \times 925}{235} = 3.66 \text{ mole}$$

$$^{238}U = \frac{.07 \times 925}{238} = 0.27 \text{ mole}$$

$$= 3.93 \text{ mole}$$

$$O_2SO_4 = 3.93 \text{ mole}$$

$$H_2O = \frac{14 \times 10^3}{18} = 778 \text{ mole}$$

$\sigma_{a(H)} = .332$ barn; $\sigma_{a(O)} = .0002$ barn; $\sigma_{a(S)} = .491$ barn

material		σ_a (barn)	mole	$\sigma_a \times$ mole
^{235}U		650	3.66	2379.00
^{238}U		2.8	0.27	0.76
moderator	H_2	0.332×2	778	516.59
	O	.0002	778	0.16
other(O_2SO_4)	O_6	.0002×6	3.93	4.7×10^{-3}
	S	.491	3.93	1.93
				2898.44

$$f = \frac{2379.76}{2898.44} = 0.821$$

for LEU fuel

$$^{235}U = \frac{.1995\times925}{235} = 0.785\text{ mole}$$

$$^{238}U = \frac{.8005\times925}{238} = 3.111\text{ mole}$$

$$U_{total} = O_2SO_4 = 3.896\text{ mole}$$

$$f = \frac{510.25+8.71}{510.25+8.71+516.75+1.92} = 0.500$$

for natural uranium

$$^{235}U = \frac{.00720\times925}{235} = .0283\text{ mole}$$

$$^{238}U = \frac{.9928\times925}{238} = 3.8586\text{ mole}$$

$$f = \frac{18.395+10.804}{18.395+10.804+516.75+1.91} = 0.0533$$

for D_2O instead of H_2O moderator

$\sigma_{a(D)}$ = ·00052 barn

$\sigma_a \times$ mole for moderator = 0·965

and $f = \frac{18{\cdot}395 + 10{\cdot}804}{18{\cdot}395 + 10{\cdot}804 + 0{\cdot}965 + 1{\cdot}91} = 0{\cdot}910$ for $U_{natural}$

can also use graphite moderation

^{12}C (·9889 abundant, σ_a = ·0034 barn)

^{13}C (·0111 abundant, σ_a = ·0009 barn)

water (H_2O) cooled graphite moderated

moderator 25% H_2O + 75 C % by volume

if $\rho_c = 2{\cdot}3\ g\ cm^{-3}$ then $(\sigma_a \times mole)_{moderator} = 135{\cdot}98$

and $f = 0{\cdot}790$

eg $L = 0{\cdot}74$, $\eta = 2{\cdot}076$, $\epsilon = 1{\cdot}01$

$p = 0{\cdot}82$, $f = 0{\cdot}79$

$k_{eff} = 1{\cdot}0051$

mass difference: $\Delta = M - A$ (in MeV)

for α decay: $Q = E_\alpha\left(1 + \frac{M_\alpha}{M_d}\right)$ where M_d is daughter mass

$E_\alpha = \frac{Q}{1 + \frac{4}{A-4}} = Q\left(1 - \frac{4}{A}\right)$ A is parent mass

for eg $^7Li(p,n)^7Be$ $E_{threshold} = \frac{m_p + m_{Li}}{m_{Li}} Q$ $-Q\frac{(M_{Be} + M_n)}{(M_{Be} + M_n - M_p)}$

decay formulæ:

α: $^A_ZX \rightarrow\, ^{A-4}_{Z-2}Y + \,^4_2He + Q$

fission: $^A_ZX = \,^{A_1}_{Z_1}Y_1 + \,^{A_2}_{Z_2}Y_2 + k\,^1_0n + Q$

β^-: $^A_ZX + e^- = \,^A_{Z+1}Y + \,^0_{-1}\beta^- + \bar{\nu} + Q$

β^+: $^A_ZX = \,^A_{Z-1}Y + \,^0_1\beta^+ + e^- + \nu + Q$

EC: $^A_ZX = \,^A_{Z-1}Y + \nu + Q$

fluorescence yield: $\omega = \frac{\lambda_X}{\lambda_X + \lambda_A}$ internal conversion coefficient: $\alpha = \frac{\lambda_e}{\lambda_\gamma}$

chain decay: $N_b = N_b(0)\, e^{-\lambda_b t} + \frac{\lambda_a N_a(0)}{\lambda_b - \lambda_a}\left(e^{-\lambda_a t} - e^{-\lambda_b t}\right)$

If $N_b(0) = 0$: $\frac{N_b \lambda_b}{N_a \lambda_a} = \frac{\lambda_b}{\lambda_b - \lambda_a}\left(1 - e^{-(\lambda_b - \lambda_a)t}\right)$ activity ratio (i.e. Mo→Tc).

decay: $N = N_0 e^{-\lambda t}$ $\lambda = \frac{\ln(2)}{t_{1/2}}$

decay via mode i in time t: $p_i = \frac{\lambda_i}{\lambda}(1 - e^{-\lambda t})$

production of radioisotopes: $N = \frac{\phi\sigma}{\lambda}\frac{maN_A}{A}(1 - e^{-\lambda t})$

Compton: $E'_\gamma = \frac{E_\gamma}{1 + \frac{E_\gamma}{m_0c^2}(1 - \cos\theta)}$

linear attenuation: $N(x) = N_0 e^{-\mu x}$ attenuation

interaction of type i for path length x: $p_i = \frac{\mu_i}{\mu}(1 - e^{-\mu x})$

$$\text{KE target} = \frac{4 m_n M \cos^2\theta}{(m_n + M)^2} E_n$$

$$\text{max KE target} = \frac{4 m_n M}{(m_n + M)^2} E_n$$

$\frac{1}{v}$ cross section $\sigma = \sigma_0 \sqrt{\frac{E_0}{E}}$

exposure rate: $\dot{X} = \frac{e}{4\pi w_{air}} \frac{N\lambda}{r^2} \sum_{i=1}^{n} (p(E_i) E_i (\frac{\mu_{en}}{\rho}(E_i))_{air})$

$$\dot{\Gamma} = \frac{e}{4\pi w_{air}} \sum_{i=1}^{n} (p(E_i) E_i (\frac{\mu_{en}}{\rho}(E_i))_{air})$$

$\lambda_E = \lambda_M + \lambda_R$ $\quad T_E = \frac{T_M T_R}{T_M + T_R}$

for internally deposited β's: $\dot{D}_0 = \frac{N_0 \lambda_R \bar{E}_\beta}{m}$

and $D = \frac{N_0 \lambda_R \bar{E}_\beta}{\lambda_E m}(1 - e^{-\lambda_E \tau})$

for internally deposited γ's: $D(50) = \frac{N_0(S) \lambda_R (1 - e^{-\lambda_E \tau})}{M_T \lambda_E} \sum_R \{AF(T \leftarrow S)_R Y_R E_R\}$

$$D_n(E) = \Phi(E) E \sum_i (N_i \sigma_i(E) f_i)$$

equivalent dose: $H_T = \sum_R (w_R D_{T,R})$

effective dose: $E = \sum_T (w_T H_T)$

broad beam attenuation: $I = B I_0 e^{-\mu x}$

primary protective barrier: $K = \frac{P d^2}{WUT}$

secondary barriers: leakage: $B = \frac{60 I P d^2}{YWT}$

scatter: $K = \frac{1000 P d^2}{fWT}$

Assignments & Tests

Note: Physics 3T03
Biology 3L03
& Med Physics 3T03

all refer to this course, which is now labelled
Med Physics 4B03/6B03

BIOLOGY 3L03/PHYSICS 3T03 DUE: NOVEMBER 22, 1994.

ASSIGNMENT #3

---

1. A researcher ingests 10^{12} atoms of ^{32}P. The ^{32}P distribution is 50% in the bone and 50% in the rest of the body. The retention function is thus characterized by a 2 component curve with half-lives of 1155 days in bone and 257 days for the rest of the body. The physical half-life for the radioactive decay of ^{32}P is 14.3 d, and the average beta decay energy is 0.695 MeV. For a skeletal mass of 7 kg and a whole body weight of 70 kg, calculate the dose to the bone and the dose to the rest of the body.

2. An X-ray machine produces 10^{15} photons/sec. Assuming the radiation field is equivalent to one with a monoenergetic spectrum at 50 keV, estimate the exposure rate in Rh^{-1} at 1 m.

3. "The amount of energy in a cup of hot tea could be fatal if absorbed by a person in the form of ionizing radiation". Do you agree? (A dose of somewhere between 4 and 6 J kg^{-1} could be fatal within 30 days of the exposure).

4. What is the specific gamma-ray emission for ^{40}K? What is the dose rate at 1 m from 1 kg of natural potassium? What is the dose rate from the ^{40}K in 130 g of natural potassium distributed uniformly in the body of a 70 kg person? The natural abundance of ^{40}K is 1.17 x 10^{-4}; it has a half life of 1.277 x 10^{9} y. ^{40}K decays by β^-(89.33%), electron capture (10.67%) and β^+ (0.001%). There is a γ-ray of energy 1.461 MeV associated with the electron capture decay, this also has a branching ratio of 10.67%.

Assignment #4

Biol.3L03/Phys.3T03 Due: Wednesday, Dec 7th, 1994
by 17:00

---

1. Consider the reaction:

$$^{37}Cl(n,\gamma)^{38}Cl.$$

What is the dose to the whole body from this reaction when the body is irradiated by a fluence of 10^8 thermal neutrons? Assume that the mass of chlorine in a 70 kg body is 100 g; ^{37}Cl is 24% abundant; the reaction cross section is 0.43 barn, and that two 3 MeV γ-rays are emitted per reaction. ^{38}Cl has a radioactive decay half-life of 37.3 minutes; it emits β^- particles with maximum energies of 4.81 Mev, 2.77 MeV and 1.11 MeV in 58%, 11% and 31% of decays respectively, and γ-rays of 2.17 MeV and 1.64 MeV in 42% and 31% of decays. Assume the biological half-life of chlorine in the body to be 10 days. Consider the doses from the prompt γ-rays and from the induced ^{38}Cl separately.

2. If a person ingests 500 kBq of ^{203}Hg, what is the dose commitment to (i) her ovaries, (ii) his testes? Use the distribution of ^{203}Hg amongst organs, the elimination constants and specific absorbed fractions given in Cember, chapter 6.

3. When cadmium is measured in liver by neutron activation there is a fast neutron dose to the liver of 25 μGy and a γ-ray dose to the liver of 50 μGy. In addition there are whole body doses of fast neutrons and γ-rays, each of which is 1% of the liver dose for the same particle. What is the equivalent dose to the liver (in μSv) and that to the whole body (in μSv)?

4. a) Find the thickness of lead required as a primary barrier for a 200 kVp X-ray installation under the following conditions:

   The distance between the target and the area is 5 m, and the occupancy factor is 0.25.

   The area is open to the general public, so an exposure of 2 mR/week is the maximum permitted.

   The workload is 15000 mA-min/week with the machine use factor of unity.

5. b) Calculate the exposure produced in the weekly operation of a 150 kVp X-ray machine at a point behind the primary barrier. The distance from the target is 2 m, and the shielding corresponds to 3 mm of lead. The machine operates 480 min. per week at a current of 2 mA.

PHYSICS 3T03/BIOLOGY 3L03

ASSIGNMENT #1 Due: **Sept. 28, 1995**

---

1. What is the most massive stable nucleus with which a 4.5 MeV α-particle can interact by crossing the Coulomb barrier?

2. Compare the energy yield per gram from fission of ^{235}U and fusion of ^{2}H. State any assumptions you make.

3. Using mass difference, Δ, calculate the energy released in the hydrogen burning cycle occurring in the sun by calculating the energy release for each of the following reactions:

$$^{1}H + {}^{1}H \rightarrow {}^{2}H + e^{+} + \nu + e^{-} \quad (x2)$$
$$^{2}H + {}^{1}H \rightarrow {}^{3}He + \gamma \quad (x2)$$
$$^{3}He + {}^{3}He \rightarrow {}^{4}He + 2\ {}^{1}H$$

given:

$\Delta(^{1}H) = 7.2890$ MeV
$\Delta(^{2}H) = 13.1359$ MeV
$\Delta(^{3}He) = 14.9313$ MeV
$\Delta(^{4}He) = 2.4248$ MeV
$m_e c^2 = 0.511$ MeV

3. Radium-224 ($^{224}_{88}Ra$) decays to radon (Rn) by α-particle emission in the manner shown in the decay scheme. The mass excess values for the Rn isotope, ^{224}Ra and $^{4}_{2}He$ are 10.599 MeV, 18.813 MeV and 2.425 MeV respectively.

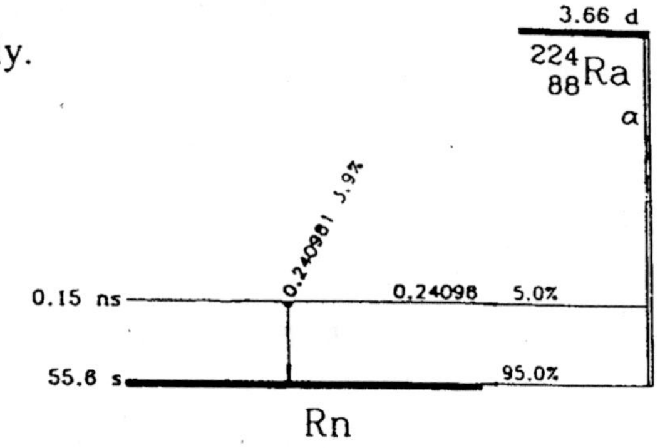

a) Write out the decay equation.

b) What are the energies of the two α-particles?

4. The disintegration scheme for ^{125}I is given below. The mass excess values for ^{125}I and ^{125}Te are -88.84 MeV and -89.019 MeV respectively. The K-shell binding energy for I is 0.033 MeV.

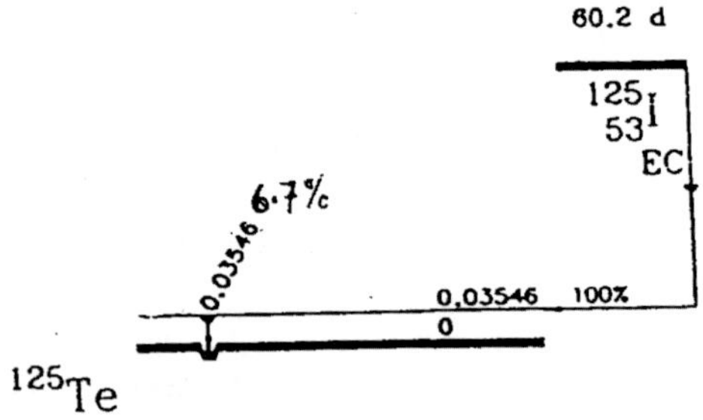

a) Write out the decay equation.

b) Use mass excess to calculate energies of any particles involved in the decay.

c) What is the internal conversion coefficient for de-excitation of the 0.035 MeV level in ^{125}Te? What is the kinetic energy of K shell internal conversion electrons?

d) Estimate the fluorescence yield in Te.

e) For a 1 MBq source of ^{125}I, what will be the emission rate (s^{-1}) of (i) 0.035 MeV γ-rays, (ii) Te x-rays, (iii) internal conversion electrons, and (iv) Auger electrons?

ASSIGNMENT #2

PHYSICS 3T03 - BIOLOGY 3L03 **Due: October 16, 1995**

---

1. A 75 Mbq aliquot of ^{99m}Tc is to be eluted from a column containing ^{99}Mo from which all ^{99m}Tc activity has been eluted 4 hours previously. What minimum activity of ^{99}Mo must be present? What activity must there have been when the ^{99}Mo was delivered to the hospital one week earlier? The half life of ^{99m}Tc is 6 hours; the half life of ^{99}Mo is 67 hours.

2. A 5 g sample of natural UO_2 was prepared (chemically separated) 2 years ago. What are the principal activities present now? List those activities $\geq$ 4kBq. What are the activities of ^{234}U and ^{235}U?

3. ^{109}Cd is produced with a specific activity of 35 PBq kg^{-1}. Assuming all the material that is not ^{109}Cd is natural Cd, what proportion of the nuclei present are ^{109}Cd? The half life of ^{109}Cd is 453 days.

4. Assuming soft tissue has the composition $O_{27}C_{6.4}H_{60}N_{1.5}$ and a density, ρ = 1g cm^{-3},

   a) what is the stopping power $\left(-\frac{dE}{dx}\right)$ of a 6 MeV α-particle is soft tissue?

   b) What is the stopping power of a 1.7 MeV β^- particle in soft tissue and in bone ($Ca_{10}(PO_4)_6(OH)_2$, ρ = 2g cm^{-3})?

ASSIGNMENT #3

PHYSICS 3T03 - BIOLOGY 3L03 Due: FRIDAY, October 27, 1995

1. A photon source is to be chosen to excite lead K x-rays. A major design consideration is that the ratio of x-ray signal to Compton scatter background is to be maximized. So the main Compton scatter 'peak' must be as far away as possible (in terms of energy) from the x-rays at 75keV and 85keV. There are two possible geometries, 90° and 180°. The angle is that through which photons are scattered in going from source to sample to detector. There are three possible sources. ^{57}Co has a γ-ray at 122keV, ^{153}Gd has γ-rays at 97keV and 102keV, ^{109}Cd has a γ-ray at 88keV.

   Which source/angle combination(s) would you choose?

2. A ^{109}Cd source decays to ^{109m}Ag, which emits a γ-ray of 88 keV. The source is found to emit 0.036 γ-rays per decay, but the intensity of Ag x-rays is 30 times this number. For a bone lead measurement the Ag x-rays are to be filtered out using copper. The linear attenuation coefficients for Ag x-rays and 88 keV γ-rays in copper are 161 cm^{-1} and 5.47 cm^{-1} respectively.

   What thickness of copper is required to transmit only 1000 Ag x-ray per second from a 1 MBq source? What percentage of 88 keV γ-rays will be transmitted through this thickness of copper?

3. A 1 μg source of ^{252}Cf is listed as having a neutron output of 2.3×10^6 neutrons s^{-1}.

   What is the average number of neutrons per fission of ^{252}Cf?

4. On average what is the relative amount of energy lost by 1 MeV neutrons in elastic scattering collisions with the carbon, hydrogen, nitrogen, and oxygen in the human body? Assume the composition of soft tissue is hydrogen (10%), carbon (23%), nitrogen (2.6%) and oxygen (61%) by mass. Take the elastic scattering cross section at 1MeV to be 4.3b, 2.6b, 2.0b and 8.0b for H, C, N and O respectively.

ASSIGNMENT #4

PHYSICS 3T03 - BIOLOGY 3L03 Due: WEDNESDAY, NOVEMBER 22, 1995

---

1. Consider a spherical cell 1 μm in diameter with a density of 1000 kg m^{-3}. Find the average dose to the cell when an incorporated tritium atom decays, assuming all the electron energy is deposited. The Q value for tritium β^- decay is 18.6 keV. If the tritium activity concentration is 10^4 Bq kg^{-1} find the fraction of cells containing a tritium atom. What is the average dose to 1 kg of tissue?

2. What is the exposure rate at a distance of 65 cm from a 15 mCi unshielded point source of ^{60}Co? What would the dose rate be in compact bone? in muscle? Values for (μ_{en}/ρ) are in m^2 kg^{-1}.

E_γ (MeV)	0.80	1.0	1.5	2.0
$(\mu_{en}/\rho)_{air}$	2.89×10^{-3}	2.80×10^{-3}	2.55×10^{-3}	2.34×10^{-3}
$(\mu_{en}/\rho)_{bone}$	3.06×10^{-3}	2.97×10^{-3}	2.70×10^{-3}	2.48×10^{-3}
$(\mu_{en}/\rho)_{muscle}$	3.18×10^{-3}	3.08×10^{-3}	2.81×10^{-3}	2.57×10^{-3}

3. For boron neutron capture therapy a boron loaded compound is arranged to concentrate in a tumour. The tumour plus healthy tissue is then irradiated with thermal neutrons. The following reaction, which has a cross section of 3838 b takes place:

$$^{10}B(n,\alpha)^7Li.$$

If a fluence of 10^{11} neutrons cm^{-2} is administered to a person, what is the equivalent dose? What concentration (μg g^{-1}) of ^{10}B must there be in the tumour to ensure that the tumour receives a total dose three times that of healthy tissue?
A thermal neutron fluence of 1 neutron cm^{-2} will result in a dose to tissue of 2.5 pGy. Radiation weighting factors are 5 for thermal neutrons and 20 for α-particles and heavy nuclei. Mass excess values (MeV) are: ^{1}n - 8.071; ^{4}He - 2.425; ^{7}Li - 14.907; ^{10}B - 12.052.

4. It has been suggested that ^{210}Pb, a decay product of ^{222}Rn, could be a significant cause of leukæmia, because it lodges in bone and produces a long term irradiation of bone marrow. ^{210}Pb has a physical half life of 22.3 years. It decays by β^- emission to ^{210}Bi, which decays by β^- emission to ^{210}Po. Both ^{210}Bi and ^{210}Po have appreciably shorter physical half lives (5 days and 138 days, respectively) than ^{210}Pb. Nearly all the dose arises from the 5.3 MeV α-particle emitted in each decay from ^{210}Po, which has w_R=20. Considering only the α-particle, what is the committed equivalent dose to bone from an activity concentration of ^{210}Pb of 1 Bq per g of bone? Assume a biological half life of Pb in bone of 30 years.
What concentration in bone (pg ^{210}Pb/g bone) would be required to produce an equivalent dose of 10 Sv in 1 year?

ASSIGNMENT # 5

PHYSICS 3T03 - BIOLOGY 3L03 **Due: WEDNESDAY, DEC 6, 1995**

1. A researcher ingests 10μCi of ^{32}P. The distribution is 66% in the skeleton and 34% in the rest of the body. The metabolic half lives are 1155d for skeleton and 257d for the rest of the body. The physical half life is 14.3d. ^{32}P is a pure β^- emitter with $\overline{E}_\beta$ = 0.695 MeV. Calculate the initial dose rates and the committed doses to both the skeleton and to the rest of the body. Assume a skeletal mass of 10kg and a total body mass of 70kg.

2. In a system designed to measure aluminum in bone, a person's hand is placed in a neutron beam, receiving a dose of 200 μGy from fast neutrons, plus 200 μGy from γ-rays. The person stands behind a shield so that the rest of the body receives a dose of only 0.1% of that received by the hand. What are the equivalent doses to the hand and to the rest of the body? Assuming the hand represents 1.5% of skin plus 1.5% of bone surfaces, what is the effective dose?

3. Calculate the specific gamma constant for ^{60}Co in units of $C m^2 kg^{-1} Bq^{-1} s^{-1}$. Express this in units of $R m^2 Ci^{-1} h^{-1}$. Determine what thickness of lead shielding is required around a 7.40×10^{13}Bq point source of ^{60}Co to reduce the exposure rate to 2.5 mR h^{-1} at a distance of 2m. The linear attenuation coefficient for lead is 68.9m^{-1} at 1.173MeV and 63.0m^{-1} at 1.332MeV.

4. The useful beam of a 300 kVp x-ray machine is directed 40% of the time normally at a hard brick wall 2.4m away. The wall, which is 10.0cm thick, separates the x-ray room from an uncontrolled hall outside. The x-ray machine is operated with a current of 14.5 mA 40 minutes per day, 5 days per week. Calculate the thickness of lead shielding that needs to be added to the brick wall for the primary protective barrier.

PHYSICS 3TO3 - BIOLOGY 3L03 ASSIGNMENT #2

Due: MONDAY, October 7, 1996

(by 17:00)

---

1. Protons are accelerated to 10 MeV and strike a lead (Pb) target. Do you expect nuclear reactions to occur? (Base any calculations you make on ^{206}Pb.) In fact, ^{206}Bi is observed. What can you deduce about what has happened?

2. Compare the energy yield per gram of natural uranium, via fission of ^{235}U, with that obtained from a gram of water from ^{2}H, ^{2}H fusion. State any assumption you make.

3. Uranium - 238 $\left(^{238}_{92}\text{U}\right)$ decays to thorium(Th) by α-particle emission in the manner shown in the decay scheme. The mass difference values for the Th isotope, ^{238}U and $^{4}_{2}He$ are 40.612MeV, 47.307MeV and 2.425MeV respectively.

   a) Write out the decay equation.
   b) What α-particle energies do you expect?

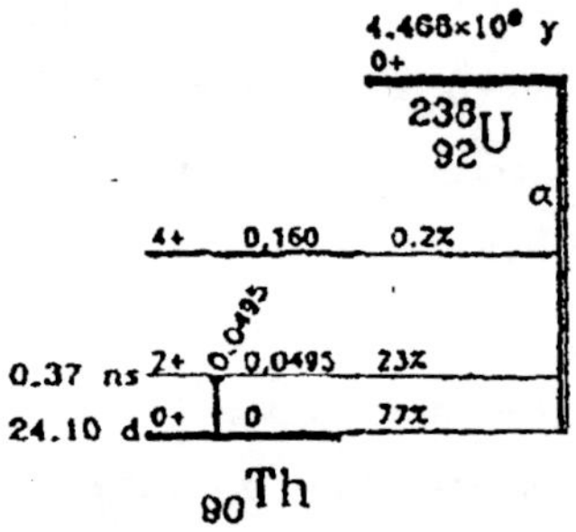

Continued on page 2...

4. A slightly simplified decay scheme for ^{126}I is given below. The mass difference values for ^{126}I, ^{126}Xe and ^{126}Te are -87.911MeV, -89.162Mev and -90.066MeV respectively.

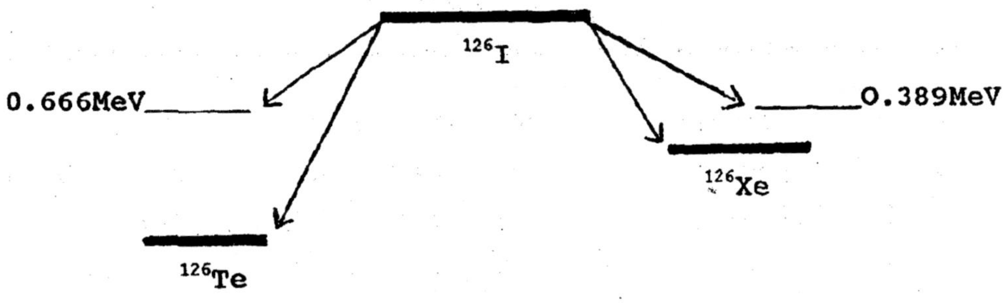

a) Write out the decay equations.

b) Use mass difference to calculate energies of any particles involved in the decays.

PHYSICS 3T03 - BIOLOGY 3L03 ASSIGNMENT #3

Due: MONDAY, November 4, 1996

(by 17:00)

1. What is the stopping power of a 7.0 MeV α-particle in water? By evaluating the stopping power also at 2.0, 0.7 and 0.2MeV, make a rough estimate of the range of the 7.0MeV α-particle in water.

2. What is the stopping power of a 1.5 MeV electron in water? What is the value for a 1.5 MeV positron. What proportion of the energy loss will be in the form of Bremsstrahlung?

3. It is desired to use a radioisotopic source for x-ray fluorescence of uranium, exciting the K series uranium x-rays. The sources available, with their principal photon energies are as follows:

source	photon energies [keV] (photon per decay)
^{109}Cd	88(.036)
^{153}Gd	97(1.0), 103(0.73)
^{57}Co	122(0.86), 136(0.11)
^{99m}Tc	141(0.89)

Two possible geometries could be used. In one the source-sample-detector angle would be 90°; in the other geometry, the angle would be 180°.

continued on next page...

Which of the above sources could you use? For the source(s) you could use, which source-geometry combinations would you choose to try? The K shell absorption edge for uranium is at 115.6 keV. The energies and relative intensities of uranium K x-rays are: $K\alpha_2$ 94.7 keV(61.9), $K\alpha_1$ 98.4 keV(100), $K_{\beta 3}$ 110.4 keV(11.6), $K_{\beta 1}$ 111.3 keV(22.0), $K_{\beta 2}$ 114.5 keV(12.3) [Consider the proximity of signal (U x-rays) to 'background' (Compton scatter)].

4. The total mass attenuation coefficient for 5 MeV γ-rays interacting with lead is $\mu/\rho = 0.044\ cm^2g^{-1}$. The mass attenuation coefficient for pair production under the same conditions is μ_π/ρ 0.022 cm^2g^{-1}. A beam of 10^5 photons is incident on a 2.5 cm thick slab.

a) How many pair production events occur in the slab.

b) What is the effective minimum energy absorbed in the slab following a pair production event?

c) What is the energy of photons emerging from the slab having undergone a single Compton scattering event through 180°?

Density of lead = 11.35 g cm^{-3}.

5. A tungsten(W) alloy shield, in which the density of tungsten is 18.1 cm^{-3}, is used to attenuate 88keV γ-rays from a 1 Gbq ^{109}Cd source. The shield is 2mm thick. ^{109}Cd emit 88 keV γ-rays following 0.036 of disintegrations. What is the flux density (γ-rays $mm^{-2}s^{-1}$) at a distance of 3.5mm? When the shield is interposed, how many γ-rays mm^{-2} are transmitted during a half-hour measurement? If the same thickness of W shield is used for 140 keV γ-rays from ^{99m}Tc, what proportion of γ-rays is transmitted? The mass attenuation coefficient for W is 6.13 cm^2g^{-1} at 88 keV and 1.90 $cm^{-2}g^{-1}$ at 140 keV.

The End

ASSIGNMENT #4

PHYSICS 3T03 - BIOLOGY 3L03 Due: 17:00, TUESDAY, NOVEMBER 26, 1996

---

1. Consider a spherical cell 1 μm in diameter with a density of 1000 kg m^{-3}. Find the average dose to the cell when an incorporated tritium atom decays, assuming all the electron energy is deposited. The Q value for tritium β^- decay is 18.6 keV. If the tritium activity concentration is 10^4 Bq kg^{-1} find the fraction of cells containing a tritium atom. What is the average dose to 1 kg of tissue?

2. What is the exposure rate at a distance of 65 cm from a 15 mCi unshielded point source of ^{60}Co? What would the dose rate be in compact bone? in muscle? Values for (μ_{en}/ρ) are in m^2 kg^{-1}.

E_γ (MeV)	0.80	1.0	1.5	2.0
$(\mu_{en}/\rho)_{air}$	2.89×10^{-3}	2.80×10^{-3}	2.55×10^{-3}	2.34×10^{-3}
$(\mu_{en}/\rho)_{bone}$	3.06×10^{-3}	2.97×10^{-3}	2.70×10^{-3}	2.48×10^{-3}
$(\mu_{en}/\rho)_{muscle}$	3.18×10^{-3}	3.08×10^{-3}	2.81×10^{-3}	2.57×10^{-3}

^{60}Co emits γ-rays of 1.33 MeV and 1.17 MeV, both with branching ratios of 100%.

3. A researcher ingests 10 μCi of ^{32}P. The distribution is 66% in the skeleton and 34% in the rest of the body. The metabolic half lives are 1155d for skeleton and 257d for the rest of the body. The physical half-life is 14.3d. ^{32}P is a pure β^- emitter with $\overline{E_\beta}$ = 0.695 MeV. Calculate the initial dose rates and the committed doses to both the skeleton and to the rest of the body. Assume a skeletal mass of 10 kg and a total body mass of 70 kg.

4. The isotope ^{111}In has a 2.83 day half-life. The biological elimination for all organs can be described by the expression

$$\frac{N(t)}{N(0)} = 0.75e^{-0.28t} + 0.25e^{-0.15t}$$

N(t) and N(0) are the quantities of ^{111}In at times t and zero. Time, t, is expressed in days. Assume the indium is distributed with 70% in red bone marrow, 20% in kidneys and 10% in liver. Calculate the red bone marrow dose in Gy for an intake of 7.5 MBq of ^{111}In. Values for specific absorbed fraction in fGy/Bq/s are given below.

target organs	source organs		
	red bone marrow	kidney	liver
red bone marrow	6.52	0.528	0.276
kidney	0.528	38.4	0.886
liver	0.276	0.886	9.46

ASSIGNMENT #5

PHYSICS 3T03 - BIOLOGY 3L03 Due: 17:00, MONDAY, DECEMBER 2, 1996

1. In a system designed to measure manganese in the liver, a person is positioned in a neutron beam such that the liver receives a fast neutron dose (E_n=1 MeV) of 15 μGy plus a γ-ray dose of 35 μGy. The beam is collimated so that the rest of the body receives neutron and γ-ray doses of 0.1% of the doses to liver. What are the equivalent doses to the liver and to the rest of the body?
What is the effective dose?

2. Calculate the specific gamma constant for ^{60}Co in units of $Cm^2kg^{-1}Bq^{-1}s^{-1}$. Express this in units of $Rm^2Ci^{-1}h^{-1}$. Determine what thickness of lead shielding is required around an 800 Ci point source of ^{60}Co to reduce the exposure rate to 2.5 mRh^{-1} at a distance of 2.5 m. The linear attenuation coefficient (μ) for lead is 68.9 m^{-1} at 1.173 MeV and 63.0 m^{-1} at 1.332 MeV.

Dose buildup factors, B, in lead.

	number of relaxation lengths (μx)						
MeV	1	2	4	7	10	15	20
1.173	1.38	1.71	2.32	3.16	3.97	5.22	6.47
1.332	1.38	1.72	2.36	3.27	4.16	5.57	7.00

3. The useful beam of a 300 kV_p x-ray machine is directed 40% of the time normally at a hard brick wall 2.4 m away. The wall, which is 10.0 cm thick, separates the x-ray room from an uncontrolled hall outside. The x-ray machine is operated with a current of 14.5 mA 40 minutes per day, 5 days per week. Calculate the thickness of lead shielding that needs to be added to the brick wall for the primary protective barrier. (Necessary data can be found in Turner or Cember.)

Physics 3T03 - Biology 3L03 **Assignment #1**

due: MONDAY, September 29th, 1997

17:00

---

1. The semi-empirical mass formula can be written:

$$M(A,Z) = 0.99389A - 0.00081Z + 0.014\,A^{2/3} + 0.083\,\frac{(A/2-Z)^2}{A}$$

$$+\ 0.000627\,\frac{Z^2}{A^{1/3}} + \delta$$

where the M is the mass in amu, A is the mass number, Z is the atomic number (charge number of nucleus) and

$\delta = 0$ for add A

$= -0.036/A^{3/4}$ for even A, even Z

$= +0.036/A^{2/4}$ for odd A, odd Z

i) What is the mass of $^{56}_{26}Fe$ in amu?

ii) If the Q value for the $^{56}Fe(n,p)^{56}$ Mn reaction is -2.913 MeV, what is the mass difference (Δ) of ^{56}Mn?

(1 amu = 931.5 MeV, $\Delta(\,^1_0n)$ = 8.071 MeV, $\Delta(\,^1_1H)$ = 7.289 MeV)

continued on page 2 ...

.. A lead (Pb) target can be bombarded with protons of energy up to 15MeV. What are the Q values for the reactions:

$^{207}Pb(p,n)^{207}Bi$	nuclide	Δ (MeV)
$^{208}Pb(p,n)^{208}Bi$	^{207}Pb	-22.463
	^{207}Bi	-20.058
	^{208}Pb	-21.759
	^{208}Bi	-18.879

What is the Coulomb barrier for these reactions?
At what energy of protons would you expect to find the effective threshold for these reactions, and why?

. If the following reaction is typical of thermal neutron induced fission of ^{239}Pu, how much energy would be released from the fission of 1 kg of ^{239}Pu?

$$^{239}_{94}Pu + {}^{1}_{0}n \rightarrow {}^{240}_{94}Pu \rightarrow {}^{111}_{45}Rh + {}^{126}_{49}In + 3x\, {}^{1}_{0}n$$

$^{111}_{45}Rh$ eventually decays to $^{111}_{48}Cd$. $^{126}_{49}In$ eventually decays to $^{126}_{52}Te$. In each case the decays take place by a succession of β^- emissions. Assume that ⅔ of the energy of each β^- decay is completely lost to the system as neutrino energy.

nuclide	Δ (MeV)
^{239}Pu	48.585
^{111}Rh	-82.53
^{111}Cd	-89.254
^{126}In	-77.90
^{126}Te	-90.066

continued on page 3 ...

4. The disintegration scheme for ^{125}I is given below. The mass difference values for ^{125}I and ^{125}Te are -88.84 MeV and -89.019 MeV respectively. The K-shell binding energy for I is 0.033 MeV.

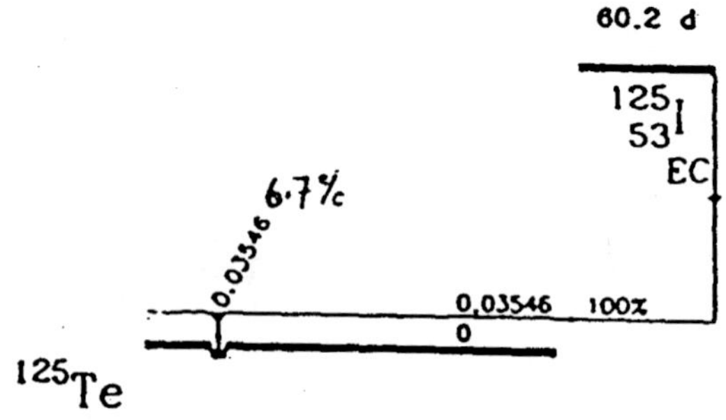

a) Write out the decay equation.

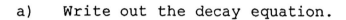

b) Use mass difference to calculate energies of any particles involved in the decay.

c) What is the internal conversion coefficient for de-excitation of the 0.035 MeV level in ^{125}Te? What is the kinetic energy of K shell internal conversion electrons?

d) Estimate the fluorescence yield in Te.

e) For a 1 Mbq source of ^{125}I, what will be the emission rate (s^{-1}) of (i) 0.035 MeV γ-rays, (ii) Te x-rays, (iii) internal conversion electrons, and (iv) Auger electrons?

THE END

Name: ______________________

Student # _______________

BIOLOGY 3L03 - PHYSICS 3T03 CLASS TEST #1

THURSDAY, OCTOBER 10, 1996

Students to answer all 3 questions

---

1. In the $^{10}_{5}B\ (n,\alpha)^{7}Li$ reaction, ^{7}Li can be formed either in the ground state or in an excited state, which has an energy 0.478 MeV greater than the ground state.
Estimate the α-particle energies in the two cases.

nuclide	Δ (MeV)
$^{1}_{0}n$	8.071
$^{10}_{5}B$	12.052
$^{7}_{3}Li$	14.907
$^{4}_{2}He$	2.425

continued on page 2 ...

2. A slightly simplified decay scheme for ^{74}As is shown below.

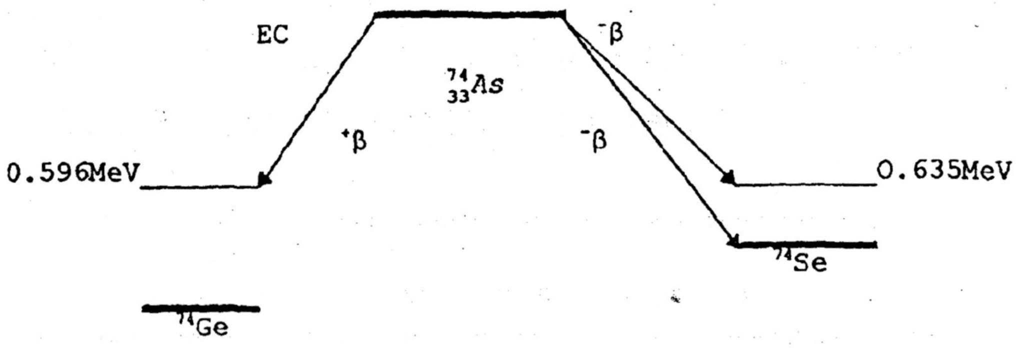

a) Write out the decay equations for EC, $^{+}\beta$ and $^{-}\beta$, specifying the atomic numbers of the product isotopes.

b) What are the maximum β-particle energies? What is the energy of the neutrino in the EC decay?

nuclide	Δ (MeV)
^{74}As	-70.860
^{74}Ge	-73.422
^{74}Se	-72.213

Atom	K shell election binding energy (MeV)
As	0.012
Ge	0.011
Se	0.013

3. ^{109}Cd is produced with a specific activity of 1000 Ci/g.

a) What is the mass of 1000 Ci of ^{109}Cd, which is entirely pure?

b) If all the material that is not ^{109}Cd is natural cadmium, what proportion of atoms are ^{109}Cd?

1Ci = 3.7×10^{10} Bq = 3.7×10^{10} disintegrations/s

half life of ^{109}Cd = 453 day

atomic weight of natural Cd = 112.41

Avogrado's number = 6.022×10^{23} atom/mole.

Name: ______________________

Student # ________________

BIOLOGY 3L03 - PHYSICS 3T03 CLASS TEST #2

WEDNESDAY, November 13, 1996

Students to answer all 4 questions

---

1. Protons of 100 MeV are used in specialized therapy of tumours of the optic nerve. From the stopping power data given below, make a crude estimate of the range of 100 MeV protons in tissue.

Ep (MeV)	-dE/dx (MeV/cm)
100	7.28
80	8.62
60	10.8
40	14.9
20	26.1
10	45.9

continued on page 2 ...

2. Calculate the energies of Compton scattered photons for the two angles 60° and 180° for each of the three energies 0.01 MeV, 1.0 MeV and 100 MeV. The rest mass of the electron is 0.511 MeV.

E_γ (MeV)	E_γ' (60°) (MeV)	E_γ' (180°) (MeV)
0.01		
1.0		
100		

3. What thickness (cm) of lead is needed to attenuate
   (i) the 88 keV γ-rays from a ^{109}Cd source by a factor of 10^6?
   (ii) the 1.33 MeV γ-rays from a ^{60}Co source by a factor of 10^3?

   The mass attenuation coefficient for lead is 6.8 cm^2/g at 88 keV and 0.057 cm^2/g at 1.33 MeV. The density of lead is 11.35 g/cm^3.

4. Manganese is to be measured in liver by using the $^{55}Mn(n,\gamma)^{56}Mn$ reaction. There is a thermal neutron fluence rate of $10^4 cm^{-2}s^{-1}$. There is a 15 minute irradiation, then a 1 hour wait and then a half hour count. How many ^{56}Mn nuclei are formed by the end of the irradiation? How many ^{56}Mn decays occur during the count if the mass of manganese in the liver is 10 mg? The half life of ^{56}Mn is 2.58 hours. The cross section for the $^{55}Mn(n,\gamma)^{56}Mn$ reaction is 13.3 barn. Avagadro's number is 6.02×10^{23} $mole^{-1}$. 1 barn ≡ 10^{-24} cm^2. All natural (stable) manganese is ^{55}Mn.

Name: ______________________________

Student #: __________________

BIOLOGY 3L03 - PHYSICS 3T03 **CLASS TEST #1**

Monday, October 25th, 2000

time: 10:30 - 11:20

Students to answer all 4 questions

Avagadro's number	6.02×10^{23} mole^{-1}
Electron rest mass	0.511 MeV.
Proton rest mass	938.3 MeV.
Ca K shell binding energy	4.04 keV

1. ^{230}Th decays to ^{226}Ra as shown in the diagram,

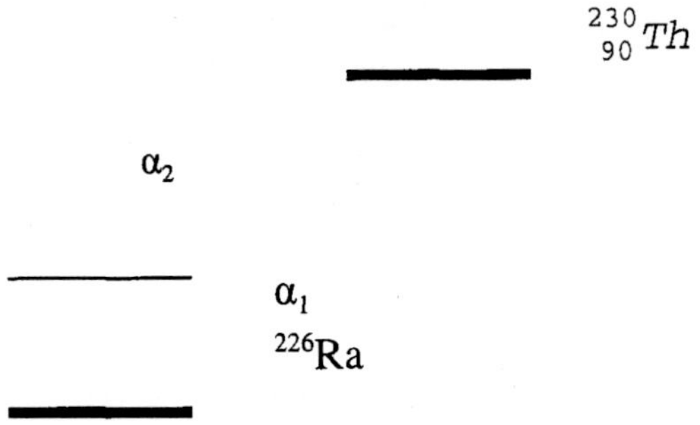

α particles of two different energies are observed. The energies are 4.688 MeV and 4.621 MeV. The mass difference (Δ) of ^{226}Ra is 23.666 MeV. The mass difference (Δ) of $^{4}_{2}He$ is 2.425 MeV.

(i) What is the atomic number of Ra?

(ii) What is the mass difference (Δ) of ^{230}Th?

(iii) What is the energy of the excited state in ^{226}Ra?

2. In a sample of natural uranium the proportions of ^{234}U, ^{235}U and ^{238}U are $5.4\text{x}10^{-5}$, $7.2\text{x}10^{-3}$ and 0.99 respectively. The half lives of these three isotopes are $2.45\text{x}10^{5}$ y (^{234}U), $7.04\text{x}10^{8}$ y (^{235}U) and $4.47\text{x}10^{9}$ y (^{238}U). The atomic mass of natural uranium is 238.0. What are the specific activities (Bq, g^{-1}) of the three isotopes in this sample of natural uranium?

3. The bremsstrahlung radiation intensity emitted as a charged particle slows down is proportional to $z^2 Z^2 / m^2$, where z is the charge number of the particle, Z is the atomic number of the medium and m is the mass of the charged particle. The radiation yield as a proportion of the total energy lost, Y, for an electron of kinetic energy T (MeV) is given by:

$$Y = \frac{6x10^{-4} Z\ T}{1 + 6x10^{-4}\ ZT}$$

What proportion of total energy lost is emitted as bremsstrahlung when 2.5 MeV electrons lose their energy in bone ash, which has an effective atomic number of 13?

What proportion of total energy lost is emitted as bremsstrahlung when 2.5 MeV protons lose their energy in bone ash?

4. a) Photons of energy 88 keV are incident on a bone sample.

(i) What is the energy of the photo electron following a photo electric interaction with a K shell electron of calcium?

(ii) What is the energy of a photon scattered thorough 160° in a Compton interaction?

b) A γ-ray of energy 1.46 MeV interacts by pair production. What is the sum of the kinetic energies of the electron and the positron?

Name: ______________________________

Student #: ___________________

BIOLOGY 3L03 - PHYSICS 3T03 **CLASS TEST #2**

Monday, Nov 20, 2000

time: 10:30-11:20

Students to answer all 4 questions

---

1 barn $\equiv 10^{-28}\ m^2$

Avogadro's number = $6.02 \times 10^{23}\ mole^{-1}$

1Ci $\equiv 3.7 \times 10^{10}$ Bq

1MeV = 1.6×10^{-13} J

1 Gy $\equiv 1\ J\ kg^{-1}$

1.

Two beams of photons of energies 50 keV and 100 keV are incident on a sample which contains both soft tissue and bone. The photon beams have to pass through 0.12 m of soft tissue and 0.04m of bone. What proportion of the 50 keV and the 100 keV photon beams pass through the soft tissue and muscle unattenuated? For soft tissue the mass attenuation coefficient (μ/ρ) is 2.264×10^{-2} m^2kg^{-1} at 50 keV and 1.693×10^{-2} m^2kg^{-1} at 100 keV. For bone the mass attenuation coefficient is 4.242×10^{-2} m^2kg^{-1} at 50 keV and 1.855×10^{-2} m^2kg^{-1} at 100 keV. The density of soft tissue is 1.06×10^3 kgm^{-3}. The density of bone is 1.92×10^3 kgm^{-3}.

2.

Neutron activation is to be used to measure manganese (Mn) in the bones of the hand. The reaction used is $^{55}Mn(n,\gamma)^{56}Mn$. There is a 5 minute irradiation with a thermal neutron fluence rate of 5×10^9 $m^{-2}s^{-1}$. If the hand contains 75 μg of Mn, how many ^{56}Mn nuclei are there at the end of the irradiation? The isotopic abundance of ^{55}Mn is 100%. The atomic mass of manganese is 54.94. The half life of ^{56}Mn is 2.58 hour. The cross section for the $^{55}Mn(n,\gamma)^{56}Mn$ reaction is 13.3 barn.

3.

^{137}Cs emits a γ-ray of energy 0.661 MeV in 85% of decays. How long does it take to accumulate a dose of 1 mGy in muscle at a distance of 5 m from a ^{137}Cs source of activity 8.3 kCi?

E (keV)	0.50	0.60	0.80	1.0
$(\mu_{en}/\rho)_{muscle}$ (m^2kg^{-1})	3.27×10^{-3}	3.26×10^{-3}	3.18×10^{-3}	3.08×10^{-3}

4.

Following ingestion there are 3.4×10^{11} ^{33}P atoms in skeleton plus 5.1×10^{11} ^{33}P atoms in muscle. The half life of ^{33}P is 25.3 days; it decays via β^- emission only, there are no γ-rays. The average energy of the β^- is 0.098 MeV. The biological half life of phosphorus in skeleton is 1150 days and the biological half life of phosphorus in muscle is 230 days. What are the committed doses to skeleton and to muscle? The mass of the skeleton is 10 kg. The mass of muscle is 28kg.

PHYSICS 3T03

DR. D. R. CHETTLE

DAY CLASS
DURATION OF EXAMINATION: 2 hours
McMASTER UNIVERSITY FINAL EXAMINATION APRIL, 1994.

THIS EXAMINATION PAPER INCLUDES 3 PAGES AND 5 QUESTIONS. YOU ARE RESPONSIBLE FOR ENSURING THAT YOUR COPY OF THE PAPER IS COMPLETE. BRING ANY DISCREPANCY TO THE ATTENTION OF YOUR INVIGILATOR.

SPECIAL INSTRUCTIONS:

Candidates may use textbook, notes and calculators.
Answer all questions.
Use examination booklet provided for all answers.

Mass Excess Values (MeV)

$^{10}_{5}B$	12.052
$^{7}_{3}Li$	14.908
$^{4}_{2}He$	2.425
$^{1}_{0}n$	8.071

continued on page 2

Marks
10

1. The specific activity of a sample of ^{109}Cd is 1000 Ci g^{-1}. If all the atoms present, other than ^{109}Cd, are natural cadmium, what proportion of the nuclei is ^{109}Cd. The atomic weight of natural cadmium is 112.4. The half life of ^{109}Cd is 453 d.

Marks
10

2. ^{36} Cl can decay in the ways shown in the diagram. The mass excess for $^{36}_{18}Ar$ is -30.231 MeV, the energy of the β^- is 0.710 MeV, and that of the β^+ is 0.122 MeV.

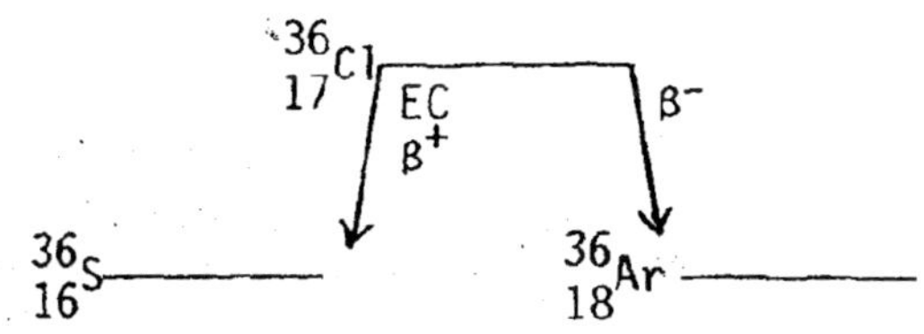

What are the mass excess values for ^{36}Cl and ^{36}S?

What is the Q value for the electron capture decay of ^{36}Cl, and how will this energy be released?

Marks
10

3. For boron neutron capture therapy a boron loaded compound is arranged to concentrate in a tumour. The tumour plus healthy tissue is then irradiated with thermal neutrons. The following reaction which has a cross section, σ, of 3838 barn takes place:

$$^{10}B(n,\alpha)^{7}Li$$

If a fluence of 10^{11} neutrons cm^{-2} is administered to a person, what is the equivalent (biological) dose? What concentration ($\mu g\ g^{-1}$) of ^{10}B must there be in the tumour to ensure that the tumour receives a total dose three times that of healthy tissue?

A thermal neutron fluence of 1 neutron cm^{-2} will result in a dose to both healthy tissue and the tumour of 2.5 pGy. Radiation weighting factors are 5 for thermal neutrons and 20 for α-particles and heavy nuclei. Mass excess values are given on page 1.

continued on page 3

Marks
10

4. The isotope ^{111}In has a 2.83 day half-life. The biological elimination for all organs can be described by the expression

$$\frac{N(t)}{N(0)} = 0.75e^{-0.28t} + 0.25e^{-0.15t}$$

N(t) and N(0) are the quantities of ^{111}In at times t and zero. Time, t, is expressed in days. Assume the indium is distributed with 70% in red bone marrow, 20% in kidneys and 10% in liver. Calculate the red bone marrow dose in Gy for an intake of 7.5 MBq of ^{111}In

S values (fGy Bq^{-1} s^{-1})

Target organs	Source organs		
	Red bone marrow	Kidney	Liver
Red bone marrow	6.52	0.528	0.276
Kidney	0.528	38.4	0.886
Liver	0.276	0.886	9.46

Marks
10

5. Design primary and secondary shielding barriers for a 150 kVp diagnostic x-ray machine. The workload is 2 x 10^4 mA min $week^{-1}$ and the use factor is 1. For the primary shield, a controlled area is 2 m from the target, has an occupancy factor of 0.5 and the maximum permissable exposure is 40 mR $week^{-1}$. For the secondary shield, the target to patient distance is 0.5 m, the maximum field size is 10 cm x 10 cm, the distance from the patient to the uncontrolled area is 2.5 m and the maximum permissable exposure is 2 mR $week^{-1}$.
There are already 10 cm thick concrete walls partially shielding each area. What is the required thickness of lead to be added to complete the primary and the secondary shield?

THE END.

BIOLOGY 3L03/PHYSICS 3T03

DAY CLASS — DR. D.R. CHETTLE
DURATION OF EXAMINATION: 2 hours
McMASTER UNIVERSITY FINAL EXAMINATION — DECEMBER 1994

THIS EXAMINATION PAPER INCLUDES 3 PAGES AND 5 QUESTIONS. YOU ARE RESPONSIBLE FOR ENSURING THAT YOUR COPY OF THE PAPER IS COMPLETE. BRING ANY DISCREPANCY TO THE ATTENTION OF YOUR INVIGILATOR.

SPECIAL INSTRUCTIONS:

Candidates may use textbook, notes and calculators.
Answer all questions.
Use examination booklet provided for all answers.

Physics Constants and Conversion Factors

e	$= 1.6 \times 10^{-19}$C
m_ec^2	$= 0.511$ MeV
1 year	$= \pi \times 10^7$ seconds
Avogadro's number	$= N_A = 6 \times 10^{23}$
1 GBq	$= 10^9$ disintegration sec^{-1}

Mass Excess Values: (MeV)

$^{220}_{86}Rn$	10.599	$^{1}_{0}n$	8.071
$^{224}_{88}Ra$	18.813	$^{31}_{15}P$	-24.440
$^{4}_{2}He$	2.425	$^{28}_{13}Al$	-16.848
$^{15}_{8}O$	2.855	$^{15}_{7}N$	0.102
$^{15}_{6}C$	9.8732		

continued on page 2...

Marks

10 1. a) When $^{224}_{88}Ra$ decays to $^{220}_{86}Rn$, 95% of decays go directly to the ground state of ^{220}Rn, 5% go to the first excited state, which has an energy of 0.241 MeV. What are the energies of the two different α-particles?

b) Oxygen-15 is a positron emitter. Write down the appropriate decay equation and calculate the maximum energy of the positron.

c) What is the Q value for the $^{31}P(n,\alpha)^{28}Al$ reaction?

10 2. Six hours after an accident involving exposure to thermal neutrons for a short time a person is found to have a whole body ^{24}Na activity of 200 Bq. To what thermal neutron fluence (number per cm^2) was the person exposed? The $^{23}Na(n,\gamma)^{24}Na$ reaction has a thermal neutron cross section of 0.53 barn; ^{24}Na has a half-life of 15 hours and there are 100 g of ^{23}Na in the human body.

10 3. A tungsten (W) alloy shield, in which the density of W is 16.8 g cm^{-3}, is used to attenuate 88 keV γ-rays from a 1 GBq ^{109}Cd source. The shield is 2 mm thick. ^{109}Cd emits 88 keV γ-rays in 0.036 of disintegrations. What is the flux density (γ-ray mm^{-2} s^{-1}) at a distance of 3.5 mm? When the shield is interposed, how many γ-rays mm^{-2} are transmitted during a half-hour measurement? If the same thickness of W shield is used for 140 keV γ-rays from ^{99m}Tc, what proportion of γ-rays are transmitted? The mass attenuation coefficient for W is 6.13 cm^2 g^{-1} at 88 keV and 1.90 cm^2 g^{-1} at 140 keV.

10 4. It has been suggested that ^{210}Pb, a decay product of ^{222}Rn, could be a significant cause of leukæmia, because it lodges in bone and produces a long term irradiation of bone marrow. ^{210}Pb has a physical half-life of 22.3 years. It decays by β^- emission to ^{210}Bi, which decays by β^- emission to ^{210}Po. Both ^{210}Bi and ^{210}Po have appreciably shorter physical half-lives (5 days and 138 days, respectively). Nearly all the dose arises from the 5.3 MeV α-particle emitted in each decay from ^{210}Po, which has w_R=20. Considering only this α-particle, what is the committed equivalent dose to bone from an activity concentration of ^{210}Pb of 1 Bq per g of bone? Assume a biological half-life of Pb in bone of 30 years.

What concentration of ^{210}Pb in bone (pg ^{210}Pb/g bone) would be required to produce an equivalent dose of 10 Sv in 1 year?

continued on page 3...

10 5. Calculate the specific gamma emission for a hypothetical electron capture radioisotope, which emits a γ-ray of energy 1 MeV in 65% of decays.

What thickness of lead (Pb) is required to reduce the dose rate to tissue at a distance of 2 m from 10^{12} Bq of this isotope to 0.5 μSv h^{-1}? Assume broad beam conditions.

THE END

PHYSICS 3T03 - BIOLOGY 3L03

D.R. CHETTLE

Day Class

Duration of Examination: 2 HOURS

MCMASTER UNIVERSITY FINAL EXAMINATION (DEFERRED) **APRIL 1996**

Before you begin, make certain that your paper is complete.
THIS EXAMINATION PAPER INCLUDES 6 PAGES and 5 QUESTIONS.
You are responsible for ensuring that your copy of the paper is complete.
BRING ANY DISCREPANCY TO THE ATTENTION OF YOUR INVIGILATOR.

SPECIAL INSTRUCTIONS

Candidates may use any calculator.
Answer all questions.
Use examination booklet provided for all answers.

Physics Constants and Conversion Factors

$e = 1.6 \times 10^{-19} C$

atomic weight Pb = 207.2

$m_e c^2 = 0.511$ MeV

at 1.0 MeV $\mu_{Pb} = 80.3\ m^{-1}$

2.0 MeV $\mu_{Pb} = 52.1\ m^{-1}$

Avogadro's number $= N_A = 6 \times 10^{23}$

1 barn $= 10^{-28} m^2$

$\rho_{Pb} = 11.3 \times 10^3 kg\ m^{-3}$

$1Ci = 3.7 \times 10^{10}$ Bq

K-shell binding energies: (keV)

$_{34}$Se 12.7 $_{35}$Br 13.5 $_{36}$Kr 14.3

continued on page 2...

MARK: 10

1. $^{80}_{35}Br$ can decay to $^{80}_{34}Se$ or $^{80}_{36}Kr$. Write down decay equations for electron capture (EC), β^+ and β^- decays. The mass excess for ^{80}Br is -75.891 MeV. The Q value for β^- decay is 2.006 MeV. The Q value for EC decay is 1.857 MeV. What are the mass excess values for ^{80}Se and ^{85}Kr. Estimate the average β^+ energy.

MARK: 10

2. ^{57}Co emits γ-rays of energies 122.1 keV and 136.5 keV. The 122.1 keV γ-ray is emitted in 85.6% of decays. The 136.5 keV γ-ray is emitted in 11% of decays.

Through what thickness (mm) of a lead shield must the radiation pass before the intensity of the 136.5 keV γ-ray is twice that of the 122.1 keV γ-ray?

(μ/ρ) Pb (m^2kg^{-1})	0.223	0.114
$E\gamma$ (keV)	100	150

continued on page 5...

MARK: 10

3. Manganese is measured via the reaction $^{55}Mn\ (n,\gamma)^{56}\ Mn$. A sample containing 50 mg of Mn is exposed to a thermal neutron fluence rate of $10^6\ cm^{-2}\ s^{-1}$ for 100s. The sample is counted for 30 minutes, starting 1.5 hours after the end of the irradiation. ^{55}Mn has a thermal neutron capture cross section of 13.3 barn. 100% naturally occurring manganese is ^{55}Mn. How many ^{56}Mn decay during the counting period? The half life of ^{56}Mn is 2.58h.

MARK: 10

4. A 10^{12}Bq point source emits 2 γ-rays in each decay. The γ-ray energies are 1.0 MeV and 2.0 MeV. What thickness of lead is required to reduce the exposure rate at a distance of 2.5m to 2.5 mRh^{-1}?

The 1.0 MeV γ-ray produces 0.54 $Rm^2\ Ci^{-1}\ h^{-1}$; the 2.0 MeV γ-ray produces 0.91 $Rm^2\ Ci^{-1}\ h^{-1}$.

Dose build up factors (B) for a point source in lead

Energy	number of relaxations lengths (μx)						
(MeV)	1	2	4	7	10	15	20
1.0	1.37	1.69	2.26	3.02	3.74	4.81	5.86
2.0	1.39	1.76	2.51	3.66	4.84	6.87	9.00

continued on page 6...

MARK: 10

5. An element has metabolic half lives of 12 hours in the kidney and 35 hours in the liver. A radioisotope of the element with a 25 hours half life is administered to a patient. Calculate the committed dose in mGy to the kidneys and liver if the administered activity was 400 MBq. Assume 20% of the activity is located in the liver (mass 1.8 kg) and 80% is located in the kidneys (mass 0.31 kg).

Energy absorbed J per disintegration is as follows:

target organ	source organ	
	kidney	liver
kidney	2.3×10^{-13}	1.3×10^{-15}
liver	1.8×10^{-16}	9.6×10^{-15}

J/disintegration

THE END

PHYSICS 3T03 - BIOLOGY 3L03

DAY CLASS **D.R. CHETTLE**

Duration of Examination: 2 HOURS

MCMASTER UNIVERSITY FINAL EXAMINATION **DECEMBER 1996**

Before you begin, make certain that your paper is complete.
THIS EXAMINATION PAPER INCLUDES 6 PAGES and 5 QUESTIONS.
You are responsible for ensuring that your copy of the paper is complete.
BRING ANY DISCREPANCY TO THE ATTENTION OF YOUR INVIGILATOR.

SPECIAL INSTRUCTIONS

Candidates may use any calculator.
Answer all questions.
Use examination booklet provided for all answers.

---

1 eV = 1.6×10^{-19} J
Avagadro's number = 6.02×10^{23} mole^{-1}
1 barn = 10^{-24} cm^2

atom/particle	mass excess (MeV)
$e^{\pm}$	0.511
${}^{1}_{0}n$	8.071
${}^{1}_{1}H$	7.289
${}^{4}_{2}He$	2.425
${}^{16}_{7}N$	5.682
${}^{16}_{8}O$	- 4.737
${}^{56}_{25}Mn$	-56.909
${}^{56}_{26}Fe$	-60.604
${}^{211}_{85}At$	-11.653

radiation	W_R
X, γ, electrons, β^+	1
neutrons: E_n<10 keV	5
10 keV<E_n<100 keV	10
100 keV<E_n< 2 MeV	20
2 MeV<E_n<20 MeV	10
E_n>20 MeV	5
protons (not recoil) E_p> 2 MeV	5
α, fission fragments non-relativistic heavy nuclei	20

 continued on next page....

MARKS **#1**

(2) a) What is the Q value for the $^{56}Fe(n,p)^{56}Mn$ reaction?

(4) b) (i) Write down the equation for the decay of $^{16}_{7}N$ to $^{16}_{8}O$.

(ii) If the decay is to an excited state of ^{16}O (E_{ex}=6.130 MeV), what maximum β± energies would you expect?

(4) c) $^{211}_{85}At$ emits a 5.866 MeV α-particle in decaying to the ground state of a daughter nucleus.
(i) What are the mass number and atomic number (charge number) of this daughter nucleus?
(ii) What is the mass excess value for the daughter nucleus?

MARKS **#2**

(5) a) An archæological sample of wood is found to contain ^{14}C with a specific activity of 7.8×10^3 Bq/kg of carbon. Wood from a piece of furniture made in 1896 has a specific activity of 14.7×10^3 Bq/kg of carbon. Estimate the age of the archæological sample. The half life of ^{14}C is 5730 years.

(5) b) ^{238}Pu decays by α-particle emission. Assume each α-particle has an energy of 5.5 MeV. What mass (kg) of ^{238}Pu is required to produce a power output of 2.0 kJ/s? The half life of ^{238}Pu is 87.7 years.

MARKS **#3**

(10) A person is exposed to a neutron beam which has 2 components. There are 10^4 thermal neutrons per cm^2 per second, plus 10^2 fast (5 MeV) neutrons per cm^2 per second. What is the dose (Sv) for a 10 minute irradiation? If a 200 μm thick cadmium shield is placed betweeen the person and the neutron source, what is the dose for a 10 minute irradiation? One thermal neutron per m^2 produces 2.4×10^{-16} Gy. One 5 MeV neutron per m^2 produces 6.0×10^{-15} Gy. The cross section for neutron absorption by cadmium is 2500 barn at thermal energies and 3 barn at 5 MeV. The density of cadmium is 8.65 g/cm^3 and its atomic weight is 112.4.

 continued on next page....

MARKS (10)

#4

40 Bq of ^{210}Pb is ingested by a person. The ^{210}Pb distributes such that 70% of it is in blood, and 30% is in bone. The masses and biological half lives of these two compartments are: blood, 5.2 kg, 35 days; bone 10 kg, 25 years. What are the initial dose rates (Sv/s) and committed doses (Sv) to each compartment? Consider only the dose to a compartment from the ^{210}Pb in that compartment. The half life of ^{210}Pb is 22.3 years. ^{210}Pb decays to ^{210}Bi, which decays to ^{210}Po. Both ^{210}Bi and ^{210}Po have relatively short half lives. Nearly all the dose comes from the 5.3 MeV α-particle emitted in each decay of ^{210}Po.

MARKS (10)

#5

A pump is contaminated with ^{110m}Ag, which emits γ-rays of energies 0.7 MeV and 1.4 MeV. The exposure at a distance of 1.5 m from the pump is 2.8 R/h from the 0.7 MeV γ-rays plus 2.2 R/h from the 1.4 MeV γ-rays. What thickness of lead (cm) is required to reduce the total exposure rate to 2.5 mR/h? μ_{Pb} is 1.105 cm^{-1} at 0.7 MeV and 0.608 cm^{-1} at 1.4 MeV.

Dose buildup factors, B, in lead.

	number of relaxation lengths (μx)						
MeV	1	2	4	7	10	15	20
0.7	1.30	1.55	1.92	2.40	2.82	3.48	3.86
1.4	1.38	1.72	2.34	3.25	4.25	5.60	7.00

THE END

PHYSICS 3T03 - BIOLOGY 3L03

DAY CLASS **D.R. CHETTLE**

Duration of Examination: 2 HOURS

MCMASTER UNIVERSITY DEFERRED **FINAL EXAMINATION** **MARCH 1997**

Before you begin, make certain that your paper is complete.
THIS EXAMINATION PAPER INCLUDES 9 PAGES and 5 QUESTIONS.
You are responsible for ensuring that your copy of the paper is complete.
BRING ANY DISCREPANCY TO THE ATTENTION OF YOUR INVIGILATOR.

SPECIAL INSTRUCTIONS

Candidates may use any calculator.
Answer all questions.
Use examination booklet provided for all answers.

---

1 eV = 1.6×10^{-19} J
Avagadro's number = 6.02×10^{23} $mole^{-1}$
1 barn = 10^{-28} m^2
1 Ci = 3.7×10^{10} Bq
at 1.0 MeV μ_{Pb} = 77.1 m^{-1}

atom/particle	mass excess (MeV)
$e^{\pm}$	0.511
${}^{1}_{0}n$	8.071
${}^{4}_{2}He$	2.425
${}^{18}_{8}O$	- 0.783
${}^{18}_{9}F$	0.873
${}^{28}_{13}Al$	-16.848
${}^{31}_{15}P$	-24.440
${}^{238}_{94}Pu$	46.161

radiation	W_R
X, γ, electrons, β^+	1
neutrons: E_n<10 keV	5
10 keV<E_n<100 keV	10
100 keV<E_n< 2 MeV	20
2 MeV<E_n<20 MeV	10
E_n>20 MeV	5
protons (not recoil) E_p> 2 MeV	5
α, fission fragments non-relativistic heavy nuclei	20

 continued on next page....

MARKS

#1

(2) a) What is the Q value for the $^{31}P(n,\alpha)^{28}Al$ reaction?

(4) b) (i) Write down the equation(s) for the decay of $^{18}_{9}F$ to $^{18}_{8}O$.

(ii) If the decay is to the ground state of $^{18}_{8}O$, what mean $\beta^{\pm}$ energies would you expect?

(4) c) $^{238}_{94}Pu$ emits a 5.398 MeV α-particle in decaying to the ground state of a daughter nucleus.

(i) What are the mass number and atomic number (charge number) of this daughter nucleus?

(ii) What is the mass excess value for the daughter nucleus?

 continued on next page....

ARKS

#2

(5) a) What is the power output (mJ/s) of 40 Ci of tritium (^3_1H) ?

What mass of tritium does this represent? The half life of

^3_1H is 12.3 years. Tritium is a pure β^- emitter with

$\bar{E}_\beta = 5.5 keV$.

(5) b) Wood from a piece of furniture made in 1797 is found to have a specific activity of ^{14}C of 14.5×10^3 Bq/kg of carbon. What specific activity of ^{14}C would you expect in modern wood (in the absence of disturbances introduced by atmospheric bomb tests and other human activity)? What specific activity of ^{14}C would you expect in a 3000 year old sample of wood? The half-life of ^{14}C is 5730 years.

 continued on next page....

MARKS

#3

(10) A beam of fast neutrons includes two energy groups. One group of 1 MeV neutrons has a fluence rate of 1.5×10^9 neutrons/m^2/s. The second group of 10 MeV neutrons has a fluence rate of 3.0×10^8 neutrons/m^2/s. The neutron beam passes through a thickness of 250 kg/m^2 of water. One 10MeV neutron per m^2 produces 8.0×10^{-15} Gy; one 1 MeV neutron per m^2 produces 3.0×10^{-15} Gy. What are the doses (Sv) from each neutron group both before and after passing through the water for a 1000s irradiation? Treat water as $^1H_2{}^{16}O$. The total interaction cross sections (in b) are:

	1 MeV	10 MeV
^1H	4.2	0.95
^{16}O	8	1.95

 continued on next page....

MARKS

#4

(10) An element has metabolic half lives of 21 hours in the kidney and 38 hours in the liver. A radioisotope of the element with a 25 hour half life is administered to a patient. Calculate the committed dose in mGy to the kidneys and liver if the administered activity was 25 MBq. Assume 25% of the initial activity is located in the liver (mass 1.7 kg) and 75% is located in the kidneys (mass 0.31kg).

Energy (J) absorbed per disintegration is as follows:

target organ	source organ	
	kidney	liver
kidney	2.3×10^{-13}	1.3×10^{-15}
liver	1.8×10^{-16}	9.6×10^{-15}

 continued on next page....

MARKS

#5

(10) An 11.6×10^6 M Bq point source of a radioisotope emits 1.0 MeV γ-rays and has a specific gamma constant of 0.36 $Rm^2\ Ci^{-1}\ h^{-1}$.

a) With the source unshielded, what is the exposure rate at 2.0m?

b) What thickness of lead is required to reduce the exposure rate at 2.0m to 2.5 mRh^{-1}? Determine this thickness so that the exposure rate is between 2.4 and 2.5 mRh^{-1}.

For Pb at 1 MeV							
number of relaxation lengths (μx)	1	2	4	7	10	15	20
B	1.37	1.69	2.26	3.02	3.74	4.81	5.86

PHYSICS 3T03 - BIOLOGY 3L03

DAY CLASS **D.R. CHETTLE**

Duration of Examination: 2 HOURS
MCMASTER UNIVERSITY FINAL EXAMINATION **DECEMBER 1999**

Before you begin, make certain that your paper is complete.
THIS EXAMINATION PAPER INCLUDES 6 pages & 5 questions.
You are responsible for ensuring that your copy of the paper is complete.
BRING ANY DISCREPANCY TO THE ATTENTION OF YOUR INVIGILATOR.

SPECIAL INSTRUCTIONS

Only the McMaster standard (CASIO-FX 991) calculator may be used.
Answer all questions.
Use examination booklet provided for all answers.

1eV = 1.6×10^{-19} J

unit charge = 1.6×10^{-19}C

Avagadro's number = 6.02×10^{23} mole^{-1}

1 barn = 10^{-28} m^2

rest mass of electron = 0.511 MeV

1Ci = 3.7×10^{10} Bq

MARKS 10

Question #1

Aluminum could be measured by any of the three reactions: ${}^{27}_{13}\mathrm{Al}(n,\gamma)^{28}Al$, ${}^{27}_{13}\mathrm{Al}(n,p)^{27}Mg$, ${}^{27}_{13}\mathrm{Al}(n,\alpha)^{24}Na$. What are the Q values for these reactions? For each reaction, and considering only mass difference, what is the minimum neutron energy required to cause the reaction to take place? Does the Coulomb barrier place any further constraints on any of these reactions?

	n	^{1}H	^{4}He	^{24}Na	^{27}Mg	^{27}Al	^{28}Al
Δ(MeV)	8.071	7.289	2.425	-8.417	-14.585	-17.194	-16.848

Coulomb barrier: potential energy = $\dfrac{k_0\, z_1\, z_2}{r}$; $k_0 = 8.99\times 10^9$ N m^2 C^{-2} ; $r \simeq 1.3\, A^{1/3} \times 10^{-15}$ m

MARKS 10

Question #2

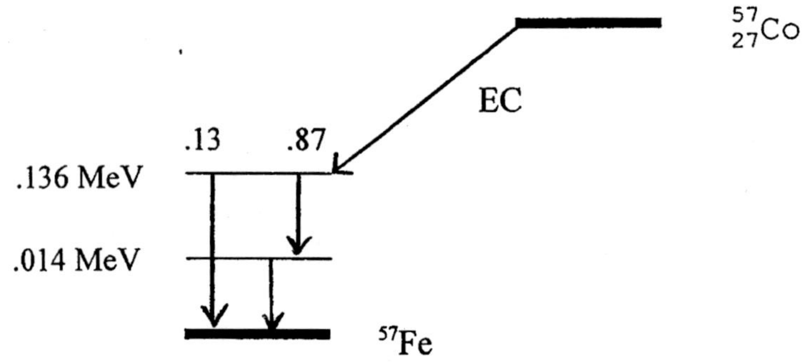

^{57}Co decays by electron capture to the second excited state (E = 0.136 MeV) of ^{57}Fe. This state de-excites to the first excited state (E=0.014MeV) of ^{57}Fe in 87% of transitions and to the ground state in 13% of transitions. γ-rays of three different energies are observed; what are these energies? Internal conversion is an alternative to γ-ray emission in each case. The internal conversion coefficient(α) for the lowest energy de-excitation is 8.5, what proportion of all transitions will result in the emissions of this γ-ray? The highest energy γ-ray is emitted in 11.1% of all transitions, the second highest energy γ-ray is emitted in 85.6% of all transitions. What are the internal conversion coefficients for these de-excitions? Using the expression for fluorescence yield:

$$\omega = \frac{z^4}{z^4 + 1.12 \times 10^6}$$

determine the proportion of ^{57}Co decays which result in emission of Fe x-rays.

MARKS **Question #3**

10

In the measurement of bone mineral, pencil beams of photons of two different energies pass through a tissue sample to a detector. The differences in attenuation allow an estimate of bone density to be made. Highly collimated beams of photons of energies 45 keV and 100 keV are incident on a person's thigh. The overall thickness of the thigh is 16 cm and it contains a bone (femur) that is 4 cm thick. Assuming the thigh contains only muscle and compact bone, what proportion of each photon beam is transmitted through the full thickness of the thigh, if the density of muscle is 1.03×10^3 kg m^{-3} and the density of compact bone is 1.20×10^3 kg m^{-3} ? What proportion of each photon beam is transmitted if the density of compact bone in 1.15×10^3 kg m^{-3} and all other factors remain the same?

mass attenuation coefficients, μ/ϱ, (m^2 kg^{-1})

photon energy (keV)	muscle	compact bone
45	5.36×10^{-3}	2.27×10^{-2}
100	2.52×10^{-3}	3.86×10^{-3}

MARKS **Question #4**

10

In an experiment in radioecology, a researcher eats a fish containing 4kBq of ^{137}Cs. Assuming all the ^{137}Cs is absorbed and distributed through the muscle, what is the committed effective dose to the person? The effective clearance rate, λ_E, for ^{137}Cs is 7.37×10^{-8} s^{-1}. When ^{137}Cs decays it emits β^- particles and internal conversion electrons with a combined average energy of 0.244 MeV per decay. Assume a mass of muscle of 25kg. ^{137}Cs also emits γ-rays.
In estimating the effective dose use radiation weighting factors of 1 for all types of radiation. Use the following tissue weighting factors: ovaries: 0.20; sensitive tissue (red marrow + lungs + stomach + colon): 0.48; other tissue: 0.27; muscle: 0.05.
In the following table are values for the energy absorbed per unit mass (J kg^{-1}) per disintegration (Bq^{-1} s^{-1}) for different tissues when ^{137}Cs is distributed in muscle.

Dose per disintegration (J kg^{-1} Bq^{-1} s^{-1})
target tissue

	ovaries	sensitive tissue	other tissue	muscle
muscle	6.05×10^{-16}	4.38×10^{-16}	4.44×10^{-16}	4.67×10^{-16}

MARKS **Question #5**

10

A source of γ-rays of energy 1.275 MeV produces an exposure rate of 6.5 Rh^{-1} at a distance of 1m when it is unshielded. What is the exposure rate at 1m when the source is shielded by 0.1m of lead? What thickness of concrete would have to surround the source in the lead container to reduce the exposure rate at 1m from the source to between 2.0×10^{-4} Rh^{-1} and 2.5×10^{-4} Rh^{-1}? The linear attenuation coefficient for lead is 63.9 m^{-1} at 1.275 MeV. The linear attenuation coefficient for concrete is 13.2 m^{-1} at 1.275MeV. Build up factors are given below for 1.275 MeV photons as a function of the number of relaxation lengths (μx) for both lead and concrete.

		μx						
	energy	1	2	4	7	10	15	20
lead								
	1.275	1.38	1.71	2.33	3.20	4.04	5.38	6.72
concrete								
	1.275	1.89	2.94	5.54	10.6	16.7	29.0	43.8

PHYSICS 3T03 - BIOLOGY 3L03

DAY CLASS **D.R. CHETTLE**

McMASTER UNIVERSITY DEFERRED **FINAL EXAMINATION**

Duration of Examination: 2 HOURS **January 2001**

Before you begin, make certain that your paper is complete.
This Examination Paper includes 5 PAGES and 5 QUESTIONS.
You are responsible for ensuring that your copy of the paper is complete.
BRING ANY DISCREPANCY TO THE ATTENTION OF YOUR INVIGILATOR.

SPECIAL INSTRUCTIONS

Only the McMaster standard (CASIO-FX 991) calculator may be used.
Answer all questions.
Use examination booklet provided for all answers.

---

rest mass of electron or positron 0.511 MeV

$$\omega_k = \frac{z^4}{1.12x10^6 + z^4}$$

$1\ R = 2.58x10^{-4}\ C\ kg^{-1}$

$1Ci = 3.7x10^{10}\ Bq$

Avagadro's number $N_A = 6.02x10^{23}\ mole^{-1}$

$w_{air} = 34\ eV$

$1eV = 1.6x10^{-19}J$

Marks:

(10) **Question #1**

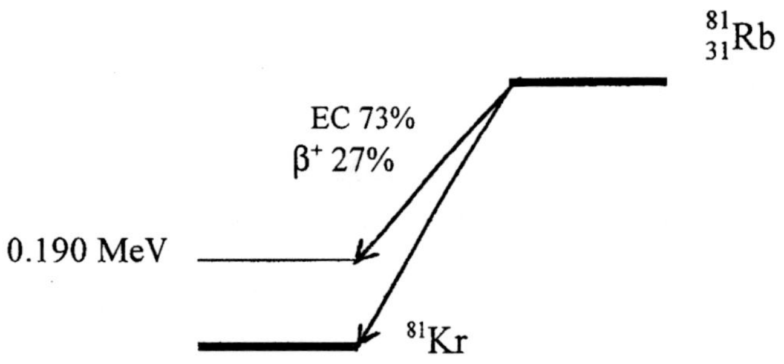

^{81}Rb decays to the first excited state of ^{81}Kr as shown. The decay is by electron capture in 73% of decays and by positron (β^+) emission in 27% of decays. The mass excess value for ^{81}Rb is -75.392 MeV. The mass excess value for ^{81}Kr is -77.654 MeV. The energy of the first excited state in ^{81}Kr is 0.190 MeV. The K electron shell binding energy in is 0.015 MeV. Internal conversion coefficient, α, for the 0.190 excited state = 0.54.

(i) What is the maximum β^+ energy?

(ii) What is the atomic number of Kr?

(iii) What is the energy of the neutrino emitted in the electron capture decay?

(iv) What photons are emitted in association with this decay and with what intensities?

Marks:

(10) **Question #2**

^{40}K is now 1.17×10^{-4} of all naturally occurring potassium atoms. Natural potassium is 2.4% of the earth's crust. The mass of the earth's crust is 1.496×10^{23} kg. Assume the earth was formed 4.5×10^9 years ago. The half life of ^{40}K is 1.277×10^9 years. The atomic mass of potassium is 39.10. The proportion of decays of ^{40}K that lead to ^{40}Ar is 0.1067. The atomic mass of argon is 39.95. The mass of the atmosphere is 5.136×10^{19} kg.

(i) What is the mass of ^{40}K in the earth's crust now?

(ii) What was the mass of ^{40}K in the earth's crust 4.5×10^9 years ago?

(iii) How many decays of ^{40}K have taken place in the last 4.5×10^9 years?

(iv) Assuming all ^{40}Ar is eventually released into the earth's atmosphere, what proportion of the earth's atmosphere is ^{40}Ar arising from the decay of ^{40}K?

Marks:

(10) **Question #3**

The most intense γ-ray emission from ^{241}Am is at 0.060 MeV in 35.7% of decays. What thickness of lead is required to reduce the fluence rate of these γ-rays to 1 $cm^{-2}s^{-1}$ at a distance of 10 cm from an ^{241}Am source of activity 10 Ci (do not make an allowance for build up)? ^{241}Am also emits γ-rays of 0.662 MeV (3.44×10^{-6} of decays) and 0.722 MeV (1.84×10^{-6} of decays). What is the fluence rate of each of these two γ-rays after the lead shield? The mass attenuation coefficient of lead is 4.93 cm^2g^{-1} at 0.060MeV, 0.106cm^2g^{-1} at 0.662 MeV, and 0.0959 cm^2g^{-1} at 0.722 MeV. The density of lead is 11.35 gcm^{-3}.

Marks:

(10) **Question #4**

^{90}Sr decays by pure β^- emission to ^{90}Y, which in turn decays by pure β^- emission to ^{90}Zr, which is stable. The physical half life of ^{90}Sr is 28.8 years; the physical half life of ^{90}Y is 64.1 hours. 1.0 μCi of ^{90}Sr is absorbed into the body; 90% of it goes to the skeleton, which has a mass of 10 kg, and 10% of the ^{90}Sr is uniformly distributed in soft tissue, which has a mass of 65 kg. The biological half life of Sr in soft tissue is 115 days. The biological clearance rate of Sr from skeleton is 2.5% per year. The average energy of the β^- emitted in the decay of ^{90}Sr is 0.196 MeV; the average energy of the β^- emitted in the ^{90}Y decay is 0.935 MeV. There are no γ-rays emitted in either decay. What are the initial dose rates (Gy per day) and committed doses to soft tissue and to skeleton?

Marks:

(10) **Question #5**

A 10 Ci source of ^{65}Zn is to be shielded by aluminum. ^{65}Zn emits a γ-ray of energy 1.116 MeV in 50.75% of decays. The mass energy absorption coefficient for air

$\left(\frac{\mu_{en}}{\rho}\right)_{air}$ is 2.74×10^{-3} m^2kg^{-1} at 1.116 MeV. What is the unshielded exposure rate

(Rh^{-1}) at 1 m from the source? Allowing for build up, what thickness of aluminum shield must be used to reduce the exposure rate to 0.5 mRh^{-1}? The linear attenuation coefficient μ for aluminum is 15.9 m^{-1} at 1.116 MeV.

Build up factors (B)	Number of relaxation lengths (μx)						
Aluminum at 1.116 MeV	1	2	4	7	10	15	20
	1.99	3.23	6.34	12.5	20.1	35.7	54.8

assignment # 3. Nov 1994

1. a) 7.85 mGy (to bone)
   b) 0.75 mGy (to rest of body)

2. 1000 R h^{-1} at 1 m

3. depending on assumptions, dose ≥ 30 Gy ⇒ fatal

4. a) 1.435×10^{-19} C m^{2} kg^{-1} Bq^{-1} s^{-1}
   b) 1.66×10^{-13} Gy s^{-1} at 1 m from 1 kg natural K
   c) 4.07×10^{-12} Gy s^{-1} (0.128 mGy y^{-1})

assignment #4, Dec 1994

1. 63 nGy

2. (i) 0·22 mGy
(ii) 76 μGy

3. (i) 550 μSv
(ii) 38·5 μSv

4. 6 mm Pb

5. 24 mR wk^{-1}

assignment #1, Sept 1995

1. ^{18}O

2. (i) $5\cdot36 \times 10^{23}$ MeV g^{-1} from ^{235}U
(ii) $5\cdot5 \times 10^{23}$ MeV g^{-1} from ^{2}H

3. 26·7 MeV

4. a) $^{224}_{88}Ra \Rightarrow {}^{220}_{86}Rn + {}^{4}_{2}He + Q$
b) 5·686 MeV, 5·419 MeV

5. a) $^{125}_{53}I \Rightarrow {}^{125}_{52}Te + \nu_e$ b) E_γ = 0·112 MeV
c) α = 13·925, E_e = 0·0035 MeV
d) ω_K = 0·867
e) (i) $6\cdot7 \times 10^{4} s^{-1}$, (ii) $1\cdot676 \times 10^{6} s^{-1}$, (iii) $9\cdot33 \times 10^{5} s^{-1}$, (iv) $2\cdot57 \times 10^{5} s^{-1}$

assignment #2, October 1995

1. 207 MBq (at beginning 1·18 GBq)

2. ^{238}U 61·4 kBq, ^{234}Th 61·4 kBq, ^{234}Pa 61·4 kBq, ^{234}U 61·4 kBq
^{234}U 2·8 kBq

3. 0·366 are ^{109}Cd

4. a) 79·8 keV μm^{-1}
b) (i) 0·181 MeV mm^{-1} (soft tissue)
(ii) 0·303 MeV mm^{-1} (bone)

assignment # 3, October 1995

1. ^{57}Co at 90°
^{109}Cd at 180°

2. 0·434 mm
78·9%

3. 3·75 neutrons per fission

4. H: ·8675; O: ·1084; C: ·0227; N: ·0015 using $f = 0{\cdot}63$ for H
·8386 ·1320 ·0276 ·0018 using ·5 Emax for all

assignment #4, November 1995

1. 1.89 Gy to cell
2.93×10^{-3}
9.92×10^{-12} Gy s^{-1} if $\lambda_B = .02 d^{-1}$ dose = 42.5 μGy

2. 3.27×10^{-9} C $kg^{-1} s^{-1}$
118 nGy s^{-1} bone
122 nGy s^{-1} muscle

3. 1.25 Sv from thermal neutrons
12.2 μg g^{-1}

4. 9.2 Sv
6.82 pg / g bone

assignment #5, December 1995

1. 2.72×10^{-9} Gy s^{-1}; 4.78 mGy skeleton
2.33×10^{-10} Gy s^{-1}; 0.394 mGy rest of body

2. 4.2 mSv hand; 4.2 μSv rest of body
E = 5.46 μSv

3. 2.49×10^{-18} C m^2 kg^{-1} Bq^{-1} s^{-1}
1.28 R m^2 Ci^{-1} h^{-1}
0.25 m

4. 7 mm Pb

assignment #2 October 1996

1. Coulomb barrier = 13.1 MeV

   Q = 5.456 MeV

2. natural U $5.5 \times 10^{8}\ J\ g^{-1}$; water $2.9 \times 10^{6}\ J$

3. $^{238}_{92}U \rightarrow ^{234}_{90}Th + ^{4}_{2}He + (E_{ex}) + Q$

   (i) 4.041 MeV; (ii) 4.150 MeV; (iii) 4.198 MeV

4. $^{126}_{53}I + e^{-} \rightarrow ^{126}_{54}Xe + ^{0}_{-1}\beta^{-} + \bar{\nu} + Q$ $\quad E_{\beta}\,max = 1.251\ MeV$ or $0.862\ MeV$

   $^{126}_{53}I \rightarrow ^{126}_{52}Te + ^{0}_{+1}\beta^{+} + e^{-} + \nu + Q$ $\quad E_{\beta}\,max = 1.133\ MeV$ or $0.467\ MeV$

   $^{126}_{53}I \rightarrow ^{126}_{52}Te + \nu + Q$ $\quad \nu = 2.123\ MeV$ or $1.457\ MeV$

assignment #3 November 1996

1. 71.4 keV/μm range ≃ 80 μm

2. β^{-} 1.87 MeV/cm; β^{+} 1.82 MeV/cm; 0.6% bremsstrahlung

3. ^{57}Co 180°; ^{99m}Tc 90°; ^{57}Co likely to be better

4. a) 3.565×10^{4}

   b) 3.978 MeV

   c) 0.243 MeV

5. $2.339 \times 10^{5}\ mm^{-2}\ s^{-1}$

   $0.097\ mm^{-2}$

   0.00103

assignment #4, Nov 1996

1. 1.89 Gy to cell
2.93×10^{-3}
9.92×10^{-12} Gy s^{-1} if $\lambda_B = .02\ d^{-1}$ dose = 42.5 μGy

2. 3.27×10^{-12} C kg^{-1} s^{-1}
118 nGy s^{-1} bone
122 nGy s^{-1} muscle

3. 2.72×10^{-9} Gy s^{-1}; 4.78 mGy skeleton
2.33×10^{-10} Gy s^{-1}; 0.394 mGy rest of body

4. 6.28 mGy

assignment #5, Dec 1996

1. 17.1 μSv

2. $\dot{\Gamma} = 1.237$ R m^2 Ci^{-1} h^{-1}
20 cm Pb

3. 7 mm Pb

assignment #1, 1997

1. (i) 55·9567 amu

(ii) $\Delta(^{56}Mn) = -36.679$ MeV

2. Q values: $^{207}Pb\,(p,n)\,^{207}Bi = -3.187$ MeV

$^{208}Pb\,(p,n)\,^{208}Bi = -3.662$ MeV

Coulomb barrier = 13·1 MeV

effective threshold = 13·1 MeV

3. 8.00×10^{13} J

4. a) $^{125}_{53}I \longrightarrow {}^{125}_{52}I + \nu$

b) $E_\nu = 0.111$ MeV

c) $\alpha = 13.9$

$KE_K = 3.46$ keV

d) $\omega_K(Te) = 0.867$

e) (i) $6.7 \times 10^{4}\ s^{-1}$

(ii) $1.68 \times 10^{6}\ s^{-1}$

(iii) $0.933 \times 10^{6}\ s^{-1}$

(iv) $0.257 \times 10^{6}\ s^{-1}$

class test 1, October 1998

. 1·78 MeV; 1·47 MeV

. ${}^{74}_{33}As \rightarrow {}^{74}_{32}Ge + \nu + Q + K_{Ge,As} + E_{ex}$ $E_\nu = 1{\cdot}954$ MeV
${}^{74}_{33}As \rightarrow {}^{74}_{32}Ge + {}_{+1}\beta^+ + e^- + \nu + Q + E_{ex}$ $E_{\beta^+ max} = 0{\cdot}944$ MeV
$e^- + {}^{74}_{33}As \rightarrow {}^{74}_{34}Se + {}_{-1}\beta^- + \bar{\nu} + Q + (E_{ex})$ $E_{\beta^- max} = 1{\cdot}353$ MeV; 0·718 MeV

. a) 0·378 g
b) ·385

class test 2, November 1996

between 7·5 cm and 9·0 cm

Eγ (MeV)	Eγ′ [60°] (MeV)	Eγ′ [180°] (MeV)
0·01	0·00990	0·00962
1·0	0·5054	0·2035
100	1·0117	0·2548

. (i) 0·179 cm
(ii) 10·68 cm

. 12,671 at end of irradiation
1,218 during count

class test #1, October 2000

1. (i) 88
   (ii) 30.862 MeV
   (iii) 0.068 MeV
2. ^{234}U: 12,245 $Bq\,g^{-1}$
   ^{235}U: 568 $Bq\,g^{-1}$,
   ^{238}U: 12,305 $Bq\,g^{-1}$
3. electrons 0.0191
   protons 5.67×10^{-9}
4. a) (i) 83.96 keV
   (ii) 65.97 keV
   b) 0.438 MeV

class test #2, November 2000

1. 50 keV: 2.160×10^{-3}
   100 keV: 2.793×10^{-2}
2. 1621
3. 3.51 s
4. skeleton: 0.522 mGy
   muscle: 0.257 mGy

exam, April 1994

1. 0.385

2. $\Delta^{34}Cl = -29.521$ MeV $\Delta^{34}S = -30.665$
1.144 MeV; neutrino, S x-ray, Auger electron

3. 1.25 Sv
12.2 $\mu g\ g^{-1}$

4. 6.28 mGy

5. primary 33 cm concrete, add 2.25 mm Pb
secondary 27 cm concrete, add 1.75 mm Pb

exam, December 1994

1 a) 5.686 MeV; 5.449 MeV
b) $^{15}_{8}O \rightarrow ^{15}_{7}N + {}_{+1}\beta^{+} + \nu + e^{-} + Q$; 1.731 MeV
c) −1.946 MeV

2. 1.48×10^{7} neutron cm^{-2}

3. 2.34×10^{5} $mm^{-2}\ s^{-1}$
0.048 mm^{-2}
0.169 %

4. 9.2 Sv
6.82 pg/g bone

5. 6.8×10^{-19} $C\ m^{2}\ kg^{-1}\ Bq^{-1}\ s^{-1}$
0.16 m

exam, April 1996

1. ${}^{x}_{35}Br \rightarrow {}^{x}_{34}Se + \nu + Q$ $\Delta\,{}^{x}Se = -77.774$ MeV

   ${}^{x}_{35}Br \rightarrow {}^{x}_{34}Se + \beta^{+} + e^{-} + \nu + Q$ $\bar{E}_{\beta^{+}} = 0.287$ MeV

   $e^{-} + {}^{x}_{35}Br \rightarrow {}^{x}_{36}Kr + \beta^{-} + Q + \bar{\nu}$ $\Delta\,{}^{85}Kr = -77.897$

2. 9 mm

3. 6.07×10^{4}

4. 0.18 m

5. $D_K = 10$ Gy

   $D_i = 35$ mGy

exam, December 1996

1. a) -2.913 MeV

   b) (i) $e^{-} + {}^{14}_{7}N \rightarrow {}^{14}_{8}O + \beta^{-} + \bar{\nu} + Q$

   (ii) 4.289 MeV

   c) (i) $A = 207$; $Z = 83$

   (ii) -20.057

2. a) 5339 y

   b) 3.6 kg

3. 1.1×10^{-4} Sv without Cd shield

   4.3×10^{-5} Sv behind Cd shield

4. blood: $\dot{H}_e = 9.13 \times 10^{-11}$ Sv s^{-1} $H = 3.97 \times 10^{-4}$ Sv

   bone: $\dot{H}_e = 2.035 \times 10^{-11}$ Sv s^{-1} $H = 1.03 \times 10^{-2}$ Sv

5. 0.133 m

exam March 1997

1. a) -1.946 MeV

b) (i) $^{18}_{9}F \rightarrow {}^{18}_{8}O + {}^{0}_{1}\beta^{+} + e^{-} + \nu + Q$

$^{18}_{9}F \rightarrow {}^{18}_{8}O + \nu + be_F$

(ii) 0.211 MeV

c) $A = 234$, $Z = 92$, $\Delta = 38.246$ MeV

2. a) 1.30 $mJ\,s^{-1}$, 4.13 mg

b) modern 14.9×10^{3} Bq/kg   3000 year old 10.3×10^{3} Bq/kg

3. 1 MeV: 90 mSv before shield; 0.1 μSv after shield

10 MeV: 24 mSv before shield; 0.96 mSv after shield

4. $D_K = 827$ mGy $D_L = 2.9$ mGy

5. a) 28.2 $R\,h^{-1}$

b) 0.25 m

exam December 1999

1. Q values: + 7.725 MeV, − 1.827 MeV, − 3.131 MeV
   minimum E_n: no minimum, 1.895 MeV, 3.247 MeV
   Coulomb barrier: no barrier, 3.319 MeV, 5.443 MeV
2. E_γ: 0.136 MeV, 0.014 MeV, 0.122 MeV
   0.014 MeV γ emitted in 0.0916 of all transitions
   $\alpha(0.136) = 0.171$; $\alpha(0.122) = 0.016$
   Fe x-rays emitted in 0.525 of all transitions
3. 45 keV: 0.173 (0.181 if density of compact bone 1.15×10^3 kg m^{-3})
   100 keV: 0.609 (0.613 if density of compact bone 1.15×10^3 kg m^{-3})
4. effective dose 25.75 μSv
5. 0.56 m concrete

exam January 2001

1. (i) 1.050 MeV
   (ii) 3.0
   (iii) 2.057 MeV
   (iv) 0.511 MeV; 0.54
   0.190 MeV; 0.649
   Kr x-rays; 0.454
2. (i) 4.20×10^{17} kg
   (ii) 4.83×10^{18} kg
   (iii) 6.79×10^{43} decays
   (iv) 9.36×10^{-3}
3. 0.330 cm Pb
   0.662 MeV: 681 cm^{-2} s^{-1}
   0.722 MeV: 378 cm^{-2} s^{-1}
4. soft tissue: 8.90×10^{-7} Gy d^{-1}; committed: 1.47×10^{-5} Gy
   skeleton: 5.21×10^{-5} Gy d^{-1}; committed: 0.354 Gy
5. 3.00 R h^{-1}
   0.755 m Al